CW00545571

Palgrave Macmillan Studies in Family and Intimate Life

'The Palgrave Macmillan Studies in Family and Intimate Life series is impressive and contemporary in its themes and approaches'—Professor Deborah Chambers, Newcastle University, UK, and author of *New Social Ties*.

The remit of the Palgrave Macmillan Studies in Family and Intimate Life series is to publish major texts, monographs and edited collections focusing broadly on the sociological exploration of intimate relationships and family organization. The series covers a wide range of topics such as partnership, marriage, parenting, domestic arrangements, kinship, demographic change, intergenerational ties, life course transitions, step-families, gay and lesbian relationships, lone-parent households, and also non-familial intimate relationships such as friendships and includes works by leading figures in the field, in the UK and internationally, and aims to contribute to continue publishing influential and prize-winning research.

More information about this series at
http://www.palgrave.com/gp/series/14676

Sarah Marie Hall

Everyday Life in Austerity

Family, Friends and Intimate Relations

Sarah Marie Hall
University of Manchester
Manchester, UK

Palgrave Macmillan Studies in Family and Intimate Life
ISBN 978-3-030-17093-6 ISBN 978-3-030-17094-3 (eBook)
https://doi.org/10.1007/978-3-030-17094-3

This Palgrave Macmillan imprint is published by the registered company Springer Nature Switzerland AG.
The registered company address is: Gewerbestrasse 11, 6330 Cham, Switzerland

Acknowledgements

The ethnographic research described in the pages of this book would not have been possible without the families and communities of 'Argleton', Greater Manchester. My first thanks go to these participants for the time, energy and generosity that they invested into the research: thank you for welcoming me into your everyday lives. Thanks also to my own family, friends and intimate relations for supporting and encouraging me to write this book. Special thanks to Ian Shone for his careful, constructive and critical feedback, and also personal thanks to Max for his encouragement, too.

I am also very grateful to friends and colleagues who have read chapters, discussed ideas with me and provided helpful advice on shaping this book, including Anna Tarrant, Clare Holdsworth, David Morgan, Helen Holmes, Laura Pottinger, Mark Jayne and Noel Castree. The research project was funded by a Hallsworth Research Fellowship in Political Economy from the University of Manchester, UK (2012–2015), during which time and since I have been based at the Geography Department and at the Morgan Centre. Thank you to colleagues from across these groups for their interest in my research and for providing a stimulating and supportive academic environment. Thank you also to friends and colleagues at the Women's Budget Group for their contributions to my understanding of gendered economies. The ideas in this book have been presented at many different seminars, talks and conferences—too many to name, in fact—but my thanks to all those people who have engaged with me and the research at those events.

I have some thanks for permissions to add, too. For the illustrations reproduced here and taken from the *Everyday Austerity* zine, thanks to Claire Stringer. For the graph and infographic reproduced here and taken from the *Women Count* booklet, thanks to Mary-Ann Stephenson and the Women's Budget Group. Chapter 2 is a revised and adapted version of 'Everyday Austerity: Towards Relational Geographies of Family, Friendship and Intimacy', *Progress in Human Geography* (2018, https://doi.org/10.1177/0309132518796280). Chapters 3 and 5 contain revised and adapted material from 'The Personal Is Political: Feminist Geographies of/in Austerity', *Geoforum* (2018, https://doi.org/10.1016/j.geoforum.2018.04.010). And Chap. 6 is a revised and adapted version of 'A Very Personal Crisis: Family Fragilities and Everyday Conjunctures Within Lived Experiences of Austerity', *Transactions of the Institute of British Geographers* (2019, https://doi.org/10.1111/tran.12300).

Contents

List of Figures

1

Introduction

Approaching Austerity

> [I]t's probably been harder that I would have thought. But then, I know for other people it's been even harder. You know, you look at the amount of people using food banks and the amount of people that are really, really struggling … I mean, it's probably worse because we've got debt. But it's hard because it's just really, the cost of living's gone up so much. (Laura, taped discussion, October 2014)

> We've not suffered any unemployment, but we have seen it around and about. You kind of see and just notice that some areas are getting a little bit more deprived than they were … all of a sudden, some of the shops shut down and they were replaced by pawn shops or pound shops, and you just kind of saw the town centre decline, really. (Zoe, taped discussion, February 2015)

'Austerity' is now a term and an experience that many people in the UK are more familiar with than before. Where once applied to times gone by, entrenched in social memories of post-war conditions, it has become a commonplace identifier for contemporary UK society and

S. M. Hall, *Everyday Life in Austerity*, Palgrave Macmillan Studies in Family and Intimate Life, https://doi.org/10.1007/978-3-030-17094-3_1

economy. In its most stripped-down form, austerity refers to a specific set of actions and policies by the state: the reduction of spending on public expenditure with the precise aim of reducing governmental budget deficit. However, and importantly, it has a dual meaning. 'Austerity' is also a term to describe a condition of severe simplicity and self-restraint. As the above quotes from two of my participants suggest, and the rest of this book will reveal in more detail, these two meanings of austerity play out in everyday life, cutting across one another as much as they do across and between spaces, times and relationships.

These two quotes also offer an insight into the relational approach I take in this book. Laura and Zoe, who we meet again in later chapters, both situate their experiences alongside those of other people they know, in the particular and familiar context of their everyday lives. In this way, this book marks a departure from many previous writings on austerity, centring on lived, felt and personal impacts of austerity as they are encountered in everyday life. It responds to the critiques about the dominance of political and economic accounts in research about contemporary austerity, while at the same time offering alternative ways for theorising, researching and understanding lived experiences in austere times. It does this in three interrelated ways.

Firstly, I conceptualise austerity as a personal and relational condition. I argue that approaching austerity as a personal and social, as much as an economic and political, condition means that lived experiences and social inequalities can come to the fore. Here austerity is reframed and scaled according to everyday relationships and practices, taken from the ground up. Seeing austerity as personal does not preclude economic or political concerns; rather it shifts how these are named and framed. Subverting the usual voices and experiences upon which discourses of austerity are built, and ultimately how they are valued, makes space for acknowledging those people and communities at the sharpest end of austerity cuts. Furthermore, acknowledging austerity as a personal condition—rather than simply an ideology or inevitability—gives credence to the fact that it has very real and tangible impacts: *a condition of severe simplicity and self-restraint.* Austerity then also becomes a form of conditioning (also see Hitchen 2016), shaping ideals, futures and horizons, with the potential to change family, friend and intimate relations, presenting opportunities as well as obstacles.

Secondly, the book centres around feminist theories, methods and praxis, applying them to everyday life in austerity in new and innovative ways. Ideas around personal lives, family, intimacy, friendship and relationality have long been fruitful spaces for feminist thought and interventions. Drawing from feminist theories regarding gendered labour and responsibilities, critiques of 'the family', social infrastructures, politics and ethics of care, and ethnographic practice, I apply and develop these concepts accordingly. Situating feminist theories of personal relationships in conversation with geographical writings about austerity also means that economic, social and cultural theories are brought together in new ways.

Thirdly, by offering fresh ways of theorising everyday life through relationality, this book provides an alternative entry point into everyday understandings of austerity. I argue that not only do we need to understand austerity as a phenomenon played out and experienced in everyday life, but that there are specific aspects of everyday life that are important to understanding austerity's effects. Austerity is more than a backdrop to the everyday lives explored in this book. Rather than being simply context, austerity becomes entwined within everyday lives and the relationships in which everyday lives are grounded.

This book therefore makes the case for thinking relationally about austerity, and of bringing together spatial and social theory as a cross-disciplinary approach. Focusing on everyday relationships and relational spaces—multiscalar and cross-spatial understandings of family, friendship and intimate relations—provides exciting opportunities for geographical approaches to everyday life in austerity. Using examples from across ethnographic research, I demonstrate how a relational approach extends current understandings of how austerity cuts through, across and between everyday spaces.

Austerity in the UK

Contemporary austerity in the UK is a particularly interesting case, inextricable from the Global Financial Crisis (GFC) and the period from 2010 onwards. When the crisis hit in 2008 (the result of a subprime mortgage crisis in the USA, based on a culture of risky lending on mortgages by banks) the impacts were felt in the financial, housing and retail sectors as much as in homes, communities and workplaces. Triggered by a 'credit crunch' and global economic recession, the UK economy officially entered into a recession that started in early 2008 and ended in late 2009. The damage unleashed by the recession on the national economy, such as unemployment, firm closures and reduced tax revenue, was adopted by the Conservative-Liberal Democrat coalition government as a justification to implement their austerity agenda, with the ostensible purpose of restabilising state finances.

Fiscal cuts to public expenditure to the tune of £83 billion were announced by the Chancellor of the Exchequer in the June 2010 Emergency Budget. Measures included 'slashing local government budgets in England by 27 per cent, benefit caps, the removal of the spare room subsidy from housing benefit ("bedroom tax") and £8 billion of cuts to the social care budget' (Hall 2017, p. 303; also see Butterworth and Burton 2013; JRF 2015; Hall et al. 2017). In 2015, the Treasury announced a further £12 billion of cuts to social security spending to be applied by 2019/2020, including reducing caps on household benefits to £20,000 a year, limiting Child Tax Credits to two children, and removing housing benefit for young people aged 18–21 (Hall 2017; HM Treasury 2015).

In the UK as well as in the USA, Republic of Ireland and parts of southern Europe, austerity remains as an economic and political condition as well as an ideology. Austerity is not a fiscal inevitability. It is a political choice and economic agenda that can have deep and long-lasting personal and social consequences. And although the personal effects of living in austerity have been skirted in most political discourse, personal responsibility was actually key to crafting the political argument for austerity following the recent recession.

More specifically, the response to the recession was named and framed as a result of the interconnections between a growing culture of personal credit reliance and government over-borrowing. Though it makes for an imprecise and misleading metaphor, individual/household and state debt became quickly conflated in political discourse on the Global Financial Crisis and recession, entangling credit users with austerity policies and creating a 'framing [that] suggests culpability on the part of those affected' (Elwood and Lawson 2013, p. 103). The UK public 'were situated as being doubly responsible; simultaneously blamed for a culture of debt, borrowing and spending on credit, while at the same time urged to consume to lift the economy out of crisis' (Hall 2015, p. 141; Hinton and Goodman 2010).

However, the impacts of austerity go beyond political and public discourse; they are real, and felt, and lived. Austerity exposes, exacerbates and exploits socio-economic unevenness. In targeting public institutions, social welfare and care infrastructures (sectors dominated by female labour and receivership), austerity is also a distinctly *gendered* ideology, process and condition. Put simply, 'women have been disproportionately affected by these cuts as a result of structural inequalities which means they earn less, own less and have more responsibility for unpaid care and domestic work' (Hall et al. 2017, p. 1; also see Charles 2000). Women are also the key beneficiaries of state welfare (also referred to as benefits or social security) and, as illustrated by Fig. 1.1, changes to these systems can lead to various gendered inequalities. Further social and structural inequalities are highlighted and aggravated by austerity, including but not limited to class, race, ethnicity, disability, sexuality, age and faith, and the points at which they intersect. In this book I touch upon some of these concerns, with focus on gender as the fulcrum upon which the social differences and inequalities in my study pivot.

In spite of the social and spatial significance of austerity, much geographical and wider social science literature continues to be heavily focused on austerity as economic, financial, political and urban. Furthermore, this analysis is commonly levelled on institutional, national, regional and international scales. Such work offers critical insight into analysing and debating the causes and aftermath of the Global Financial Crisis and recession, particularly problems of broader economic systems,

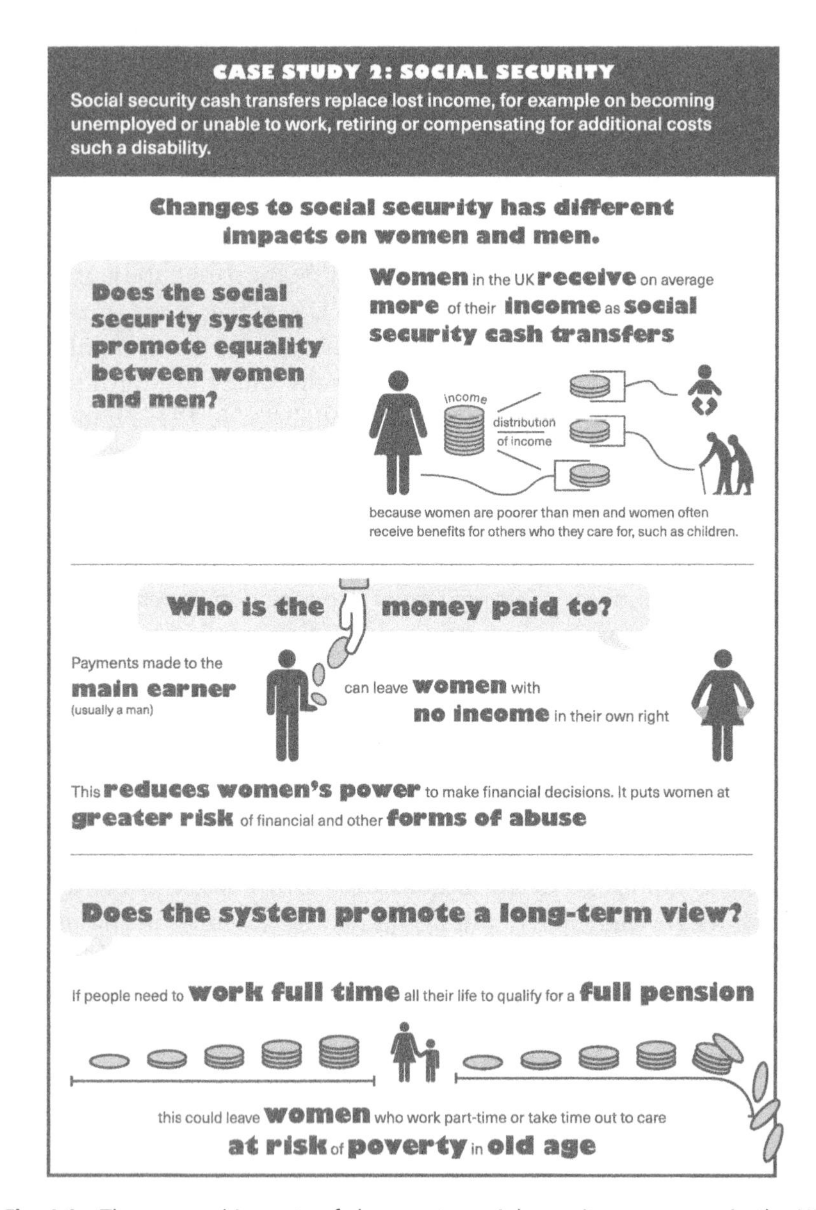

Fig. 1.1 The unequal impacts of changes to social security on women in the UK (from *Women Count* (2018) by the Women's Budget Group, see https://women-count.wbg.org.uk/)

their governance and organisation, and how austerity policies play out in global markets and city politics. I expand upon this in further detail in Chap. 2. Suffice to say there are important contributions to be made pertaining to the everyday impacts of the economic downturn and subsequent period of austerity in the UK. I now explain the importance of a focus on everyday life, and the influential ideas and literatures that have shaped my own approach to the everyday.

Everyday Life

The everyday is an interdisciplinary endeavour—crossing geography, sociology, anthropology, philosophy and further—and it falls in and out of favour and fashion quite readily. Writers on the everyday argue that everyday life is a space of possibility, comprised as much by material environments as political encounters. While without a specific disciplinary home, contemporary writings on everyday life often cite one of two authors, which for many reading this book will likely have already sprung to mind.

First is the French Marxist philosopher and social theorist Henri Lefebvre, author of the classic *Critique of Everyday Life* (1991 [1947]). He argued that *la quotidienne* is characterised by routine, repetition and regularity, punctuated by occasional breaks that made tasks bearable. Drawing upon the example of capitalist workplaces (e.g. factories, workhouses), he saw everyday life here as structured by cyclical rhythms—starting times, scheduled breaks, clocking off—which had the effect of alienating people from the true condition of their existence. As Hemmings et al. (2002, p. 272) explain,

> The democratic and industrial revolutions of the eighteenth and nineteenth centuries gave rise to an increasing concern with the ordering of ordinary people's everyday lives, not just as citizens and workers, but also with regard to aspects of their private or domestic lives.

Framing his critique around classed labour, Lefebvre conceptualised everyday life as inherently temporal, regulated by space-time, habitual living day by day. That it is neither a benign nor a residual category, but an important realm to study in its own right (Scott 2009).

Secondly, Michel de Certeau, also a French philosopher and social theorist, placed his focus instead on the significance of how people 'do' or 'practice' everyday life (see de Certeau 1984). While this might mean following certain norms, rules, laws and traditions, he argued that everyday life can nevertheless also be understood as tactical resistance to the strategies of the powerful—tactics that are creative, adaptive, defiant. He argued that individuals can subvert authority by breaking minor rules, or what he called 'making do'. Both Lefebvre and de Certeau's theorisations of the everyday have featured heavily in geographical writings, from research on urban walking (see Bridge 1997) to informal economies in post-Soviet societies (see Round et al. 2008). Both theorists certainly shaped my own early academic understandings of and readings about everyday life.

However it was upon reading Cindi Katz's essay on 'Major/Minor' theory that I started to question my own gravitation towards the work of two relatively privileged, white, male, European scholars. Katz (1996, p. 166) makes the following observation, which in many ways still remains true of much academic scholarship today. That our

> sights are trained sharply and astutely on what I will clumsily call meta-theorists of great accomplishment (I would rather call them "big boys" though they are not all necessarily men). They are "major" theorists because they define and excel at a mode of inquiry that remains dominant in the academy and that is quite tightly bounded.

More recent interventions, such as by Sara Ahmed, likewise critique well-worn exclusionary citational practices. Citations, she explains, are

> academic bricks through which we create houses. When citational practices become habits, bricks form walls. I think as feminists we can hope to create a crisis around citation, even just a hesitation, a wondering, that might help us not to follow the well-trodden citational paths. (Ahmed 2017, p. 148)

In light of these important and insightful critiques, and in response to the overwhelming dominance of particular philosophers ('big boys') and their ideas about the everyday, I now outline how I came to craft theories of everyday life by instead engaging with the work of feminist scholars and activists.

Crafting Feminist Theories of Everyday Life

The significance of the everyday is in the fabric of feminist writings, in part, I think, because of who and what feminist theory credits and values. By and large, adopting a feminist approach is about seeing the world through a lens focused on acknowledging and recognising social difference. This includes but is not limited to gender, and how social differences are ingrained in both micro and macro scales of economy, politics and culture. This involves paying attention as much to embodiment, corporeality and self-positioning, as to structural inequalities in law, trade or institutions. Moreover, a feminist approach often involves thoughtful methodologies and considered empirical approaches to collecting data that acknowledge and try to address power relations and social locations, giving rise to marginalised voices and experiences (e.g. Oakley 1981; Stacey 1988).

Indeed, this is a point Katz (1996, p. 166) also makes in her reckoning of 'big boy' theories, whereby a refocused approach

> could sight a new terrain of figures, hitherto spectral, who produce theory that is deliberately and decidedly not "big boy" theory. These scholars produce theory that is interstitial with empirical research and social location, that self-reflexively interpolates the theories and practices of everyday historical subjects—including, but not restricted to, scholars. This is not "master theory" so much as it is "minor theory".

She also acknowledges the power of bringing together theory and experience, academic and subject knowledges, and breaking down the divisions between. This is also about crafting theory; seeing theory not as top down ('master') but ground up ('minor'), as emerging from (rather than applied to) the world. This is where my understandings of everyday life are also situated. I place combinations of theory into conversation, with one another and with empirical material, to synthesise, create and weave theories of everyday life. This involves bringing together the work of feminist, social and economic scholars from across disciplinary perspectives. Indeed, the mechanisms of crafting theory in this way are also calibrated to a feminist approach of appreciating difference.

In this book I draw upon and thread together lots of different and variously sourced feminist approaches to the everyday, including gendered politics and ethics of care (Hanisch 1970; Held 1993; Tronto 1993), critiques of the family as an institution (Beck and Beck-Gernsheim 2002; Stacey 1990), intimacy and corporeality (Twigg 2006; Zelizer 2005), social infrastructures and social reproduction (Charles 2000; Pearson and Elson 2015), and feminist methods and praxis (England 1994; Roberts 1981). Wherever possible, I also moderate my use of language, citational benchmarks and assumptions about the world. I make efforts not to reproduce typically (and often unconsciously) gendered, classed and racialised norms within my writing and analysis, such as considering an author's work to be 'central' rather than 'seminal'. And rather than veer towards metaphors like networks or assemblages, where possible I employ everyday gendered phraseologies like crafting, weaving and tapestries, to try and decentre long-standing masculine geographical norms.

However, underpinning all of this is a sense of the personal and relational. I approach the everyday—and everyday life in austerity—as a relational project, where identities, spaces and experiences are formed through interactions with others (Massey 2004). These interactions are everyday relationships, intimacies and social encounters. As I explore further in Chap. 2, one way to think about this is through the relationship between family, friends and intimate relations: that is to say, core, significant everyday social relationships. Moreover, a relational approach is also a political one; it recognises difference and between-ness of people, places and practices. Everyday life in austerity, as I now go on to discuss, is characterised by difference and unevenness, where a relational approach helps shed light on the differences between what it means to live *in* and live *with* austerity.

Living in and Living with Austerity

The lived experience of austerity, like all elements of social life, is characterised by difference. Austerity impacts on individuals, families and communities in different ways, at different times and at different magnitudes. Doing social research in this context may therefore involve people living in and through a period of economic austerity, but with subtle or stark variations in their experiences. It includes those already living in or close to poverty and hardship, those witnessing family and friends struggle and offering their support, and those largely insulated from the consequences. This means that living in austerity—in a time of deep social, political and economic change—is not necessarily the same as *living with* austerity, that is, bearing the everyday brunt of the impacts of austerity policies. This is an important distinction to make, as it affects how people relate to austerity, the place it has in their lives, and how it can impact on their social relationships. I'll give an example to illustrate.

Barbara is a woman in her early 60s living with her husband and carer, Chris. They live together in a council-owned house, where they raised their children. Barbara receives disability allowance, after having a stroke some ten years before, though for most of her adult life she has been financially supported by state welfare. In 2013 a policy is introduced where the government cut housing benefit allowance for households deemed to be living beyond their spatial requirements. Barbara and Chris have two rooms 'too many'; under this policy as a couple they should be sharing one bedroom, but they live in a three-bedroom house. Sometimes they need to sleep in separate rooms because of Barbara's health conditions. And one of the 'spare' bedrooms has a lift going through it so Barbara can get upstairs, but the council say it is still a 'working' bedroom. So they face a choice: lose a quarter of their housing benefit and have to make up the difference using their other benefits payments, or move house. They already struggle for money and since neither of them is able to earn extra or work, they have little option but to move.

Out of the blue Chris becomes very sick and, shortly after being hospitalised, he passes away. Barbara is devastated, as are their children, family and friends. Barbara has lost her life partner, her best friend and her carer. Now she will also lose her home, because she cannot pay the extra for the two 'spare' bedrooms on her own. A bungalow became available shortly before Chris' passing, and they had agreed to move into it. But now moving does not feel like such a great prospect, because the new house is relatively far away from her friends and family on whom she has been reliant recently. Moreover, the moving date given to her by the council falls in the same week as Chris' funeral, with a very narrow window of time to pack. Barbara can't change the date without being charged extra to stay in the old house, and she cannot stay at the old house indefinitely because that would require paying for the extra for the two 'spare' bedrooms on her own. So her close family rally around, helping her pack up, cleaning her current home, clean the new home, moving in and making it feel like home. Her first night in the new bungalow is the night of Chris' funeral. This is a really frantic time, and one of Barbara's sisters, Susan, is very involved with the physical parts of the house move, as well as comforting her sister for her loss and trying to steady her nerves about living alone in a new part of town. Susan has children herself, and while they are not physically present to help with the house move, they are at the other end of the phone listening, comforting, advising their mum as she supports her sister.

In this example the personal and relational are interwoven, and it is difficult to extract individual stories and experiences because they are jumbled together in a knot of emotion, response and circumstance. Inter- and intra-generational relations, gendered care responsibilities and life-course trajectories are all tangled together. There are also relational geographies at work, of extended kinships, affective connections, proximities and propinquities. The impacts of austerity are being felt in a range of ways—for some more sharply, while for others they are moderated—though always situated within everyday relationships. Barbara and her late husband Chris felt the implementation of the policy to reduce cuts to welfare most acutely. It impacted on their financial circumstances, living arrangements and intimate co-habitational practices. But these effects also ricocheted off to affect family and friends, who also turn to their loved ones for care and support.

This example forefronts the personal and relational lens that I apply throughout this book in another way, too. The names are changed, and the example is not taken from my ethnographic research but from my own personal life. I am one of Susan's children, and it was in witnessing this very situation from the sidelines that I started to think relationally about austerity in everyday life, and everyday life in austerity.

In addition, the example also highlights the interconnectedness of personal and social conditions of austerity. For some, the realities of austerity are intrinsically connected to experiences of poverty, precarity and insecurity, disproportionately impacting on those already struggling (also see Jupp 2013b; JRF 2015). Austerity policies can therefore intensify already-existing hardships, particularly for those living in and around poverty. Public spending cuts have been levelled at welfare and social care, meaning vulnerable people, families and communities are doubly hit, by the continuation and acceleration of difficult personal and social conditions, or what Harrison (2013, p. 105) terms 'more of the same'. Likewise austerity can lead to precarity and poverty, whether because of the lack of job security, threats to social and housing benefits, or cuts in mental health services and social care. Austerity policies can therefore be both a cause and a catalyst for hardship and deprivation. But it is important not to synonymise austerity with these different concepts. Although they can coexist, overlap and intersect, they are not always coupled.

For it is possible to be impacted by austerity but not necessarily be (or define oneself as) living in poverty or a personal condition of austerity. It is also possible to be living in poverty, or a personal condition of austerity, during a period of economic prosperity. So while the term 'austerity' can also refer to a personal condition of severe simplicity, there is no generalised personal condition of austerity. Austerity as a socio-economic condition can, however, be a point of relationality, commonality and mutuality: something that many people may be living in (i.e. living in times of austerity policies) but not living with (i.e. they are not hit by austerity cuts). With this book I wish to explore these personal and social similarities and differences, to tease out the lived experiences of austerity by forefronting the voices and lives of those impacted.

How and by whom are austerity policies felt on the ground?
How might everyday relationships be subject to change or continuity in times of austerity?

How does austerity impact on personal and shared experiences in the present, and the lives people imagine themselves leading?

These are the questions that shape the research study and chosen methodologies, and which I address throughout this book.

Researching Everyday Life in Austerity: An Ethnographic Approach

An academic interest in the impact austerity makes on people's everyday lives, how it is lived in and lived with, also leads to particular methodological approaches. Ethnographic research has a long history of gathering in-depth personal, relational and experiential data concerning socially significant issues. For Susie Scott (2009, p. 193), 'the most obvious way of understanding somebody else's everyday life is to go to their locale and experience it directly'. Ethnography is a 'personal and intimate interaction' (Hall 2009, p. 264) in which the researcher enters the social and cultural worlds of others, developing 'ongoing relations' with participants (Emerson et al. 1995, p. 1). A rich literature claims the importance of 'being in' the lives of research subjects in order to understand change and continuity. Ethnography therefore 'emphasises the experiential' (Stacey 1988, p. 22), and the role of the ethnographer is to explore 'the tissue of everyday life' in 'fine grained detail' (Herbert 2000, p. 551).

Initially developed within anthropology, gaining increased credibility within sociology, human geography and cultural studies, ethnography is a widely used, accepted and regarded methodological approach within the social sciences today. While a traditional reliance on observational methods remains, particularly participant observation, ethnographic studies typically also include combinations of interviewing, conversations, sketches, photographs, archival material, videos and more (Davies 2008; Herbert 2000). This extended toolkit of methods makes ethnography particularly appealing to social researchers, a way to comprehend the complexity of the everyday and gather various forms of data to do so. In particular, when combined these methods move beyond recollected spoken accounts, examining the tensions between narrative and practice. Often attributed to the anthropologist Margaret Mead, the use of multiple techniques helps unveil inconsistencies in how 'what people say, what people do, and what they say they do are entirely different things'.

An ethnographic approach is also conducive to the positionings and assumptions I have already set out in this introduction. My ontological approach, what 'the social world consists of' (Scott 2009, p. 184), is shaped by the personal and relational, centring social connections as the basis for understanding the everyday. And my epistemological stance, what 'counts as valid knowledge' (ibid.), is deeply rooted in experience, giving voice to and acknowledging lived truths as told by those affected by austerity in various ways. Using ethnography to explore everyday social relations is therefore also a political statement that personal stories of austerity matter, as valued and valid knowledge. Ethnography also enables insight into everyday life over time, to bear witness to lives as they are lived, as well as allowing for rapport and relationships to form.

My ethnographic approach is further shaped by engagement with the writings of feminist researchers who question the ethics of power and positionality within the research process. Such authors make a strong case for valuing empathy, care and compassion within qualitative enquiry (England 1994; Stacey 1988). What might better be called 'critical feminist praxis', such authors work from unquestioned assumptions about who and what ethnography involves. This has the effect of destabilising taken-for-granted ways of doing ethnographic research and the power relations exposed therein. For instance, Judith Stacey (1988, p. 21) famously questioned whether there can ever be a feminist ethnography, when at the essence of ethnographic research are 'exploitation, betrayal, and abandonment by the researcher'. She goes on to argue that

> while there cannot be a fully feminist ethnography, there can be (indeed there are) ethnographies that are partially feminist, accounts of culture enhanced by the application of feminist perspectives. There also can and should be feminist research that is rigorously self-aware and therefore humble about the partiality of its ethnographic vision and its capacity to represent self and other. (Stacey 1988, p. 26)

Ann Oakley (1981, p. 38) similarly described the process of interviewing women as a 'contradiction in terms', whereby 'objectivity, detachment, hierarchy', positivist and masculine traits once revered in social research do not account for when participants ask questions back. These critical reflections on the very bricks and mortar of ethnographic enquiry have significantly altered empirical practice today, whereby social location, positionality and reflexivity are considered core elements of high-quality ethnographic research.

Other important shifts and innovations include the move to ethnographies 'at home', which likewise have strongly influenced my own ethnographic practice. In the late 1980s, within the discipline of anthropology a debate erupted about the legitimacy of ethnography closer to 'home' (see Jackson 1987). Traditional anthropological study rested on the assumption that cultural, if not geographical, distance was a requirement in ethnographic research of cultural worlds, and therefore researching one's own culture was not a justifiable ethnographic practice (Jenkins 1984). However, some scholars were making the case that while ethnography 'at home' entails studying a culture with which one is already acquainted, with access to shared languages and sources of information (Davies 2008), 'the exotic might only be five miles away' (Jackson 1987, p. 8).

Here, and in previous work, I have referred to my own ethnographies 'at home' as 'ethnographies on my doorstep' (see Hall 2014). Doorstep ethnographies add an unusual ingredient to traditional ethnography, because the researcher does not leave the field in ways typical of early anthropological work. Nor are they always entirely unfamiliar with the culture of the group with whom they research. The ethnographic fieldwork described in this book was carried out close to where I live and work, hence 'on my doorstep'. The result of this, I argue, is a more nuanced understanding of reflexivity in research praxis, encouraging researchers to confront their responsibilities around confidentiality and disengagement, though it also potentially presents additional ethical complications (see Hall 2014). It also complements the personal and relational focus of the research, with my emplacement 'in', if not 'with', everyday life in austerity for my participants.

In addition, research by family sociologists provides an important base for my own 'family ethnographies' approach. Where traditional ethnographies typically focused on communities or groups, with the work of Bott (1957), Young and Willmott (1957), Stacey (1990) and Edwards (2000), to name but a few, came an approach centred on kinship relations. For 'while ethnographers regularly encounter families, the focus has for the most part been on the communities to which families belong [...] consequently, discussions around the ethical and methodological challenges of doing ethnography with families continue to be limited' (Hall 2014, p. 2177). I have often wondered if one of the reasons for an increased demand for family ethnographies (e.g. see Valentine 2008a; Valentine et al. 2012) is that they are notoriously difficult to develop and maintain. Because while an ethnographer may become part of a community, such as a social club, workplace or hobbyist organisation, 'it is nearly impossible to become a member of a family' (Hall 2014 p. 2177). That said, family ethnographies offer incredible possibilities for empirical articulations of social relations that might be overlooked when the primary focus of research is placed on specific spaces, locations or other types of social gathering. With this in mind, I now describe the ethnographic research that forms the basis of this book.

Ethnography in Argleton, Greater Manchester

Choosing where to carry out an ethnography about austerity in everyday life was shaped by a few different factors. Social and economic differences were important to consider, given the unevenness of austerity, so a range of income distributions, class dynamics, ethnic and racial diversity, and a generational spread were necessary. Communities where austerity had made an impact were also of interest, and this was particularly pronounced in the north of England, where by 2017 cuts to public spending amounted to £696 billion in real terms since 2012, compared to growth by £7 billion in the south (see Rhodes 2017).

Greater Manchester was chosen as the site for this research, as a large and diverse urban area that has experienced significant austerity cuts: 'between 2010–2017 cuts of up to £2 billion have been made to local government and over £1 billion of social benefit income is being made annually as a result of welfare reforms' (Etherington and Jones 2017, p. 5). Like other conurbations in England, Greater Manchester is characterised by areas of extreme poverty as well as extreme wealth, sometimes in very close proximity. Greater Manchester was also selected by the UK government as the trial location for Universal Credit—an overhaul in how social security and benefit payments are distributed to citizens, intertwined with prevailing conservative politics of austerity and in particular severe cuts to welfare (Hall 2017).

At the same time, I was acutely aware that certain parts of Greater Manchester had been saturated by social researchers in recent years, something that became clear to me from conversations with local communities and activists well before my research began. I wanted to balance my desire to go somewhere 'ordinary', somewhere that was as typical of Greater Manchester as I could find, while at the same time remaining realistic and grounded in the knowledge that the point of ethnographic research is not to generalise. It is not to develop all-encompassing, oversimplified, widely applicable findings, but to understand intricacies, nuances and depths.

Ethnographic research is also difficult to carry out. It requires dedication, concentration, and emotional, mental and physical energy. There is also a certain power and privilege to doing this type of fieldwork—the resources and time to become immersed in a far-away community, which are not available to all scholars. Doing research close to where I lived and worked, on my doorstep in Greater Manchester, certainly meant that I was able to complete the ethnography to its fullest potential with the financial resources available to me, while also attending to my own personal and relational care responsibilities. The spatial dynamics of such research does mean that the everyday spaces of researchers and respondents can intersect. Sometimes I bumped into participants on the bus or when I was out shopping. Researching one's culture means that the researcher is in some ways already immersed in the field (Reed-Danahay 2009).

The research took place in the town of 'Argleton', Greater Manchester, from September 2013 to October 2015. I apply a pseudonym to the town here, as I do for all participants from the research, to preserve the confidentiality of their personal lives. Argleton is a town of average socio-economic status in terms of home ownership and renting, markers of wealth and impoverishment, and ethnic and racial diversity, when compared to national statistics. It contains pockets of affluence and economic comfort, disadvantage and precarity. Local residents commonly describe the town as being 'cut in half' by a main road, making a 'posh' part (with larger houses, cars on the drive and leafier surroundings) and a 'rough' part (with smaller, terraced housing, and litter on the streets from rows of fast-food outlets). Participants and their wider social networks were strewn across both parts of the 'divide', albeit a divide that held some ground both in the descriptive elements of my field diary entries and in the focus of austerity cuts to community services (typically on the 'rough' half). Each of these descriptions also served as a byword for simmering class tensions within Argleton, a form of place-making and people-placing. However, to reproduce these in my descriptions of participants as characteristics or geographical markers would only serve to reify such representations, when in reality their everyday experiences were far more complex.

The two years of ethnographic research within Argleton focused around the community and in particular six families, given the focus of my study on social relations. These families (defined as two or more people living together who regard themselves as 'family') were approached through community-based gatekeepers and by attending local activities, such as playgroups, coffee mornings, advice centres, exercise classes, social housing community get-togethers and reading groups—anything that would enable me to meet people living nearby. These spaces remained a key part of the ethnography, and over the two years I became a regular face in and around the town.

The six families were varied in their socio-economic backgrounds. Some were reliant on social security and welfare. Some worked cash-in-hand, some worked full-, fixed- or part-time hours, and some were retired. There was also a range of different familial compositions: unmarried heterosexual couples, families with and without children, and lone-parent families. They were all self-selecting, and took part in the research for between eight and fifteen months. When recruiting I suggested a participation timeframe of around one year, and this varied depending upon personal and relational circumstances. Although not all families or family members felt themselves to be personally impacted by current austerity measures, all described living 'in it' as a social condition: knowing kith and kin who have been affected, or had themselves experienced previous hardships that informed their understandings. This will be expanded upon in later chapters. As is usual in ethnography, participants were not paid to take part in the research. Gratitude was instead expressed through small offerings such as a pint of milk, a packet of biscuits or the bus fare to town covered—'neither a grand nor costly gesture, [which] can be easily absorbed without the obligation to reciprocate' (Hall 2017, p. 306). I address this further in Chap. 5 when discussing the politics of presence.

Methodologically, the focus was on participant observation, spending time with families in their everyday lives and doing the things they would normally do day to day. This worked out as anything between a few hours and a whole day at a time, and although I asked participants not to change their plans or patterns, they inevitably did, even in small ways. As a result I participated in and observed a whole array of everyday practices with various combinations of family members. This included doing the school run, cooking and preparing food, eating meals together, supermarket shopping, playing in the park, cleaning and tidying, family outings or helping run a coffee morning. Sometimes it was just a case of having a cup of tea and a chat, or sitting together in silence watching television—perhaps the ultimate sign of familiarity. Where possible, like Stacey (1990, p. 32), I also 'responded with some spontaneity to invitations, crises, and other ethnographic "opportunities"'. Getting to know participants over time, gaining and sustaining familiarity of personalities and performances, seeing and hearing contradictions and equivocations also helped to break down presentations of self and family relations.

As well as accompanying and observing participants, some of our discussions were also taped. These were a combination of single and group interviews, on a range of topics, and families took part in between two and five of these across the ethnography. Referring to them as discussions rather than interviews is more representative of how they took place, because they were often for clarification purposes based on something I had observed or been mulling over, or about which we had already had a brief discussion. These conversations therefore allowed for more in-depth dialogue about participants' interpersonal relationships, including personal and shared experiences of austerity.

Participatory tasks also formed part of the ethnography, including photograph elicitation. Participants were given a disposable camera (although they often used their own mobile phone cameras instead) to take pictures 'of anything that you think will give me a better idea of how you get by day to day'. The task was deliberately left open to interpretation, to elicit different types of data forms and conversations about the photographs. The films or files were collected from participants, then photographs were printed as hard copies and taken along to the next visit. Talking through the photographs in a taped discussion prompted participants to show, describe and reflect upon their own everyday lives. Some of these photographs are reproduced in this book. Anchored by observations but supported by taped discussions, photographs and collected materials, this research is therefore largely typical of long-term ethnographies that draw 'on a wide range of sources of information' (Hammersley and Atkinson 1983, p. 2). Consent to participate, including the various activities and methodologies, was an ongoing and openly negotiable process.

The research also adopts a light auto-ethnographic perspective in that my observations were also about 'doing ethnography in [my] own society' (Reed-Danahay 2009, p. 30), in which one's social location is central (Lumsden 2009). Being a young female researcher from a working-class background (with a distinctly Northern English accent) and having family and friends deeply impacted by austerity certainly shaped my place in the lives of participants. This is not the focus of my research per se, but to ignore the role of the researcher in intimate ethnographic encounters would be an oversight and would present a disingenuous view of the research.

Contents of the Book

With a focus on the everyday personal and relational impacts of austerity, this book works towards developing new theoretical perspectives using rich empirical accounts. The next chapter explains the conceptual framework I use for thinking geographically about 'everyday austerity'. I illustrate that despite decades of research from sociologists, human geographers and feminist economists on previous economic crises, recessions and austerity, because of the scale and focus in such work (leaning more often towards financial, economic and urban analysis) very little is known about the social impacts of the economic downturn and subsequent period of austerity *on* and *in* everyday life.

In this chapter I identify how such an understanding might be established and expanded. In particular, a relational geographical approach is outlined. This accounts for the impact that contemporary conditions of austerity—as both a personal and a societal condition—might have on personal relationships, ordinary practices and imaginaries of the future. Using examples of care and support and mundane mobilities, peppered with empirical examples, I argue that focusing our attentions on significant social relationships, and the relational spaces of austerity—that is, geographies of family, friendship and intimate relations—provides new ways of thinking about everyday austerities.

Taking forward this framework, in Chap. 3 I provide a more detailed introduction to the six families from Argleton, weaving together current literatures and empirical material. By thinking about care as an everyday, relational practice this chapter considers the everyday social infrastructures required to sustain people and society in austere times. The metaphor of the 'tapestry' is also employed—intricate hand-woven designs with visible as well as hidden threads.

The chapter draws on feminist theories of social infrastructures largely developed within political literatures, and brings these together with work on the politics and ethics of care, and body-work. Using empirical findings I offer a critique of how we think about and enact care in everyday life—particularly in the context of a retreating, austere state. I illustrate that family, friends and intimate others form entanglements of inter- and intra-generational exchanges. These infrastructures are open to change with time and circumstances, and different aspects of care are sought from various combinations of family, friends and intimate relations. This care can be formal or informal, paid or unpaid, regular or one-off.

Chapter 4 then shifts in focus to explore intimacies between and beyond kith and kin in austere times. Mindful of feminist critiques of the family as an institution and arguments of a move towards individualisation, I build upon this work by arguing that we must also not romanticise friendships or acquaintanceships, and that intimacy in everyday life can take many shapes. Taking the conceptual framework outlined in Chap. 2, here I tease apart how intimacy is formed, galvanised or disrupted in austere conditions. Intimate relationships between and beyond family and friends emerged with the empirical research as important forms of emotional and sometimes embodied support and care.

A whole range of 'intimate others' make up the tapestry of everyday social lives, such as staff at the local store, regular faces at a coffee morning, cleaners, nannies, families nannied for, social workers, nursery staff, hairdressers, masseuses and so on. While not all, many of these relationships involve some kind of exchange of money, and many also involve intimate practice, and close corporeality. They might also intersect and blur with kith and kin networks. However, access to or affordability of some of these relations, or the services/organisations/communities through which they are mediated, can be limited as a result of austerity. These intimate relationships can also have very different characteristics and origins; from monetary, to momentary, to more-than-human, and material. But what binds them together is that they sit outside of what are typically considered the realm of intimate relations, and it is a focus on the condition of austerity that brings them to light.

In Chap. 5 I draw upon writings by feminist scholars and activists to explore the everyday politics of austerity. Using ideas of the personal as political, I develop connections to burgeoning literature on quiet politics and activisms, applying them to the personal and political consequences of austerity. The everyday geographies of austerity, I show, are also distinctly relational, because austerity remains a socially uneven process and condition, and this unevenness follows into everyday politics, too.

With empirical examples from my time with families and communities in Argleton, I show how a smile, a nod, a mutter of encouragement or a conversation over a counter is an important political moment. These quiet, subtle and implicit activisms are instantiations of the everyday politics of austerity. Mundane niceties and micro-aggressions form the basis of social relations in austerity, and are just as important as disruptive and noisy political performances. Quieter moments of life in austerity should therefore not be dismissed as trivial, but as reminders that the personal is political.

Chapter 6 builds upon the notion of austerity as a personal condition, and extends this to concepts of crises. Drawing also on research in the social sciences regarding the lifecourse and personal lives, the chapter explores how austerity is couched within everyday life; that it does not sit aside from personal matters, but becomes knotted within. We might understand lived experiences of austerity as moments of crises and conjuncture, which can significantly alter an individual's lifecourse trajectory—and of those around them. Moments of crisis, such as austerity, can be revealing of fragilities within familial and personal relations.

Participants frequently described the effects of living in austerity as disruptions in their lifecourse. They reported strong feeling that their life was going 'off course', that they were being taken off a path they were once travelling down. This can lead to uncertainty about the future and feelings of a very personal crisis. In addition, the personal effects of austerity are compounded in that they can take place at the same time as other significant life events and personal circumstances. Crises are therefore important for not only how they feel but also what they represent, and participants discuss these moments of personal and familial crisis as something that they reflect upon, for their relational qualities.

Closing the book, in Chap. 7 I draw together the arguments contained, providing a summative and speculative conclusion. Firstly, noting the ever-shifting socio-political-economic climate, which undoubtedly will have changed since the writing of this book began, I offer suggestions for taking forward work on everyday austerity. Playing with the claim that austerity is 'over', and building from findings in Chap. 6, I propose that prospective research adopt long-term, lifecourse and futures-based approaches. Despite the claims, austerity does not seem to be going away any time soon, and the effects on people's lives in the longer term should be documented for future scholarship. Relational spaces of everyday life—the substance of social relationships, and the spaces that they themselves create—can provide deep insight into ways and means of getting by in crisis-stricken times. An austere economic climate is not 'out there', but deeply affects academic research. I make a plea for social scientists not to abandon long-term, ethnographic, in-depth research, as I fear they might, in favour of more frugal or supposedly efficient methods. There is much to be gained by an ethnographic and longitudinal approach to unveil the lived experience of austerity in the contemporary age.

Bibliography

Ahmed, S. (2017). *Living a Feminist Life*. Croydon: Duke University Press.

Beck, U., & Beck-Gernsheim, E. (2002). *Individualization*. London: Sage.

Bott, E. (1957). *Family and Social Network: Roles, Norms, and External Relationships in Ordinary Urban Families*. London: Tavistock Publications.

Bridge, G. (1997). Towards a Situated Universalism: On Strategic Rationality and "Local Theory". *Environment and Planning D: Society and Space, 15*, 633–639.

Butterworth, J., & Burton, J. (2013). Equality, Human Rights and the Public Service Spending Cuts: Do UK Welfare Cuts Violate the Equal Right to Social Security? *Equal Rights Review, 11*, 26–45.

Charles, N. (2000). *Feminism, the State and Social Policy*. Basingstoke: Palgrave.

Davies, C. A. (2008). *Reflexive Ethnography: A Guide to Researching Selves and Others*. London: Routledge.

de Certeau, M. (1984). *The Practice of Everyday Life*. Berkeley, CA: University of California Press.

Edwards, J. (2000). *Born and Bred: Idioms of Kinship and New Reproductive Technologies in England*. Oxford: Oxford University Press.

Elwood, S., & Lawson, V. (2013). Whose Crisis? Spatial Imaginaries of Class, Poverty, and Vulnerability. *Environment and Planning A, 45*, 103–108.

Emerson, R., Fretz, R., & Shaw, C. (1995). *Writing Ethnographic Fieldnotes*. Chicago, IL: University of Chicago Press.

England, K. V. L. (1994). Getting Personal: Reflexivity Positionality and Feminist Research. *The Professional Geographer, 46*, 80–89.

Etherington, D., & Jones, M. (2017) *Devolution, Austerity and Inclusive Growth in Greater Manchester: Assessing Impacts and Developing Alternatives*. Hendon: CEEDR, Middlesex University. Retrieved July 13, 2018, from www.mdx.ac.uk/__data/assets/pdf_file/0030/368373/Greater-Manchester-Report.pdf.

Hall, S. M. (2009). "Private Life" and "Work Life": Difficulties and Dilemmas When Making and Maintaining Friendships with Ethnographic Participants. *Area, 41*, 263–272.

Hall, S. M. (2014). Ethics of Ethnography with Families: A Geographical Perspective. *Environment and Planning A, 46*(9), 2175–2194.

Hall, S. M. (2015). Everyday Ethics of Consumption in the Austere City. *Geography Compass, 9*(3), 140–151.

Hall, S. M. (2017). Personal, Relational and Intimate Geographies of Austerity: Ethical and Empirical Considerations. *Area, 49*(3), 303–310.

Hall, S. M., McIntosh, K., Neitzert, E., Pottinger, L., Sandhu, K., Stephenson, M.-A., Reed, H., & Taylor, L. (2017). *Intersecting Inequalities: The Impact of Austerity on Black and Minority Ethnic Women in the UK*. London: Runnymede and Women's Budget Group. Retrieved from www.intersecting-inequalities.com.

Hammersley, M., & Atkinson, P. (1983). *Ethnography: Principles in Practice*. London: Routledge.

Hanisch, C. (1970). The Personal Is Political. In S. Firestone & Koedt (Eds.), *Notes from the Second Year* (pp. 76–78). New York: Published by Editors.

Harrison, E. (2013). Bouncing Back? Recession, Resilience and Everyday Lives. *Critical Social Policy, 33*(1), 97–113.

Held, V. (1993). *Feminist Morality: Transforming Culture, Society and Politics*. Chicago, IL: University of Chicago Press.

Hemmings, S., Silva, E., & Thompson, K. (2002). Accounting for the Everyday. In T. Bennett & D. Watson (Eds.), *Understanding Everyday Life* (pp. 271–315). Oxford: Blackwell Publishers.

Herbert, S. (2000). For Ethnography. *Progress in Human Geography, 24*, 550–568.

Hinton, E., & Goodman, M. (2010). Sustainable Consumption: Developments, Considerations and New Directions. In M. R. Redclift & G. Woodgate (Eds.), *The International Handbook of Environmental Sociology* (pp. 245–261). London: Edward Elgar.

Hitchen, E. (2016). Living and Feeling the Austere. *New Formations, 87*, 102–118.

HM Treasury. (2015). *Summer Budget 2015*. Retrieved July 13, 2015, from http://www.gov.uk/government/publications/summer-budget-2015/summer-budget-2015.

Jackson, A. (Ed.). (1987). *Anthropology at Home*. London: Tavistock Publications.

Jenkins, R. (1984). Bringing It All Back Home: An Anthropologist in Belfast. In C. Bell & H. Roberts (Eds.), *Social Researching: Politics, Problems, Practice* (pp. 147–164). London: Routledge and Kegan Paul.

JRF. (2015). *The Cost of the Cuts: The Impact on Local Government and Poorer Communities*. Retrieved July 17, 2015, from http://www.jrf.org.uk/sites/files/jrf/CostofCuts-Full.pdf.

Jupp, E. (2013b). "I Feel More at Home Here than in My Own Community": Approaching the Emotional Geographies of Neighbourhood Policy. *Critical Social Policy, 33*, 532–553.

Katz, C. (1996). Towards Minor Theory. *Environment and Planning D: Society and Space, 14*, 487–499.

Lefebvre, H. (1991). *Critique of Everyday Life Volume I [1947]*. New York: Verso.

Lumsden, K. (2009). "Don't Ask a Woman to Do Another Woman's Job": Gendered Interactions and the Emotional Ethnographer. *Sociology, 43*(3), 497–513.

Massey, D. (2004). Geographies of Responsibility. *Geografiska Annaler B, 86*(1), 5–18.

Oakley, A. (1981). Interviewing Women: A Contradiction in Terms. In H. Roberts (Ed.), *Doing Feminist Research* (pp. 30–61). London: Routledge.

Pearson, R., & Elson, D. (2015). Transcending the Impact of the Financial Crisis in the United Kingdom: Towards Plan F—A Feminist Economic Strategy. *Feminist Review, 109*, 8–30.

Reed-Danahay, D. (2009). Anthropologists, Education, and Autoethnography. *Reviews in Anthropology, 38*(1), 28–47.

Rhodes, D. (2017). North of England Hit Hardest by Government Cuts. *BBC News*. Retrieved July 13, 2018, from www.bbc.co.uk/news/uk-england-42049922.

Roberts, H. (Ed.). (1981). *Doing Feminist Research*. London: Routledge.

Round, J., Williams, C. C., & Rodgers, P. (2008). Everyday Tactic of Spaces of Power: The Role of Informal Economies in Post-Soviet Ukraine. *Social & Cultural Geography, 9*, 171–185.

Scott, S. (2009). *Making Sense of Everyday Life*. Cambridge: Polity Press.

Stacey, J. (1988). Can There Be a Feminist Ethnography? *Women's Studies International Forum, 11*(1), 21–27.

Stacey, J. (1990). *Brave New Families: Stories of Domestic Upheaval in Late-Twentieth-Century America*. Berkeley, CA: University of California Press.

Tronto, J. (1993). *Moral Boundaries: A Political Argument for an Ethic of Care*. London: Routledge.

Twigg, J. (2006). *The Body in Health and Social Care*. Basingstoke: Palgrave Macmillan.

Valentine, G. (2008a). The Ties that Bind: Towards Geographies of Intimacy. *Geography Compass, 2*(6), 2097–2110.

Valentine, G., Jayne, M., & Gould, M. (2012). Do as I Say, Not as I Do: The Affective Space of Family Life and the Generational Transmission of Drinking Cultures. *Environment and Planning A, 44*(4), 776–792.

Women's Budget Group. (2018). A "Jam Tomorrow" Budget': Women's Budget Group Response to Autumn Budget 2018. Retrieved December 19, 2018, from https://wbg.org.uk/wp-content/uploads/2018/11/WBG-2018-Autumn-Budget-full-analysis.pdf.

Young, M., & Willmott, P. (1957). *Family and Kinship in East London*. London: Routledge and Kegan Paul.

Zelizer, V. (2005). *The Purchase of Intimacy*. Princeton, NJ: Princeton University Press.

2

Family, Friendship and Intimacy: A Relational Approach to Everyday Austerity

In this chapter I outline what a relational approach to everyday life in austerity looks like and how it can be employed. Bringing work around economic, urban and financial geographies into conversation with ideas about family, friendship and intimacy, I develop a conceptual framework for the more empirically detailed chapters of this book. Throughout this discussion, I use the phrase 'everyday austerity' to encompass the lived elements of contemporary austerity. This term also acknowledges that time, place and context are important in shaping what austerity means in different spaces and moments. I show how the everyday elements of living in and through austerity have the potential to enhance and extend current geographical understandings, and across sub-disciplinary divides, as to the contextualised and multiscalar experience of austerity (see Pimlott-Wilson and Hall 2017).

Austerity measures imposed by the state typically involve a rolling-back of public spending on housing, welfare, local government, education and cultural institutions, and so on. This is certainly the case in the UK (Hall 2015). *Imposed* is the operative term here, because austerity is a purposeful, exacting political and economic agenda, carrying with it a romanticised, nostalgic discourse that works to temper public mood and

S. M. Hall, *Everyday Life in Austerity*, Palgrave Macmillan Studies in Family and Intimate Life, https://doi.org/10.1007/978-3-030-17094-3_2

shift responsibility from state to citizens (Hall and Jayne 2016). Austerity policies can cut deeply or scratch the surface, bleeding into the very fabric of everyday geographies—the spaces in which people live, meet, work, play.

Key to unlocking the complexity of lived austerity is understanding everyday relationships, or the relational spaces within which and across austerity takes place. As noted in Chap. 1, geographers have long been interested in the realm of the 'everyday', as a 'largely taken-for-granted world that remains clandestine', and the routine, mundane and unremarkable elements of human (and non-human) activity (Gardiner 2000, p. 2). For Pain and Smith (2008, p. 2), the everyday represents 'the feelings, experiences, practices and actions of people outside the realm of formal politics'. Everyday life encompasses 'affect and emotions, bodily experience and practical knowledges, the role played by "lived" time and space in the constitution of social experience, language and intersubjectivity, and interpersonal ethics' (Gardiner 2000, p. 3). The everyday is often implicitly taken to refer to geographical scale, a 'microscale' that it sits beneath—rather than alongside or part of—'global' concerns (Pain and Smith 2008, p. 6). Studying the everyday can often seem an overwhelming task since it refers to a vast terrain, characterised by difference and diversity (Askins 2015; Horton and Kraftl 2009). This includes households, workplaces, leisure spaces and community spaces (Jupp 2013b; McDowell 2012; Smith and Stenning 2006), and a host of relationships and relational interconnections.

Doreen Massey's work on relational space is pertinent to these discussions. Massey (1991) argues that social relations are central to geographical understandings of the world, and how identities, experiences and relationships can create, subvert and move through and across space. To consider space as relational is to recognise that spaces, like identities, are made through interactions with others, ongoing possibilities that are unbounded and ever-changing (Massey 2004). Building on this, I argue that a closer inspection of relational geographies—particularly family, friendships and other intimate relations—offers interesting possibilities for understanding austerity in everyday life, in that together they represent the core of significant everyday social relationships. I show how a relational approach to 'everyday austerity' therefore involves paying close attention to geographies *of* everyday life, by attending to questions of difference through, across and between spaces (see Massey 2004). It also encompasses geographies *in* everyday life, by addressing the interactions, relationships and spatial practices that configure and are configured by the everyday.

In the rest of this chapter I outline how economic, financial and urban geographical literatures have been moving towards a consideration of the lived impacts of austerity. After this, I work through topical debates on family, friendships and intimate relations, drawing from work within geography and the wider social sciences. Taking forward a relational approach, I then identify two broad themes—care and support, and mundane mobilities—to start to unpick geographies of everyday austerity. Here I also briefly introduce the six families from Argleton upon which the ethnography was based, though you will get to know them better throughout the rest of the book. My aim is to show that, when taken together, a focus on family, friends and intimate relations can enable nuanced relational and multiscalar understandings of austerity and everyday life.

Geographies of Austerity: Economic, Financial, Urban

As already noted, austerity is often characterised foremost as an economic condition. It comes as no surprise, then, that economic geographers have provided valuable insights into the governance, regulation and structure of global financial markets and their role in the recent Global Financial Crisis (GFC) (e.g. Martin 2011; Hall 2010; Lee et al. 2009). Since the Global Financial Crisis and protracted period of austerity, economic geographers have undertaken analysis of how austerity policies have been deployed in city, regional and national governance (Ballas et al. 2017; MacLeavy 2011; Pike et al. 2018), the gendered nature of capital (Pollard 2013) and the impact of spending cuts on academic institutions (Christopherson et al. 2014). The financial crisis has been declared 'a highly geographical crisis', and one that 'evolved and impacted unevenly in part because it occurred against the ineluctable backdrop of—indeed, was surely in part a result of—a long history of uneven geographical development' (Christophers 2015, p. 206).

Questions regarding the socio-spatial unevenness of austerity, urban and regional concerns have been at the forefront of geographical writing. Ideas about 'austerity urbanism' (Peck 2012)—a term used to describe the challenges faced by cities and urban regions in the current economic climate—have been readily taken up and widely deployed within geography. Contributors working on austerity urbanism have sought to conceptualise austerity as 'a particularly urban phenomenon' (Donald et al. 2014, p. 12), with their analysis typically levelled at the regional and city scale (Davidson and Ward 2014; Kitson et al. 2011). Urban space, they argue, is the main stage upon which the impacts of austerity—wealth and power, inequality and impoverishment—are thought to play out (Hall 2015). One of the key influences of this work is that it has shaped current geographical debates on austerity, wherein 'the urban' has become a significant frame of reference for the contemporary context, though ostensibly removed from everyday, personal and lived experiences.

Bringing these elements into dialogue has enormous potential to ground economic, financial and urban geographies in the 'messiness of everyday life', encouraging intra-disciplinary links between 'the economy' and 'culture' (Hall 2016a, p. 326). As emerging research shows, the quotidian spaces of austerity matter, as do the day-to-day rhythms, routines and relations in and upon which austerity is placed (Hall 2017). For instance, in work on post-crisis youth identities, McDowell (2012, p. 580) contends that 'the new era of austerity' brought with it 'material inequalities in the labour market and … discourses of disadvantage'. The service industry, she argues, is a more competitive and precarious workplace than ever, with high unemployment levels pitting graduates and non-graduates against one another for the same, temporary, low-paid, body-intensive labour. Jupp's (2013a, p. 173) study of 'UK Sure Start Children's Centres … as particular kinds of spaces' similarly identifies heightened social and spatial unevenness in the impact of welfare cuts. Horton's (2016) work on cuts to public services also focuses on a particular sphere, this time youth groups, revealing that anticipation and anxieties surrounding austerity are potentially more devastating than the reality.

Geographical literature on foodbanks in the UK, USA and across Europe has likewise typically identified these as spaces of austerity, and of emotion, ethics and encounter (Cloke et al. 2016; Lambie-Mumford and Green 2015; Garthwaite 2016). Such studies focus on foodbanks as liminal spaces of institutional and structured responses (by communities, third-sector organisations and faith groups), rather than informal spaces and practices with which they, and austerity, are bound up (Hall 2015). Similarly, studies of community services facing closure have considered libraries as therapeutic spaces (Brewster 2014), and have noted the strain placed on non-governmental organisations of support, such as Citizens Advice Bureaus (Kirwan et al. 2016). In these examples, spaces of austerity are institutionalised and formalised (workplaces, childcare centres, youth groups, foodbanks, libraries, citizens' advice bureaus) where connections are founded foremost on geographical grouping and physical proximity, with relational consequences. Many of these literatures have also started to use spaces of austerity (households, youth groups, workplaces) to think about how everyday experiences 'talk up' to economic policy.

Furthermore, a rich pocket of literature on austere post-Soviet states and everyday socio-economic relations also makes an important contribution here. This includes the following: studies of everyday tactics used by poor households in urban Ukraine in response to economic marginalisation (Round et al. 2008); simultaneous transitions to adulthood and post-socialism for young people (Burrell 2011); and interrelationships between housing, mobility, leisure and consumption for everyday geographies in Poland (Stenning 2005). In the capitalist development of post-socialist societies, when formal and informal economies were acquiring new meaning and place, Smith and Stenning (2006, p. 197) identify the role of 'family, friends and acquaintances in the formal economy', as a means by which ordinary people sought to overcome state-imposed austerity and access goods, services and information. They argue for households as an entry point, 'a networked space, "nested" with other geographies including other homes, workplaces, community venues, the housing block, the street, the familial home, perhaps in a distant location, sites of work abroad, and so on' (ibid., p. 202).

Towards a Relational Approach to Austerity

My reading of the literature discussed above is that it makes an important contribution to considerations of spaces of everyday austerity, albeit remains somewhat static in its thinking about the properties of space as bounded and nested. I suggest that paying more attention to social relations and relational geographies can help to address this, by exploring the ways in which everyday austerity cuts through, across and between spaces (Hall 2016a; Massey 2004). There are examples of literature on everyday geographies that do speak to some of these ideas of relational space. Examples include Waters' (2002) work on doing transnational family life across places and scales, Blunt (2005) on the home and home-making as relationally constituted space, and Conradson (2003) on emerging relational practices of care within therapeutic practice. However, I argue for further exploration and application of relational thinking and everyday lives.

The term 'relational' is therefore being deployed here to connect two ideas. Firstly, in the literal sense of social relations and how relational geographies are being reworked by and through austerity. For Morrison et al. (2012, p. 513) in their work on the geographies of love, relational space refers to 'relations and spaces *between* and among individuals, groups and objects': that is, the spaces created by and through relationships. Secondly, and taking from Massey (1991, p. 24), relational space also refers to politics and spaces created by the 'geographical stretching-out of social relations': that is, the spaces produced (and power, inequality and difference therein) as a result of the changing socio-material constitution of everyday life (technology, mobility, communication).

Here, I seek an understanding of the everyday that is not place-bound, but which conceives of everyday life as relational space (Massey 2004). I suggest that relational geographies—of family, friendship and intimate relations—are a useful starting point to conceptualise everyday austerity. Together they represent the core of everyday social relationships; the many obligations, practices, emotions and so on that shape how austerity is experienced and encountered through, across and between everyday spaces. This is what Massey (2004, p. 5) describes as 'think[ing] space relationally'. Developing this three-part framework, I now turn to literatures on family, friendship and intimate relations, before illustrating how a cohesive conceptual approach to social relations can reveal relational geographies of everyday austerity.

Family Geographies

It is a well-known argument that the notion of family is deeply rooted in how most governments convey messages of responsibility and distribute social benefits to citizens (Edwards and Weller 2010; Harker and Martin 2012; Oswin and Olund 2010). As Edwards and Gillies (2012, p. 63) note, 'it would be hard to find any aspects of family life and relationships that stand outside of "culture" and are not "political" in some shape or form'. This role of family as a political institution is of particular significance in the current context of cuts to public expenditure.

Despite the centrality of kinship to socio-political life, family has commonly been described as an 'absent presence' within the geographical discipline (Valentine 2008a, p. 2098). Where earlier writings focused on 'geographies of social reproduction' (Valentine et al. 2012, p. 777), recent years have seen renewed interest in geographies of familial relations, or at least a recognition that family, including the challenges faced in austere times, has been 'rather unrepresented' (Harker and Martin 2012, p. 769). In giving further attention to routine, unspectacular elements of everyday family life (Valentine et al. 2012), geographers should be wary of romanticising familial relationships. As later chapters in this book confirm, familial relations can be defined as much by emotional closeness as tension, unhappiness or abuse, which may become exacerbated by tumultuous economic and political contexts (Morrison et al. 2012; Pinkerton and Dolan 2007).

Regarding this lack of an explicit focus on families within geography, there are some recent attempts of redress. Using the concept of caringscapes, or the time-space dimensions of care, Bowlby (2012) has interrogated social relationships within familial and intergenerational caring practices. Looking at the ways caring responsibilities and needs change across the lifecourse, this work also recognises how shifting policy landscapes can shape everyday relationships. Evans (2012) has also explored multiple dimensions of family relationships, specifically sibling relationships in youth-headed households in Tanzania and Uganda, revealing that young people's lifecourse transitions are notably altered by sibling caring responsibilities. In research on intergenerationality and grandparenthood, Tarrant (2010, p. 190) describes 'how the transition to the identity of a grandparent is intersected by space, place and intergenerational relations', including care responsibilities for younger kin.

Much of this work around family geographies also speaks to sociological debates on family practices and intimate lives (Morgan 2011; Smart 2007), where there has been a notable shift away from 'the family' and associated heteronormative prescriptions (Aitken 1998). A retreat away from families in favour of personal lives, intimacy, kinship, intergenerationality and relatedness can be noted in a range of sociological and geographical literatures (e.g. Jamieson 1997; Nash 2005; Valentine 2008a; Vanderbeck 2007). As Smart (2007, p. 6) explains, 'sociology has periodically tried to rid itself of the conceptual and political straitjacket that the concept of "the family" imposes, by talking instead of "households", or by introducing "families of choice", by preferring the term "kinship", or by conceptualising relationships more in terms of practices than institutions or structures'.

Nevertheless, a growing number of scholars have argued for a defence and retention of 'family' as an important conceptual tool for grasping everyday social realities and relationalities (Edwards and Gillies 2004; Morgan 2011). Such calls do not necessarily mark a move away from personal life, intimacy or kinship. Nor do they dismiss changing family formations, obligations and living arrangements that may counter traditional ideas of family (Aitken 1998; Beck and Beck-Gernsheim 2002). Rather, they recognise that despite social and demographic variations, family still matters and has 'public political' resonance, particularly when family is at the centre of austere policy-making (Edwards and Gillies 2012, p. 64; Pimlott-Wilson and Hall 2017).

Moreover, many non-traditional families or 'families of choice' (Weeks et al. 2001) use the term 'family' to 'emphasise the strength of their kin-like social networks and commitments to their partners' (Jackson 2009, p. 3), representing 'a range and mix of blood, partner and friendship ties and commitments that stretch beyond the conventional couple' (Edwards and Gillies 2012, p. 65; Valentine 2008a; Wilkinson and Ortega-Alcázar 2017). Hence, there are ways of 'doing' family that might not subscribe to the 'heterosexual, cohabiting, two-point-four-children family' model, but for which the notion of family is still significant in everyday practice and parlance.

Furthermore, while the socio-spatial dynamics of family are changing, this is not to say that the concept of family has become redundant. Familial relations are practised over increasingly distant scales, bending and stretching relational spaces (Massey 2004). However, there is often an assumption 'about the intensification of mobility at the expense of family', that people are moving further away from family (Holdsworth 2013, p. 1). But this is not the same as dispersal; 'we cannot all be moving away from each other, as at the same time this mobility will mean we are moving closer to others' (ibid., p. 2). Broadbent (2009) similarly rejects claims that the process of individualisation is deteriorating the importance of contemporary family life (Beck and Beck-Gernsheim 2002), arguing that people now have more contact with their family than ever before, largely due to personal communication technologies. Relational geographies of family are shown here to operate on multiple scales.

Geographical literature on migrant workers also reveals the obstacles created by spatial distance to maintaining familial relationships (Pessar and Mahler 2003; Pratt 1997). Parrenas (2005, p. 317) shows how Filipino migrant mothers living abroad engage in a variety of intergenerational transnational communications, including 'flow of ideas, information, goods, money and emotions', allowing the transgression of spatial and relational barriers in gendered care practices. As Popke (2006, p. 506) describes, care responsibilities 'may stretch across both territorial boundaries and familial generations'; imagined and practiced over various time-space configurations (Bowlby 2012; Dyck 2005). Waters' (2002) work on 'astronaut' families (migrant wives left to settle in a new country with their children) and lone mothers in Vancouver likewise reveals the flexibility of familial relations, enacted across great distances by exchanging material things and developing new kin-like relations.

In these and other examples it is common for authors to refer not only to family members (i.e. those related by blood, marriage or adoption), but to 'friends and family', or what is sometimes called 'kith and kin', as a distinct set of social relations. Spencer and Pahl (2006, pp. 213–214) describe this as a 'suffusion of roles', building on Wellman's (1990) earlier work on 'kinfolk', and the fuzzy boundaries between kin and personal communities. This coupling is applied so often that it is rendered a given and rarely troubled. So while family has geographical significance, it is part of broader relational geographies of austerity.

Friendship

Although occupying a central position in contemporary space and society, friendship has tended to remain the reserve of sociological and anthropological study (see Bowlby 2011; Bunnell et al. 2012; Coakley 2002). Here, friendships have been understood as a form of 'social glue' (Spencer and Pahl 2006, p. 213), providing 'social and emotional support and a sense of collectivity' (Edwards and Gillies 2004, p. 631). With overlaps in relational networks of family and friends, or 'friends as family' and 'family as friends' (Allan 1989; Pahl 2000; Powdermaker 1966; Smart 2007; Wellman 1990), these relationships are also part of the fabric of everyday austerity.

Focused attention on geographies of friendship is a relatively recent but necessary consideration, since 'friendship is a means through which people across the world maintain intimate social relations both proximate and at distance' (Bunnell et al. 2012, p. 490; Conradson and Latham 2005). That said, there have been some murmurings within geography about the overlapping relational possibilities with kinship, and sexual relationships, and whether friendship may be distinguished (Bunnell et al. 2012; Valentine 1993; Valentine 2008a). Thinking about the context of austerity, these contributions are particularly important because they identify how various relationalities work against heteronormative assumptions that underpin family-centric state welfare policies (Brown 2015; Pimlott-Wilson and Hall 2017; Wilkinson and Ortega-Alcázar 2017).

However, and despite the prominence of work on families of choice (Jackson 2009; Weeks et al. 2001), the ties that bind friendship are often argued to be discernible from kinship. This is because friendships are not based on consanguinity or law (which are core ideals of family and kinship), but choice, entered into voluntarily, and founded upon shared values or experiences (Bowlby 2011; Morrison et al. 2012; Weeks et al. 2001). Within friendships it is usual to witness interdependency and reciprocity, and 'some degree of emotional involvement', that are typically absent in acquaintanceships (Bowlby 2011, p. 608; Morgan 2009). This indicates a wider variation in social relations beyond family and friends. Friendships are also discernible from communities, though may share some similar traits. People often create their own personalised communities (Bowlby 2011; Spencer and Pahl 2006; Wellman 1990), though they 'tend to form their social networks from people brought together for reasons other than geographical proximity of residence' (Smith 1999, p. 28).

Where geographers have considered friendship, it is largely as a result of examining other spatial-temporal practices. For instance, work on the geographies of care-giving illustrates that 'social networks of friends and relatives [are] involved in informal care relationships', which are in turn 'influenced by social relationships beyond those spaces' (Bowlby 2012, p. 2103). Jupp (2013a, p. 182) argues that people actively seek out caring relationships, with children's centre as the locus of where friendships were nurtured in her research. Friendships were also seen to alter the rhythms and patterns of usage and presence, as well as experiences of the centre, whether between users or users and staff. Here, friendships are shown not to be static, but varying over time and space. Regarding transnational friendships, Conradson and Latham (2005, p. 301) show that friendships have a certain temporal and spatial resilience, which 'shape and give form' to people's mobility. And regarding local childcare, an increasingly politicised issue during austerity (Holloway and Pimlott-Wilson 2014; Jupp 2013b), Holloway (1998, p. 39) identifies gendered and classed geographies of friendship, whereby mothers gravitated towards those with whom they shared similar social characteristics. Valentine (1993, p. 110) likewise found that intersections of gender and sexuality are formative in shaping how and where friendships are made, with lesbian women resorting to 'looking for clues in dress or body language' to ascertain similarities and differences.

On geographies of social difference, Askins' (2015) study of a befriending scheme for asylum seekers in North East England also reveals how close physical proximities are part of the spatialities from which friendships flourish, albeit with positionalities and identities to navigate in the process. On spatialities of crafting, Hall and Jayne (2016) examine how practices of dressmaking simultaneously create convivial spaces for friendships to develop. Social similarities and differences act as surfaces upon which friendships (or tensions) are built (Browne 2003; Hall 2017; Wilson 2013). Mirroring warnings about familial relations, friendships can also be contested. They may involve arguments, bullying, exclusion or dissolution, as well as pleasure, comfort and companionship (Bowlby 2011; Bunnell et al. 2012; Morris-Roberts 2001; Morris-Roberts 2004; Newman et al. 2006; Valentine 1993).

There is also a clustering of research on friendships within children's geographies (Andrews and Chen 2006; Neal and Vincent 2013). Examples span global and socio-political contexts, from street children in Accra, Ghana, for whom friendship is a 'survival strategy' (Mizen and Ofosu-Kusi 2010, p. 441; Hörschelmann and van Blerk 2012; van Blerk 2011) to teenage girls in the Rhondda Valley in South Wales, UK, who 'use the streets as places of leisure', a relational space of togetherness (Skelton 2000, p. 69). Spaces of friendship have been a particular concern for children's geographers—bedrooms, beaches, schools, streets or parks—as part of befriending processes and developing personal and relational identities (Bartos 2013; Morris-Roberts 2001; Morris-Roberts 2004). Moreover, children's friendship may intersect with and create opportunities for friendships between parents (and vice versa), such as encounters in playgrounds (Wilson 2013), schools (Neal and Vincent 2013), parenting classes (Holloway and Pimlott-Wilson 2014), Sure Start centres (Jupp 2013a), mother and baby groups (Holloway 1998), or virtual parenting in chat rooms, blogs and forums (Madge and O'Connor 2006). As will be discussed, austerity can reshape the significance of these relational spaces, and other spaces and relations may emerge during testing times.

The time taken to build up friendships, including rapport, familiarity and sharing intimate details, has also been reflected upon in geographical writings on fieldwork (Blake 2007). As Browne (2003, p. 133) describes, friendships alter the space of the field, which 'incorporate more than spaces where information is gathered/formed'. Fieldwork friendships can also lead to researchers inadvertently caring for research subjects through acts of gratitude and by their very presence, particularly during austere times (Hall 2017). Friendship can also mean different things in different moments, at different points in time, and because of different personal and generational biographies. Space-time dimensions also emerge when considering the everyday doings of friendship, which may be defined by the frequency, rhythm or regularity of contact, whether physical, telephonic or virtual, across days, weeks, months or years (see Bowlby 2011; Coakley 2002).

What much of this prior research also affirms is that doings and makings of friendship are shaped by intersecting social positions, such as class and gender, as well as sexuality, race, ethnicity, intra- and intergenerationality (Bowlby 2011; Browne 2003; Coakley 2002; Holloway 1998; Leach et al. 2013; Morris-Roberts 2004; Valentine 1993). Such similarities and differences work as the surfaces upon which friendships are built or, in some cases, in which people come into conflict (Browne 2003; Hall 2017; Wilson 2013). Indeed, it is important not to assume that all friendships are enjoyable, dependable or mutual. In assessing the everyday importance of care work between friends, Bowlby (2011) remarks that power imbalances can emerge, and that inequalities in the exchange of care can change spaces of friendship and friendly relations.

Extending Spencer and Pahl's (2006) 'social glue' metaphor, then, friendships have different consistencies and adherences depending on the people, places, distances and temporalities in question; social, political and economic context matters. Relational geographies of friendships, and how they extend, bend and map onto familial relations and other intimate relations, are also of interest (Bowlby 2011; Morgan 2009; Valentine 2008a), particularly in periods of political and economic turbulence such as austerity (Smith and Stenning 2006). It is to this that I now turn.

Intimate Relations

Writings on intimate geographies have applied 'key spatial concepts like proximity and distance' (Harker and Martin 2012, p. 770), reflecting on the complex interplay between proximity and propinquity (Oswin and

Olund 2010). Foundational work within the discipline, influenced by feminist scholars, concentrated on spaces of intimacy such as the home as domestic, gendered space (Blunt 2005; Milligan 2003) and the body (Johnson and Longhurst 2010; Longhurst 2008), shaping preceding geographical enquiry. As Price (2012, p. 578) explains in a piece on the fleshiness of skin in lived experiences of race and ethnicity, '[h]uman geography is undergoing a turn to the intimate, wherein bodies and encounters figure prominently', meaning the social differences that emerge as a result of such intimacy also come to the fore (see Wilson 2017).

Geographies of intimacy may seem like a contradiction in terms, since the notion of intimacy beholds an inherent spatial form, suggesting that which is near, close and corporeally proximate. As Mitchell (2007, p. 716) argues, 'intimacy is about connections that are embodied and lived', and likewise Holdsworth (2013, p. 114) describes how 'being intimate necessitates being close to others, both physically and emotionally'. For Morgan (2009, p. 2) there are three key manifestations of intimacy: physical/embodied intimacy, emotional intimacy and intimate knowledge, which 'do not necessarily co-exist in all interpersonal relationships'. So it follows, 'intimacy' not only refers to placed or material entities but it is also a social metaphor, describing multiple relationships to and with others. Intimacy, then, may be a result as well as a catalyst, a cause and an outcome, in the production, maintenance or disassembly of relational spaces of austerity.

Questions about framing intimacy within geography, and the need for relational thinking, have been raised. Valentine et al. (2012, p. 790), for instance, emphasise the need 'for geographers to pay more attention to the spatial concepts of proximity and distance'. In such discussions, ideas about 'intimate relations' continue to assume a certain level of closeness and familiarity, founded on love or mutuality. This is at best romanticised, and at worst ignorant. Valentine (2008a, p. 2015) concurs that there is a real need to pluralise geographical understandings of intimate relations: 'by focusing only on relationships in the domestic, we miss out on the complex web of intimate relationships that span different spaces and scales'. Recent conceptual discussions about intimacy have worked to 'unfix' the scale of intimate relations, broadening understandings of relational space. It is argued that 'intimate relations cannot be considered synonymous with the body or the household, locations which then simply mirror larger social relations through their capacity to oppress or liberate at closer physical proximity' (Oswin and Olund 2010, p. 60).

Intimacy and intimate relations are also not necessarily bound by family or friendship, nor are there set ways for intimacy to develop. Familiarity is not a prerequisite. Geographical research on domestic workers illustrates this very point. For example, in Cox and Narula's (2003, p. 333) study of au pairing in London, relationships between employers and domestic workers—cleaners, housekeepers, nannies, au pairs and ironing 'ladies'—may develop into 'false kin relations', which are neither 'of equal benefits nor one constructed by both parties'. In similar work exploring differences between British and Filipina nannies, Pratt (1997, p. 165) describes these intimate others as 'someone who might be folded into one's own family for a period of time'. Notwithstanding, intimacy is not always reciprocal, meaning intimate relations can be founded on unidirectional propinquities. Moreover, intimacy does not always equate to pseudo-familial relations borne out of domestic practices, whereby the spatial and relational dimensions of being or feeling close to others may result from unfamiliarity.

Indeed, the centrality of the body in service work (as a form of gendered, racialised, classed, low-waged and undervalued labour) has been widely acknowledged within the social sciences as an example of intimate corporeal practice that is not preceded (or necessarily succeeded) by prior relations (see Zelizer 2005). With a move towards embodiment, senses and emotions, so too have geographers made important contributions to this field. Recent, notable examples include Jayne and Leung's (2014, p. 265) work on massage in urban China, wherein 'massage allows suspension of social norms of "closeness" and interaction' in the 'encounters between customer and practitioner'. Similarly Holmes (2015, p. 479), investigating the materialities of hairdressing, describes the hair salon as a space of '"intimate service encounter" [...] which may be somewhat prolonged: where you feel obliged to talk, to break the uncomfortable silence with the person working upon your body'.

While relations may bloom and friendships strike up over time, such relations are initiated (and sometimes purely based) on monetary exchanges, as examples of where intimacy is not always reciprocal (Cohen

2010; Morgan 2009). I explore these ideas in more detail in Chap. 4. Finally, and in the context of austerity cuts and reduced employment opportunities, McDowell's (2012, p. 578) research on classed and gendered youth identities in the service economy identifies how 'service provider and the purchaser are co-present'. Understandings of intimate relations are herein reconfigured, for such (often precarious) labour is deeply entrenched in close corporeality and 'acceptable' bodily politics, performance and display (Crang 1994).

These examples each speak to a different type of interpersonal service engagement through which social relations—whether friendship, acquaintanceship, corporeal closeness and undefined sorts of intimacy—develop at different rates and tempos, in turn shaping possibilities of/for relational space. Thus, non-familial and non-friendship, yet intimate and significant relationships and everyday spatial practices are 'embedded in wider social and political formations' (Bunnell et al. 2012, p. 492). To segregate them is to offer an artificial representation of everyday life. Crucially, the possibilities, capacities and spatialities of such relations are at risk of change, transformation and reinstatement in times of austerity. By giving due attention to family, friendship and intimate relations (and the connections between) I now show how nuanced geographical understandings of everyday austerity and relational geographies can be developed.

Everyday Austerity: Relational Spaces of Family, Friendship and Intimacy

Taking a relational approach to everyday austerity offers further opportunities for exploring austerity as a lived and personal condition. It relates not only to relationships between individuals, but also according to the politics and spaces created by and through these relations (Massey 2004; Morrison et al. 2012). The discussion below is grouped into two themes according to their cross-spatial and interrelational properties: care and support, and mundane mobilities. Using literature and empirical examples, I illustrate that by focusing on relational geographies of family, friendship and intimate relations, cutting through, across and between spaces, scales and practices, everyday geographies of austerity can be seen anew.

Care and Support

The provision of care and support is a messy endeavour, entangled within intra-personal relationships and responsibilities. Changes to household and family structures, alongside an increase in women's workforce participation and intensified mobility, have reshaped everyday care provision towards formal institutions (Holdsworth 2013; McDowell et al. 2005; Smith 2011). This is particularly pronounced within austerity, when these institutions and welfare provision are being cut back, and responsibility for care falls back onto women in families and communities (Jupp 2013b; Pearson and Elson 2015). Research shows that family and kinship still matter with regard to everyday support (Finch and Mason 1993; Valentine 2008a), and as much as ever during times of austerity (Hall 2016a). As Heath and Calvert (2013, p. 1121) demonstrate, the role of family in providing material and financial support entails 'complex intergenerational negotiations relating to obligations and responsibilities, indebtedness and gratitude, dependency and independence, fairness and equality'.

Indeed, there are various kinds of support and care beyond material and financial that are required (given or received) in austerity: when local services have been cut, social care and welfare budgets slashed, and personal spending and lending curbed (England 2010; Hall 2015). This includes everyday practical support, such as childminding, help carrying bags from bulk shopping and offering lifts to appointments (because local transport services have been axed). There is also emotional support, such as providing comfort and counsel, as well as a 'loving' environment to see through these changes (Edwards and Gillies 2004; Pinkerton and Dolan 2007; Morrison et al. 2012; Thomson et al. 2010). These practices and interactions involve particular, and often embodied, intercorporeal spatial practices; 'small acts, words and gestures which can instigate and reciprocate/reproduce such care' (Horton and Kraftl 2009, p. 14). They are also spatially diverse (across home, workplaces, towns, cities), involve multiple relationships (familial, friendship and other intimate relations) and have the capacity to reshape relational spaces of care.

To explain, care work, paid or unpaid, is a significant part of how everyday relationships are understood and maintained (also see Chap. 3). As Conradson (2003, p. 453) puts it, 'care is woven into the fabric of particular social spaces and communities, at times supporting individuals and facilitating their well-being; at times breaking down and leaving significant gaps; and often requiring very significant amounts of effort'. The current context of austerity has raised concerns about how and by whom care and support are administered, enacted and received (the relational politics of care) when both public and personal expenditure are curtailed (Hall 2016a). As the well-known feminist mantra goes, and as explored further in Chap. 5, the personal is political.

Families, especially female members, are often responsible for enacting day-to-day care-giving for young, elderly and disabled kin. This is a responsibility commonly juggled with paid employment and domestic tasks (Evans 2012; Gillies 2005). In austerity, the sustainability of this care comes under intense threat, as seen in the UK with billions of pounds worth of cuts to the social care budget alone (Pearson and Elson 2015). This creates a growing care gap (England 2010) with funding for elderly day-care activities, children's groups, and community centres slashed. This gap is typically filled by unpaid, female labour across generational divides. The social unevenness of this care provision becomes even more stark when considering that care work (especially cleaning, food and laundry, when waged) is gendered, classed and racialised. Pearson and Elson (2015) likewise demonstrate that women are hit harder by austerity, namely due to public services, benefits and social care cuts where women form the majority of employees, recipients and benefactors. Recent research also reveals that austerity cuts have the greatest impact on black, Asian and minority ethnic women in the UK (Hall et al. 2017). Figure 2.1, for instance, developed from work on the intersecting inequalities of austerity (see Hall et al. 2017), illustrates the cumulative impact of changes to personal taxes and social security benefits in the UK from 2010 to 2020. This reveals that when gender, race and poverty are intersected, black and Asian women from the poorest third of households are likely to lose the highest proportion of their incomes.

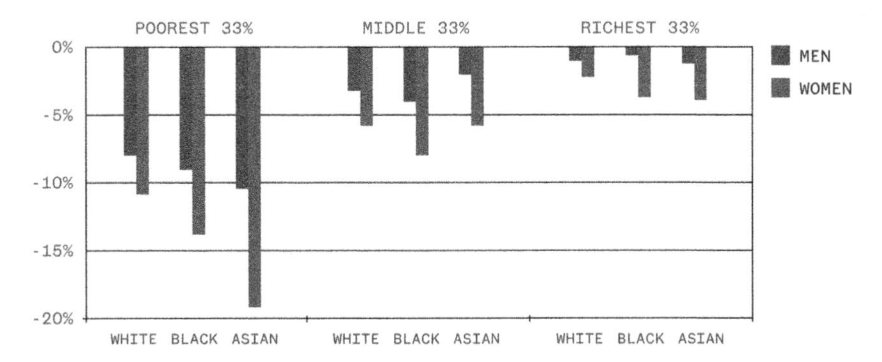

Fig. 2.1 The cumulative impact in April 2020 of changes to taxes and benefits announced between June 2010 and March 2016 by income, gender and ethnicity as a proportion of net individual income, UK (from *Women Count* (2018), by the Women's Budget Group; see https://womencount.wbg.org.uk/)

Current literatures that identify the uneven impacts of austerity as multiscalar (Davidson and Ward 2014; Kitson et al. 2011; MacLeavy 2011) may be developed with a relational approach. For Massey's (2004) conceptualisation of relational space is founded on the premise that identities are formed in and through social relations, of various kinds, which make way for political responsibilities to others. A reconsideration of relational geographies in times of austerity raises questions about whether and how care needs of/for parents and adult children, in-laws, grandparents and grandchildren can reshape everyday, gendered care responsibilities. Exploring grandfathering, Tarrant (2013, p. 193) notes that 'increasingly grandparents are playing significant caring roles in contemporary families and are responding to care demand'. When everyday caring responsibilities expand due to financial curtailments, such as in austerity (Hall 2016a), 'wider familial networks' (Valentine 2008a, p. 2101)—siblings, step-siblings, aunties, uncles, nieces, nephews, cousins and so on—may also enter to provide support. In their study of Internet gambling within families, Valentine and Hughes (2011) describe how both vertical (parents, children, grandparents) and horizontal kin relations (partners, siblings) are commonly relied-upon mechanisms of practical, financial and emotional support.

Pauline, for instance—retired and living with husband George in their own home—regularly looked after her grandchildren on days and evenings when her daughter-in-law was working. Both Pauline and George were in their mid-60s and had gone into retirement only within the last two years, although childcare was a responsibility that increasingly fell to Pauline since finishing work. Their adult sons were both married and had children, and Pauline would look after the grandchildren of her younger son, who also lived in Argleton. Their older son lived in Blackpool, over an hour away by car or train, but they 'made a conscious effort to visit often so that their grandson grows up knowing his family' (field diary, September 2014). It seemed as though Pauline was dividing her time between her sons and grandchildren to ensure that distance was not an obstacle to performing these gendered familial caring responsibilities. I discuss this and similar examples further in Chap. 3.

However, the significance placed on family for care and support during times of hardship (in both academic writing and policy-making) means far less attention has been paid to friendships and other intimate relations in everyday geographies of austerity. Yet it is well recognised that friendships are central to social networks, financial stability and personal well-being (Harrison 2013; Spencer and Pahl 2006), shaped by 'differential social positioning regarding gender, class and ethnicity' (Edwards and Gillies 2004, p. 627). In their study of young people's support networks, Pinkerton and Dolan (2007, pp. 219–220) refer to 'internal emotional worlds' such as 'social support network membership' as channels through which support for 'troubled or troublesome' young people is best provided. Stenning (2005, p. 122), writing on research in post-Soviet Poland, also identifies 'networks of acquaintance and support … as a relatively undocumented part of the complex social and economic relationships which are increasingly recognized as important for managing lives under socialism and post-socialism'. Meanwhile, the current economic climate has the potential to 'reconfigure the dependencies within the family' (Thomson et al. 2010, p. 155), as well as how much people rely on or contribute support to friends and other 'kinfolk' (Wellman 1990).

Herein lie possibilities for extending ideas about the relational geographies of austerity, at a time when heavier reliance on long-standing kinship ties and friendships, reconnecting with old kin and friends, or constructing new affective links is necessary. The extension of caring-cared, supporting-supportive roles to wider intimate relations has the potential to shift the temporalities and spatialities of everyday relationships (Bowlby 2012), whether by bringing people emotionally or physically closer, in more regular contact, or enhancing proximities and propinquities of care. Notwithstanding, with such changes in interpersonal interactions comes the possibility of added strains on familial and friend relationships, particularly if excessive or inappropriate support is sought (Hall 2016a; Heath and Calvert 2013). After all, care-giving regularly takes place in the context of already intimate relationships, defined as much by love, trust and compassion as power, dominance and oppression (Cox and Narula 2003; Morrison et al. 2012).

The example of Kerry and her relationship with her sister was one such example in which extended support in austerity led to strained relationships. Kerry was a stay-at-home mum in her late 20s, living with her partner Dan and four young sons. They lived in a privately rented three-bedroom house relatively close to the centre of Argleton where most of their immediate family also lived, including Kerry's sister, and Dan worked as a mechanic nearby. Kerry's sister became pregnant during the ethnography, and Kerry described feeling pestered by the constant barrage of WhatsApp text messages, Facebook notifications, telephone calls and emails with questions about pregnancy, giving birth and looking after a baby. Kerry recognised that having had four children and previously worked as a childminder and au pair she was a trusted source of information, but this soon wore thin. In the middle of a taped discussion Kerry picked up her phone, frantically punched letters on the touch screen, then sighed, 'I'm just Facebook replying to my sister's stupid messages' (September 2014). In particular, she was 'shocked and a bit concerned that [her sister] didn't know half of these things' (field diary, January 2014). Furthermore, her sister was impatient, would ask the same question on multiple devices and would contact Kerry when she said she was busy. These sibling tensions started to bubble over when money lending and other financial arrangements entered into the mix, as discussed in Chaps. 3 and 4.

Research following the recent financial crisis in Europe shows that 'informal loans from friends and families are one of the ways for families to cover their debts, but many families (especially those out of work) find it hard to pay these back' (Eurofound 2014, p. 30). Moreover, the provision of (and responsibility to enact) care is not necessarily reciprocal in nature, and nor are family and friends always in a position to provide support. Relational geographies of austerity are then shaped by factors such as class, social mobility and employment status (Horton 2017; Pimlott-Wilson 2017). As Bowlby (2011, p. 608) explains, 'caring between friends involves both giving and receiving and the expectation of some sort of reciprocation. [...] Nevertheless, persistent inequalities in the exchange of care between friends may lead to the loss of the friendship.'

The current context of austerity—as backdrop, mechanism and affective environment—provides additional layers to the already gendered and culturally contingent values and norms that encircle everyday caring relations (McDowell et al. 2005). If the personal and political condition of austerity has the potential to redefine kin and familial relationships, this can ricochet to other social and intimate relations: neighbours, health and social care professionals, nannies, childcare and childminders, workmates and colleagues, and community members (Cox and Narula 2003; Emmel and Hughes 2010; Harrison 2013; McDowell et al. 2005; Valentine 2008a; Wellman 1990). Such relationships, while not necessarily based on familial or friendship ties, may still be intimate, often involving close or sustained engagement in everyday routines and practices. With cuts to welfare, increasing rents, added pressure on public services, increasing unemployment and precarious working conditions, the care and support offered by such other intimate relations signal a change in everyday relational geographies. The question of where care is performed, and by whom, transcends everyday geographies of home, workplace, community or leisure spaces. It intersects with everyday relationalities, as well as social identities and difference.

Married couple Sharon and Bill, for example, spoke about how they had provided and sought emotional support from work colleagues as such intimate others. Both were in their early 50s at the start of the research, living together in their own home, and working in professional employment (Sharon as a project manager in the housing sector, Bill as a public sector accountant). They have lived in and around Argleton for most of their lives, with family and close friends mostly living nearby. In her role as a project manager, Sharon found that she was a source of support and strength for her colleagues:

> I am the only manager with any ... real people skills. And that's not me being big-headed, that's what people have told me. A lot of people have told me that, because I do naturally talk to people. I don't want to know their personal lives, but if they're looking worried or they're upset, can I help? Let me know, kind of thing, and deal with stuff. And when we lost our dear colleague last year, it was me they all came to, to sort out stuff. Because you've got half your female team in tears and you've got to deal with it, it's me that dealt with it and dealt with the people, and also dealt with the funeral stuff. Things like that. (Sharon, taped discussion, January 2014)

Likewise, when Sharon was diagnosed with breast cancer, Bill 'talked to people at work', particularly a woman he knew well who 'had either known or had similar situations' (taped discussion, January 2014). In many examples throughout the ethnography there were gendered trends of women being caregivers in terms of support, advice and performing embodied gestures of reassurance. These social infrastructures will be discussed in more detail in Chap. 3. When changes to employment hit as a result of austerity, such care-filled intimacies too are changed.

However, in the face of austerity, new care-full relationships and opportunities for sociability emerge, giving form to and possibilities for relational space. Users and providers at foodbanks or Citizens Advice Bureaus may develop intimacies and relationships that extend the physical and social boundaries (and expectations) of institutionalised spaces (Cloke et al. 2016; Kirwan et al. 2016). Shoppers at 'nearly-new' sales (selling heavily discounted children's clothes) may meet other new parents in their local area (Waight 2018). While not all can or may become friendships, due to norms and regulations around client/service provider associations, these relations can still be intimate (Jayne and Leung 2014; Holmes 2018), involving the sharing of private details, personal moments and material things. They can also offer a sense of belonging or conviviality, be emotionally and affectively charged (Askins 2015; Massey 2004), and offer an example of relational spaces of care in the everyday geographies of austerity. Be that as it may, these possibilities should not be romanticised, emerging as they do from sometimes difficult and painful situations.

In the context of austerity opportunities for sociability and intimacy might also, conversely, become agitated or limited, because of funding cuts and closures of relied-upon community services like Sure Start centres, libraries, sports centres and youth groups. They may also be strengthened by rallying efforts to save these and similar amenities (Horton 2016; Jupp 2013b). Additionally, leisure activities, hobbies and provision of self-care, and relationships with those encountered as a result are also likely to be implicated. Pleasures, treats, pamperings—of whatever scale or frequency, from a haircut or massage, to holidays—are typically 'cut back' in austere times (Hall 2015). Relational spaces of care can also contract, dissolve and reshape during austerity. As Massey (2004, p. 6) notes, 'propinquity needs to be negotiated'.

Considering everyday relational spaces of austerity requires thinking about emerging intimate relationships with the potential for friendship, as well as the breaking down of kin relations, friendships and other intimate relations. These examples of everyday geographies of care in austerity cut through, across and between 'nested' spaces and scales (see Smith and Stenning 2006), whether because of changing living or working circumstances, service closures or the inaccessibility of certain activities. In what follows, I reflect more on these mundane mobilities and how they too can be reconsidered in light of a relational approach to everyday austerity.

Mundane Mobilities

If conceptualising everyday austerity, as I situate it, requires understanding the relational nature of space, then mundane mobilities—the 'everyday voyages' of 'commonplace and regular occurrence not generally conceived as extraordinary or special trips through time and space but enmeshed with the familiar worlds we inhabit, constituting part of the unreflexive, habitual practice of everyday life' (Binnie et al. 2007,

p. 165)—are important to this discussion. I suggest that changing mundane mobilities—where people live, who they live with or near, how far they have to travel for work, logistics of leisure, relaxation and socialising—as a result of austerity cuts are in turn (re)shaping familial, extra-familial, friendship and other intimate relations. Where people live and who they live near are also pivotal to everyday care and support (Holdsworth 2013). As Smith (1999, p. 26) argues, 'the strength of obligation as well as desire to care for others may depend on where as well as who they are': a combination of geographical proximity *and* propinquity. The impacts of economic downturns on mobility, spatial and social, have been noted, albeit typically foregrounding family rather than friendships and intimate relations.

In a longitudinal study of motherhood during the recent UK recession, Thomson et al. (2010, p. 152) found that '"moving" was a common subject of conversation … involving projections into the future in terms of finding areas with good public services [and] proximity to family support'. While economic upheaval may produce shifts in emotional and physical proximities of social relations, these are not always shared experiences (Hall 2017). An example comes from Edwards and Gillies (2004, p. 638), who identify that 'differential lived experience of parenting' are significantly shaped by social class, 'with middle-class parents experiencing less close-knit, more geographically dispersed, families'. In a protracted period of austerity, there are likely further repercussions to mundane mobilities that shape, or are shaped by, familial, friend and intimate relations, and the social identities and differences (such as gender, race, disability, sexuality) with which they are bound.

For Laura and her family these ideas about mundane mobilities being shaped by everyday austerity were a lived reality. Laura and Rich were a young couple in their early 30s, both from white working-class backgrounds. They lived in a privately rented house together with their two young sons, Lucas (aged five) and Isaac (aged two). Laura was on maternity leave for part of her participation and then returned to part-time work, while Rich worked full time as a mental health nurse. Their decision to live where they did was heavily shaped by Laura's desire to live near to her mum and dad. She had a close relationship with them and wanted to be physically close as a result, but they also chose the house and the area because they needed support from Laura's mum with looking after the boys (similar to the aforementioned example of Pauline looking after her grandkids).

However, this notion of living 'close' was more complicated once we talked it through. Laura and Rich cannot afford a car, and so they need to live somewhere that is 'close to everything they need'—shops, schools, work—and that is 'well networked' (field diary, October 2013). Their current house was within walking distance from the shops and Lucas' school, a bus ride for Laura and Rich to get to work and a few streets away from a train station; Laura would often tell me that 'it's all about location' (taped discussion, May 2014). From this station, Laura could get a train to her parents' house, and while as the crow flies it was over 20 miles away, it made her *feel close* to them knowing she could be there within half an hour. Laura discussed how they 'could live somewhere cheaper, but she wanted to be near the train line' (field diary, October 2013). In practice, however, Laura rarely took the train to see her parents, and they would always drive to Argleton visit her. But it was the *possibility* that was important for Laura, that if she needed to in an emergency, or decided to on a whim, she could get the train to see them quite easily. It was for this reason that they paid more to rent their house, an example of everyday decision-making that has intricacies of intimacy at its core. Chap. 3 discusses such everyday social infrastructures in further detail.

Another resounding feature of mundane mobilities in contemporary austerity is the precariousness of the housing market. Private rental prices are increasing, homeownership is the reserve of older generations and strict cuts levelled at housing benefits restrict the type of property and with whom claimants can live (Hall 2016b; Wilkinson and Ortega-Alcázar 2017). These austere conditions limit where and whom people can live near, move to or even move away from. Individuals and families might be forced to stay living where they once had hoped to sell their home, or continue renting when they had hoped to buy. Tensions between fixity and mobility in the housing market have very real, knock-on effects, shaping job opportunities, education and childcare options (Aalbers 2009; Holloway 1998; McDowell et al. 2005; Smith 2011). These effects are also multiscalar (Davidson and Ward 2014; Kitson et al. 2011; Peck 2012), impacting on certain sections of society and geographical regions (Christophers 2015; Pearson and Elson 2015; Pollard 2013).

Such mundane mobilities have a geography of their own, and may in turn be shaped by the social and economic characteristics of an area; 'residents living in disinvested parts of cities fall back on what they know and what they have—each other' (Slater 2013, p. 376). In Poland, where social relationships are central features of coping in post-socialism, Stenning (2005, p. 122) likewise observes that 'low levels of housing mobility and the association of housing tenure with the workplace have meant that networks of acquaintance and friendship tend to be long-standing and stable'. Class dynamics are important here, whereby a close sense of working-class 'community' is often accentuated by 'intergenerational continuity, with many families who can trace back their roots over multiple generations' (Harrison 2013, p. 102; Pahl 1984; Wellman 1990). Uprooting homes and lives as a result of austerity has differently felt impacts according to various social groups, and an austere economy is inextricably tied up with a sense of place and social 'locatedness' (Hall 2017; Skeggs 2004).

These impacts are felt by not only the people who have to move, but those who they might move away from. Zoe and her husband Stuart lived with their children Isobel (aged nine) and Ryan (aged seven) in their own home. Zoe worked in a few different part-time jobs over the course of the research, as well as studying for a non-teaching assistant qualification and being Ryan's primary carer. Stuart worked full time in a construction business that he part owned. They regularly talked about moving house, but were very much on the fence. Zoe explained, 'we really would like to move. Although we do love it here and we love the neighbours, we just feel we are slightly outgrowing the house' (taped discussion, January 2014). Their ability to move was predicated on forthcoming changes to disability payments for Ryan which would have an impact on their overall income. It was also entangled with emotional connections with their next-door neighbours, as the quote from Zoe above suggests. The following field diary extract, taken during a visit to their home a few months later, provides more detail:

> "The kids love the neighbours", Zoe explained, and while that was a reason to stay living where they were it probably wasn't enough of a reason. They were an older couple, "like a third set of grandparents" to Isobel and Ryan. They've got a key to their garden gate, and Isobel often goes next door after school, on weekends or in the holidays to help them with their gardening. For the last few years these neighbours have been frequently asking them "you're not going to move, are you?"—and regularly enough to make Zoe feel guilty for thinking of moving. (field diary, May 2014)

In talking about their neighbours and the emotional entanglements bound up with decisions to move house, kin-like relations emerge in this example of Zoe's neighbours being 'like a third set of grandparents' to her children (also see Jackson 2009; Valentine 2008a). The intimate relations described here therefore touch on kinship, community as well as a complicated mixture of emotional and physical proximities, being and feeling close to intimate others, which would be affected by residential mobility.

Connected to this, the precarious and ever-changing austere job market (Harrison 2013; Pimlott-Wilson 2017), including increased unemployment, rising self-employment, extensions of working-age, and the proliferation of fixed and zero-hours contracts, also shapes the rhythms of relationalities in everyday life. Such conditions result in people commuting over longer distances, adapting to different working practices, environments or forms of transport, or changing caring duties and patterns (Henwood et al. 2010; Holdsworth 2013; Smith 2011), with repercussions for relational geographies. An example of how these interweaving impacts of austerity play out in and through relational space can be seen in the case of younger generations reporting increasing financial dependence on their parents. Resulting from a toxic mix of soaring youth unemployment rates in Europe following the GFC, rising personal debt and everyday living costs (Heath and Calvert 2013), research by Eurofound (2014) found that almost half of young European adults aged 18–35 were living with their parents. The same report also notes a distinct trend of lone parents and their children moving in with relatives due to unemployment, albeit it neglects to mention the role of friends and other intimate relations. Prolonged or returned living with parents and family serves to entrench aforementioned processes of (gendered and intergenerational) responsibilisation and familialisation (Heath and

Calvert 2013; Wilkinson and Ortega-Alcázar 2017), with the potential to strain or strengthen these and other relations, impacting on relational spaces of home, work and leisure. Meetings with friends, intimates and sexual partners may be altered by these revised living arrangements, whereby the home may not offer suitable privacy (Morrison et al. 2012; Robinson et al. 2004).

In the UK, these impacts on mundane mobilities, particularly related to housing and employment, have been compounded by cuts to welfare. As part of a suite of austerity policies, individuals who are single and under the age of 35 are entitled to financial support for housing only in bed-sit accommodation or a single room in shared accommodation (Brown 2015). The removal of the spare room subsidy, colloquially known as the 'bedroom tax'—whereby housing benefit allowance has been reassessed according to 'spatial requirements'—has resulted in changing living and personal circumstances, with occupants forced to either pay the difference out of their social security payments, or be placed in alternative housing (Brown 2015; Hall 2016b; Wilkinson and Ortega-Alcázar 2017; also see Chap. 1). Austerity cuts have also been especially sharp for vulnerable groups dependent on social care (England 2010), once again highlighting the uneven, intersectional impacts of austere policy-making (Hall et al. 2017). Changes in monetary allowances and access to resources/support likewise expose relational spaces of austerity to alteration; with individuals requiring further support from family, experiencing a reduction in contact with paid care providers, even moving to new care facilities and leaving behind friendships or intimate relations formed with staff and fellow residents.

Selma is one such example of where austerity cuts had impacted on already-marginalised and vulnerable groups, with an influence on her everyday mobilities. Selma was a single mum in her mid-30s, living with her 8-year-old daughter, Mya. Selma and Mya are originally from Iran (they are both ethnically Arabic and speak Persian as their first language), and moved to the UK a few years before taking part in the research. During the eight months of taking part in the research Selma was looking for paid work, as well as volunteering opportunities but with little success; she struggled to find work to fit around Mya's school hours. They were completely financially dependent on social security, as well as help from family and friends, and lived in a two-bed social housing flat near Mya's school. Both Selma and Mya sorely missed their family living in Iran, where the distance became more pronounced by the fact there were few means of communicating with them. When they moved to the new flat there was no telephone line, and Selma worried about paying for the installation and a contract she couldn't afford.

Selma had a cousin who lived in London, who she and Mya would visit once every few months, returning with small trinkets and furnishings for the flat to make it feel more homely. Her cousin, knowing how much she missed family, took out an all-inclusive smartphone contract for her, paying the £39 per month. This was life-changing for Selma. It meant she could speak to her family and friends 'by texts [WhatsApp] or by internet [Skype], every day' (taped discussion, May 2014), and for free. It also meant she could call or message her cousin if she needed help or just someone to talk to; they had become a lot emotionally closer as a result. The role of virtual spaces of communication and intimacy may then acquire new meaning and face new struggles in austerity, when access to these technologies and services is limited because of rising costs in relation to income alongside the closure of local libraries as a hub for online communications (see Brewster 2014; Madge and O'Connor 2006; Parrenas 2005; Waters 2002). Some of these themes are continued in Chap. 4.

Austerity policies therefore have a direct impact on mundane mobilities, whether in residency, neighbourhoods, commuting, practical logistics, communications or daily movement for socialising, which then affect how these relations are reconstituted in and through austerity. Relational geographies of austerity are revealed; the spaces through, across and between which these relationships are enacted, maintained or usurped; stretching, bending, twisting and shrinking the spatialities and relationalities of family, friendship and intimacy.

Conclusions

My aim in this chapter has been to lay the groundwork for conceptualising everyday life in austerity through a relational approach, bringing together ideas about family, friendship and intimate relations as core social relations. Developing such relational thinking about austerity has involved bringing often disparate geographical discussions—economic, financial and urban, lived, felt and personal—into conversation with one another (Hall 2016a). Through discussions of relational geographies of care and support, and mundane mobilities, and supported by snippets of ethnographic stories, everyday life is shown to not be tethered to particular spaces, but a terrain that cuts across various and overlapping spaces, relationships and practices.

One way to advance a relational approach is to consider how social relationships are configured through and across space. Such an approach illustrates how austerity is manifest in everyday life, developed through interaction and relationality, creating spaces of mobility, fixity, care, support, tension, difference and similarity. Emphasis on relational geographies of everyday life also brings to light how these relations are themselves reconstituted in and through austerity. In the chapters that follow the lives of the six families and the broader community in Argleton are fleshed out in further detail. I pick up where this chapter leaves off by thinking about everyday relationships as they are practiced and experienced in times of austerity, particularly regarding social infrastructures of care.

Bibliography

Aalbers, M. (2009). The Sociology and Geography of Mortgage Markets: Reflections on the Financial Crisis. *International Journal of Urban and Regional Research, 33*(2), 281–290.

Aitken, S. C. (1998). *Family Fantasies and Community Space*. New Brunswick, NJ: Rutgers University Press.

Allan, G. (1989). *Friendship: Developing a Sociological Perspective*. Brighton: Harvester and Wheatsheaf.

Andrews, G. J., & Chen, S. (2006). The Production of Tyrannical Space. *Children's Geographies, 4*(2), 239–250.

Askins, K. (2015). Being Together: Everyday Geographies and the Quiet Politics of Belonging. *ACME: An International E-Journal for Critical Geographies, 14*(2), 470–478.

Ballas, D., Dorling, D., & Hennig, B. (2017). Analysing the Regional Geography of Poverty, Austerity and Inequality in Europe: A Human Cartographic Perspective. *Regional Studies, 51*(1), 174–185.

Bartos, A. E. (2013). Friendship and Environmental Politics in Childhood. *Space and Polity, 17*(1), 17–32.

Beck, U., & Beck-Gernsheim, E. (2002). *Individualization*. London: Sage.

Binnie, J., Edensor, T., Holloway, J., Millington, S., & Young, C. (2007). Mundane Mobilities, Banal Travels. *Social & Cultural Geography, 8*(2), 165–174.

Blake, M. K. (2007). Formality and Friendship: Research Ethics Review and Participatory Action Research. *Acme, 6*(3), 411–421.

Blunt, A. (2005). Cultural Geography: Cultural Geographies of Home. *Progress in Human Geography, 29*(4), 505–515.

Bowlby, S. (2011). Friendship, Co-presence and Care: Neglected Spaces. *Social & Cultural Geography, 12*(6), 605–622.

Bowlby, S. (2012). Recognising the Time-Space Dimensions of Care: Caringscapes and Carescapes. *Environment and Planning A, 44*, 2101–2118.

Brewster, L. (2014). The Public Library as Therapeutic Landscape: A Qualitative Case Study. *Health & Place, 26*, 94–99.

Broadbent, S. (2009). How the Internet Enables Intimacy. *Technology, Entertainment, Design (TED) Talks*. Retrieved August 28, 2015, from www.ted.com/talks/stefana_broadbent_how_the_internet_enables_intimacy.

Brown, G. (2015). Marriage and the Spare Bedroom Tax: Exploring the Sexual Politics of Austerity in Britain. *ACME: An International e-Journal for Critical Geographies, 14*(4), 975–988.

Browne, K. (2003). Negotiations and Fieldworkings: Friendship and Feminist Research. *ACME: An International E-Journal for Critical Geographies, 2*(2), 132–146.

Bunnell, T., Yea, S., Peake, L., Skelton, T., & Smith, M. (2012). Geographies of Friendships. *Progress in Human Geography, 36*(4), 490–507.

Burrell, K. (2011). Opportunity and Uncertainty: Young People's Narratives of "Double Transition" in Post-Socialist Poland. *Area, 43*(4), 413–419.

Christophers, B. (2015). Geographies of Finance II: Crisis, Space and Political-Economic Transformation. *Progress in Human Geography, 39*(2), 205–213.

Christopherson, S., Gertler, M., & Gray, M. (2014). Universities in Crisis. *Cambridge Journal of Regions, Economy and Society, 7*, 209–215.

Cloke, P., May, J., & Williams, A. (2016). The Geographies of Food Banks in the Meantime. *Progress in Human Geography*. https://doi.org/10.1177/0309132516655881.

Coakley, L. (2002). "All Over the Place, in Town, in the Pub, Everywhere": A Social Geography of Women's Friendships in Cork. *Irish Geography, 35*(1), 40–50.

Cohen, R. L. (2010). When It Pays to Be Friendly: Employment Relationships and Emotional Labour in Hairstyling. *Sociological Review, 58*(2), 197–218.

Conradson, D. (2003). Geographies of Care: Spaces, Practices, Experiences. *Social & Cultural Geography, 4*(4), 451–454.

Conradson, D., & Latham, A. (2005). Friendship, Networks and Transnationality in a World City: Antipodean Transmigrants in London. *Journal of Ethnic and Migration Studies, 31*(2), 287–305.

Cox, R., & Narula, R. (2003). Playing Happy Families: Rules and Relationships in Au Pair Employing Households in London, England. *Gender Place and Culture, 10*, 333–344.

Crang, M. (1994). It's Showtime: On the Workplace Geographies of Display in a Restaurant in Southeast England. *Environment and Planning D: Society & Space, 12*, 675–704.

Davidson, M., & Ward, K. (2014). "Picking Up the Pieces": Austerity Urbanism California and Fiscal Crisis. *Cambridge Journal of Regions, Economy and Society, 7*(1), 81–97.

Donald, B., Glasmeier, A., Gray, M., & Lobao, L. (2014). Austerity in the City: Economic Crisis and Urban Service Decline? *Cambridge Journal of Regions. Economy and Society, 7*(1), 3–15.

Dyck, I. (2005). Feminist Geography, the "Everyday", and Local-Global Relations: Hidden Spaces of Place-Making. *The Canadian Geographer, 49*, 233–245.

Edwards, R., & Gillies, V. (2004). Support in Parenting: Values and Consensus Concerning Who To Turn To. *Journal of Social Policy, 33*(4), 627–647.

Edwards, R., & Gillies, V. (2012). Farewell to Family? Notes on an Argument for Retaining the Concept. *Families, Relationships and Societies, 1*(1), 63–69.

Edwards, R., & Weller, S. (2010). Trajectories from Youth to Adulthood: Choice and Structure for Young People Before and During Recession. *Twenty-First Century Society, 5*(2), 125–136.

Emmel, N., & Hughes, K. (2010). "Recession, It's All the Same to Us Son": The Longitudinal Experience (1999–2010) of Deprivation. *Twenty-First Century Society, 5*(2), 171–181.

England, K. (2010). Home, Work and the Shifting Geographies of Care. *Ethics, Place & Environment, 13*(2), 131–150.

Eurofound. (2014). *Third European Quality of Life Survey—Quality of Life in Europe: Families in the Economic Crisis.* Luxembourg: Publications Office of the European Union.

Evans, R. (2012). Sibling Caringscapes: Time-Space Practices of Caring Within Youth-Headed Households in Tanzania and Uganda. *Geoforum, 43*(4), 824–835.

Finch, J., & Mason, J. (1993). *Negotiating Family Responsibilities*. London: Routledge.

Gardiner, M. (2000). *Critiques of Everyday Life*. London and New York: Routledge.

Garthwaite, K. (2016). *Hunger Pains: Life Inside Foodbank Britain*. Bristol: Policy Press.

Gillies, V. (2005). Meeting Parents' Needs? Discourses of "Support" and "Inclusion" in Family Policy. *Critical Social Policy, 25*, 70–90.

Hall, S. (2010). Geographies of Money and Finance I: Cultural Economy, Politics and Place. *Progress in Human Geography, 35*, 234–245.

Hall, S. M. (2015). Everyday Ethics of Consumption in the Austere City. *Geography Compass, 9*(3), 140–151.

Hall, S. M. (2016a). Everyday Family Experiences of the Financial Crisis: Getting by in the Recent Economic Recession. *Journal of Economic Geography, 16*(2), 305–330.

Hall, S. M. (2016b). Family Relations in Times of Austerity: Reflections from the UK. In S. Punch, R. Vanderbeck, & T. Skelton (Eds.), *Geographies of Children and Young People: Families, Intergenerationality and Peer Group Relations*. Berlin: Springer.

Hall, S. M. (2017). Personal, Relational and Intimate Geographies of Austerity: Ethical and Empirical Considerations. *Area, 49*(3), 303–310.

Hall, S. M., & Jayne, M. (2016). Make, Mend and Befriend: Geographies of Austerity, Crafting and Friendship in Contemporary Cultures of Dressmaking. *Gender, Place & Culture, 23*(2), 216–234.

Hall, S. M., McIntosh, K., Neitzert, E., Pottinger, L., Sandhu, K., Stephenson, M.-A., Reed, H., & Taylor, L. (2017). *Intersecting Inequalities: The Impact of Austerity on Black and Minority Ethnic Women in the UK*. London: Runnymede and Women's Budget Group. Retrieved from www.intersecting-inequalities.com.

Harker, C., & Martin, L. L. (2012). Familial Relations: Spaces, Subjects, and Politics. *Environment and Planning A, 44*(4), 768–775.

Harrison, E. (2013). Bouncing Back? Recession, Resilience and Everyday Lives. *Critical Social Policy, 33*(1), 97–113.

Heath, S., & Calvert, E. (2013). Gifts, Loans and Intergenerational Support for Young Adults. *Sociology, 47*, 1120–1135.

Henwood, K., Shirani, F., & Coltart, C. (2010). Fathers and Financial Risk-Taking During the Economic Downturn: Insights from a QLL Study of Men's Identities-in-the-Making. *Twenty- First Century Society, 5*(2), 137–147.
Holdsworth, C. (2013). *Family and Intimate Mobilities*. Basingstoke: Palgrave Macmillan.
Holloway, S. L. (1998). Local Childcare Cultures: Moral Geographies of Mothering and the Social Organisation of Pre-school Education. *Gender, Place & Culture, 5*, 29–53.
Holloway, S. L., & Pimlott-Wilson, H. (2014). "Any Advice is Welcome Isn't It?": Neoliberal Parenting Education, Local Mothering Cultures, and Social Class. *Environment and Planning A, 46*(1), 94–111.
Holmes, H. (2015). Transient Craft: Reclaiming the Contemporary Craft Worker. *Work, Employment and Society, 29*(3), 479–495.
Holmes, H. (2018). Transient Productions; Enduring Encounters: The Crafting of Bodies and Friendships in the Hair Salon. In L. Price & H. Hawkins (Eds.), *Geographies of Making, Craft and Creativity*. London: Routledge.
Hörschelmann, K., & van Blerk, L. (2012). *Children, Youth and the City*. Abingdon: Routledge.
Horton, J. (2016). Anticipating Service Withdrawal: Young People in Spaces of Neoliberalisation, Austerity and Economic Crisis. *Transactions of the Institute of British Geographers, 41*(4), 349–362.
Horton, J. (2017). Young People and Debt: Getting on with Austerities. *Area, 49*(3), 280–287.
Horton, J., & Kraftl, P. (2009). Small Acts, Kind Words and "Not Too Much Fuss": Implicit Activisms. *Emotion, Space and Society, 2*(1), 14–23.
Jackson, P. (2009). Introduction: Food as a Lens on Family Life. In P. Jackson (Ed.), *Changing Families, Changing Food* (pp. 1–16). Basingstoke: Palgrave Macmillan.
Jamieson, L. (1997). *Intimacy: Personal Relationships in Modern Societies*. Cambridge: Polity Press.
Jayne, M., & Leung, H. H. (2014). Embodying Chinese Urbanism: Towards a Research Agenda. *Area, 46*(3), 256–267.
Johnson, L., & Longhurst, R. (2010). *Space, Place and Sex: Geographies of Sexualities*. Plymouth: Rowman and Littlefield.
Jupp, E. (2013a). Enacting Parenting Policy? The Hybrid Spaces of Sure Start Children's Centres. *Children's Geographies, 11*(2), 173–187.
Jupp, E. (2013b). "I Feel More at Home Here than in My Own Community": Approaching the Emotional Geographies of Neighbourhood Policy. *Critical Social Policy, 33*, 532–553.

Kirwan, S. F., McDermont, M. A., & Clarke, J. (2016). Imagining and Practising Citizenship in Austere Times: The Work of Citizens Advice. *Citizenship Studies, 20*(6–7), 764–778.

Kitson, M., Martin, R., & Tyler, P. (2011). The Geographies of Austerity. *Cambridge Journal of Regions. Economy and Society, 4*(3), 289–302.

Lambie-Mumford, H., & Green, M. A. (2015). Austerity, Welfare Reform and the Rising Use of Food Banks by Children in England and Wales. *Area*. https://doi.org/10.1111/area.12233.

Leach, R., Phillipson, C., Biggs, S. and Money, A. (2013) 'Babyboomers, consumption and social change: the bridging generation?', *International Review of Sociology, 23*(1), 104–122.

Lee, R., Clark, G. L., Pollard, J., & Leyshon, A. (2009). The Remit of Financial Geography—Before and After the Crisis. *Journal of Economic Geography, 9*, 723–747.

Longhurst, R. (2008). The Geography Closest In—The Body … The Politics of Pregnability. *Australian Geographical Studies, 32*(2), 214–223.

MacLeavy, J. (2011). A "New" Politics of Austerity, Workfare and Gender? The UK Coalition Government's Welfare Reform Proposals. *Cambridge Journal of Regions, Economy and Society, 4*, 355–367.

Madge, C., & O'Connor, H. (2006). Parenting Gone Wired: Empowerment of New Mothers on the Internet? *Social & Cultural Geography, 7*(2), 199–220.

Martin, R. (2011). The Local Geographies of the Financial Crisis: From the Housing Bubble to Economic Recession and Beyond. *Journal of Economic Geography, 11*, 587–618.

Massey, D. (1991, June). A Global Sense of Place. *Marxism Today*, pp. 24–29.

Massey, D. (2004). Geographies of Responsibility. *Geografiska Annaler B, 86*(1), 5–18.

McDowell, L. (2012). Post-Crisis, Post-Ford and Post-Gender? Youth Identities in an Era of Austerity. *Journal of Youth Studies, 15*(5), 573–590.

McDowell, L., Ray, K., Perrons, D., Fagan, C., & Ward, K. (2005). Women's Paid Work and Moral Economies of Care. *Social & Cultural Geography, 6*, 219–235.

Milligan, C. (2003). Location or Dis-Location? Towards a Conceptualization of People and Place in the Care-Giving Experience. *Social & Cultural Geography, 4*(4), 455–470.

Mitchell, K. (2007). Geographies of Identity: The Intimate Cosmopolitan. *Progress in Human Geography, 31*(5), 706–720.

Mizen, P., & Ofosu-Kusi, Y. (2010). Asking, Giving, Receiving: Friendship as Survival Strategy Among Accra's Street Children. *Childhood, 17*(4), 441–454.

Morgan, D. (2009). *Acquaintances: The Space Between Intimates And Strangers: The Space Between Intimates and Strangers*. Maidenhead: McGraw-Hill Education (UK).
Morgan, D. (2011). *Rethinking Family Practices*. Basingstoke: Palgrave Macmillan.
Morrison, C., Johnston, L., & Longhurst, R. (2012). Critical Geographies of Love as Spatial, Relational and Political. *Progress in Human Geography, 37*(4), 505–521.
Morris-Roberts, K. (2001). Intervening in Friendship Exclusion? The Politics of Doing Feminist Research with Teenage Girls. *Ethics, Place & Environment, 4*(2), 147–153.
Morris-Roberts, K. (2004). Girls' Friendships, "Distinctive Individuality" and Socio-Spatial Practices of (Dis)identification. *Children's Geographies, 2*(2), 237–255.
Nash, C. (2005). Geographies of Relatedness. *Transactions of the Institute of British Geographers, 30*(4), 449–462.
Neal, S., & Vincent, C. (2013). Multiculture, Middle Class Competencies and Friendship Practices in Super-Diverse Geographies. *Social & Cultural Geography, 14*(8), 909–929.
Newman, M., Woodcock, A., & Dunham, P. (2006). "Playtime in the Borderlands": Children's Representations of School, Gender and Bullying Through Photographs and Interviews. *Children's Geographies, 4*(3), 289–302.
Oswin, N., & Olund, E. (2010). Governing Intimacy. *Environment and Planning D: Society and Space, 28*(1), 60–67.
Pahl, R. (1984). *Divisions of Labour*. Oxford: Blackwell.
Pahl, R. (2000). *On Friendship*. Cambridge: Polity Press.
Pain, R., & Smith, S. (2008). *Fear: Critical Geopolitics and Everyday Life*. Abingdon: Ashgate.
Parrenas, R. (2005). Long Distance Intimacy: Class, Gender and Intergenerational Relations Between Mothers and Children in Filipino Transnational Families. *Global Networks, 5*(4), 317–336.
Pearson, R., & Elson, D. (2015). Transcending the Impact of the Financial Crisis in the United Kingdom: Towards Plan F—A Feminist Economic Strategy. *Feminist Review, 109*, 8–30.
Peck, J. (2012). Austerity Urbanism: American Cities Under Extreme Economy. *City, 16*(6), 626–655.
Pessar, P. R., & Mahler, S. J. (2003). Transnational Migration: Bringing Gender In. *International Migration Review, 37*(3), 812–846.

Pike, A., Coombes, M., O'Brien, P., & Tomaney, J. (2018). Austerity States, Institutional Dismantling and the Governance of Subnational Economic Development: The Demise of the Regional Development Agencies in England. *Territory, Politics, Governance, 6*(1), 118–144.

Pimlott-Wilson, H. (2017). Individualising the Future: The Emotional Geographies of Neoliberal Governance in Young Peoples' Aspirations. *Area, 49*(3), 288–295.

Pimlott-Wilson, H., & Hall, S. M. (2017). Everyday Experiences of Economic Change: Repositioning Geographies of Children, Youth and Families. *Area, 49*(3), 258–265.

Pinkerton, J., & Dolan, P. (2007). Family Support, Social Capital, Resilience and Adolescent Coping. *Child and Family Social Work, 12*(3), 219–228.

Pollard, J. S. (2013). Gendering Capital: Financial Crisis, Financialization and an Agenda for Economic Geography. *Progress in Human Geography, 37*, 403–423.

Popke, J. (2006). Geography and Ethics: Everyday Mediations Through Care and Consumption. *Progress in Human Geography, 30*(4), 504–512.

Powdermaker, H. (1966). *Stranger and Friend: The Way of an Anthropologist*. New York: WW Norton & Company.

Pratt, G. (1997). Stereotypes and Ambivalence: The Construction of Domestic Workers in Vancouver, British Columbia. *Gender, Place and Culture, 4*(2), 159–178.

Price, P. L. (2012). Race and Ethnicity II: Skin and Other Intimacies. *Progress in Human Geography, 37*(4), 578–586.

Robinson, V., Hockey, J., & Meah, A. (2004). "What I Used to Do … On My Mother's Settee": Spatial and Emotional Aspects of Heterosexuality in England. *Gender, Place & Culture, 11*(3), 417–435.

Round, J., Williams, C. C., & Rodgers, P. (2008). Everyday Tactic of Spaces of Power: The Role of Informal Economies in Post-Soviet Ukraine. *Social & Cultural Geography, 9*, 171–185.

Skeggs, B. (2004). *Class, Self and Culture*. London: Routledge.

Skelton, T. (2000). "Nothing to Do, Nowhere to Go?": Teenage Girls and 'Public' Space in the Rhondda Valleys, South Wales. In S. L. Holloway & G. Valentine (Eds.), *Children's Geographies: Playing, Living, Learning* (pp. 69–85). London: Routledge.

Slater, T. (2013). Your Life Chances Affect Where You Live: A Critique of the 'Cottage Industry' of Neighbourhood Effects Research. *International Journal of Urban and Regional Research, 37*(2), 367–387.

Smart, C. (2007). *Personal Life*. Cambridge: Polity Press.

Smith, D. M. (1999). Geography, Community and Morality. *Environment and Planning A, 31*, 19–35.

Smith, D. P. (2011). Geographies of Long-Distance Family Migration: Moving to a "Spatial Turn". *Progress in Human Geography, 35*(5), 652–668.

Smith, A., & Stenning, A. (2006). Beyond Household Economies: Articulations and Spaces of Economic Practice in Post-Socialism. *Progress in Human Geography, 30*(2), 190–213.

Spencer, L., & Pahl, R. (2006). *Rethinking Friendship: Hidden Solidarities Today*. Princeton, NJ: Princeton University Press.

Stenning, A. (2005). Post-Socialism and the Changing Geographies of the Everyday in Poland. *Transactions of the Institute of British Geographers, 30*, 113–127.

Tarrant, A. (2010). Constructing a Social Geography of Grandparenthood: A New Focus for Intergenerationality. *Area, 42*(2), 190–197.

Tarrant, A. (2013). Grandfathering as Spatio-Temporal Practice: Conceptualizing Performances of Ageing Masculinities in Contemporary Familial Carescapes. *Social & Cultural Geography, 14*(2), 192–210.

Thomson, R., Hadfield, L., Kehily, M. J., & Sharpe, S. (2010). Family Fortunes: An Intergenerational Perspective on Recession. *21st Century Society, 5*, 149–157.

Valentine, G. (1993). Desperately Seeing Susan: A Geography of Lesbian Friendships. *Area, 25*(2), 109–116.

Valentine, G. (2008a). The Ties that Bind: Towards Geographies of Intimacy. *Geography Compass, 2*(6), 2097–2110.

Valentine, G., & Hughes, K. (2011). Geographies of 'Family' Life: Interdependent Relationships Across the Life Course in the Context of Problem Internet Gambling. In L. Holt (Ed.), *Geographies of Children, Youth and Families: An International Perspective* (pp. 121–135). London: Routledge.

Valentine, G., Jayne, M., & Gould, M. (2012). Do as I Say, Not as I Do: The Affective Space of Family Life and the Generational Transmission of Drinking Cultures. *Environment and Planning A, 44*(4), 776–792.

van Blerk, L. (2011). Managing Cape Town's Street Children/Youth: The Impact of the 2010 World Cup Bid on Street Life in the City. *South African Geographical Journal, 93*(1), 29–37.

Vanderbeck, R. M. (2007). Intergenerational Geographies: Age Relations, Segregation and Re-engagements. *Geography Compass, 1*(2), 200–221.

Waight, E. (2018). "Hand-Me-Down" Childrenswear and the Middle-Class Economy of Nearly New Sales. In A. Ince & S. M. Hall (Eds.), *Sharing*

Economies in Times of Crisis: Practices, Politics and Possibilities (pp. 96–109). London: Routledge.

Waters, J. L. (2002). Flexible Families? "Astronaut" Households and the Experiences of Lone Mothers in Vancouver, British Columbia. *Social & Cultural Geography, 3*(2), 117–134.

Weeks, J., Heaphy, B., & Donovan, C. (2001). *Same Sex Intimacies: Families of Choice and Other Life Experiments*. London: Routledge.

Wellman, B. (1990). The Place of Kinfolk in Personal Community Networks. *Marriage & Family Review, 15*(1/2), 195–228.

Wilkinson, E., & Ortega-Alcázar, I. (2017). A Home of One's Own? Housing Welfare for 'Young Adults' in Times of Austerity. *Critical Social Policy, 37*(3), 1–19.

Wilson, H. F. (2013). Collective Life: Parents, Playground Encounters and the Multicultural City. *Social & Cultural Geography, 14*(6), 625–648.

Wilson, H. F. (2017). On Geography and Encounter: Bodies, Borders, and Difference. *Progress in Human Geography, 41*(4), 45–471.

Women's Budget Group. (2018). A "Jam Tomorrow" Budget': Women's Budget Group Response to Autumn Budget 2018. Retrieved December 19, 2018, from https://wbg.org.uk/wp-content/uploads/2018/11/WBG-2018-Autumn-Budget-full-analysis.pdf.

Zelizer, V. (2005). *The Purchase of Intimacy*. Princeton, NJ: Princeton University Press.

3

Everyday Social Infrastructures and Tapestries of Care in Times of Austerity

Getting by in times of austerity often requires intricate tapestries of care, carefully woven fabrics of familial and extra-familial relationships, or what I describe here as 'everyday social infrastructures'. Where in Chap. 2 I outlined what a relational approach to everyday austerity might look like, in this chapter I start to apply this framework and weave these ideas together with more detailed empirical accounts. Ethnographic examples from the families and communities in Argleton include crying on friend's shoulders, carrying out extra care-giving duties for family, gaining trusted financial advice, and the integration of researchers as intimate others. Intimate and significant others, such as childcare workers, social club volunteers and even researchers, also play important roles in everyday social infrastructures. These interpersonal connections also bring to light social differences, similarities and tensions, including inter- and intra-generationality, class and gender. The dynamics of these everyday social infrastructures are prone to change in times of austerity.

To situate these ethnographic findings, feminist concepts of care, particularly care ethics and social infrastructures of care, are applied and extended. I illustrate the extent to which austerity transforms relational geographies of care (who does what, for whom and where), whether

S. M. Hall, *Everyday Life in Austerity*, Palgrave Macmillan Studies in Family and Intimate Life, https://doi.org/10.1007/978-3-030-17094-3_3

inter- or intra-familial, within friendships and other intimate relationships. While proponents of care ethics typically prioritise where care takes place or how care changes over time, I advocate a closer look at the relational qualities of care: how care is embedded within, and has the potential to shape, everyday social infrastructures. Starting with an overview of literature on feminist politics of care, gendered labour and social infrastructures, the chapter is arranged around three key themes that emerged from analysis of the empirical data: intergenerational and gendered infrastructures, tangled, knotty and textured infrastructures of care, and fieldwork as care work.

A note on language is also required here. Rather than applying notions such as 'assemblages', 'bricolage' or 'networks' (e.g. see Anderson and McFarlane 2011; Braun 2006; Jones 2009) the metaphor of the 'tapestry' is instead used to describe the warp and weft of support, care and advice that give people help, guidance and grounding in their everyday lives. Tapestries are intricate, colourful and textured. Tapestries take much time, effort, consideration, embodied work, visceral connection and attention, and are also often associated with feminised, domestic labour and skill, whether paid or pastime.

Recent writing by Nelson (2018, p. 1) has explored how metaphors are deployed within geographical writing, thinking of tapestries as 'a riot of overlapping threads running over and under one another to form blurring, edgeless patterns'; though he fails to acknowledge the cultural and gendered norms that pervade the language we choose and thus the ideas, world views and assumptions we then propagate (also see Ellegard and De Pater 1999; Strong 2018). Moreover, the visible design of a tapestry does not always represent the full picture. Rather, it can hide behind it a messiness of threads, knots and loose ends. And while different tapestries might portray different scenes, the threads within, much like patterns of social relationships, are interwoven, each stitch dependent on the one before. I therefore use the concept of tapestries to unravel the lived experiences of everyday social infrastructures. I show how the variously colourful threads are stitched together to create a fuller, carefully crafted picture, but often with an untidy underside and fraying edges that sometimes require maintenance.

Feminist Politics of Care, Gendered Labour and Social Infrastructures

In considering care in everyday life, theories of an 'ethics' or 'politics' of care provide a useful starting point. Ideas around the spatialities, ethics and politics of care blossomed as a result of influential writings and insights from feminist scholars such as Joan Tronto, Virginia Held and Carol Gilligan. As a concept, ethical standpoint and applied philosophy, feminist politics of care ultimately posit caring (and the spaces, politics and relationalities of this care) as a moral disposition. The emphasis is placed on:

> the concerns and implications of *caring*: caring for children, caring for the ill or infirm, caring about the feelings of others, and understanding how to care for human beings, including ourselves, enmeshed as we are in human relationships. (Held 1993, p. 30; italics in original)

Four key facets to a politics of care have been identified. These are '*caring about* (recognizing a need), *taking care of* (assuming responsibility for an identified need), *care-giving* (the direct meeting of a need) and *care-receiving* (the object of care responds to care received)' (Hall 2016b, p. 1020; also see Fisher and Tronto 1990; Tronto 1993). Care thus becomes 'embedded in relations of attentiveness and responsiveness', interdependence and mutuality, and indicative of 'the collectivity to which one belongs' (Barnett and Land 2007, p. 1067; Lawson 2007; Massey 2004).

The politics of care are, therefore, grounded in and actively build upon social and interpersonal relations and connection. This is also Popke's (2006, p. 505) argument for 'reclaiming "care" as a social, and thus political, relation'. Proposing a feminist politics of slow scholarship, Mountz et al. (2015, p. 1251) likewise state that 'a feminist ethics of care is personal and political, individual and collective. We must take care of ourselves before we can take care of others. *But we must take care of others.*' Care is therefore, by extension, inherently political, interpersonal and relational, because it almost always involves another (Barnett and Land

2007). The exception here, as I have argued in earlier writing, is self-care. For while Tronto (1993, p. 102) claims that care requires 'reaching out to something other than the self', and Barnett and Land (2007, p. 1067) argue that care 'cannot be solely self-referential or monological', care for self and others is in practice not so clear-cut. In fact, rather than being competing ethical and political motivations, self-care can also be 'a conduit to caring for others' (Hall 2016b, p. 1036).

Care is therefore 'a politics founded on interdependence as a human condition' (Smith 2005, p. 15). It also has a place, both in society at large and in everyday routines, relationships and practices, though most commonly associated within the personal and domestic space of home (England and Dyck 2011; Power and Hall 2018). Notwithstanding, a politics of care can also trouble 'the conventional distinction between a public realm, viewed as the site of politics and justice, and the private spaces of emotion, care and welfare' (Popke 2006, p. 507). Inspection of the practicalities and realities of care ultimately raises questions about the role of care in society and economy, the labour required and the value (or lack thereof) attributed to care work.

As a field of feminist philosophical and political theory, the politics of care have been especially influential in human geography, resulting in widespread and eclectic theoretical engagement (Lawson 2007; Popke 2006). Care has been shown to be spatially contingent, 'woven into the fabric of particular social spaces and communities' (Conradson 2003, p. 453), as well as geographical writing, institutions and fieldwork (England 1994; Hall 2017; McDowell 2017; Mountz et al. 2015). Care as gendered, reproductive labour has also attracted heightened socio-political interest in recent years. As McDowell et al. (2005, p. 219) point out, 'the care of children and older people has moved to the forefront of current policy debates in a way that was unimaginable only a decade ago'. Such care responsibilities are also not evenly distributed, since 'policy shifts [...] have placed the burden of care increasingly onto individuals and families' as opposed to the state (Popke 2006, p. 506; Jensen and Tyler 2012).

For instance, Millar and Ridge (2013), in their study of working lone mothers in the UK, identify familial and other social relationships as an important source of support in relation to childcare. Grandparents, aunts, uncles and cousins provided essential help, and employers and co-workers were significant in terms of negotiating flexible working around childcare responsibilities, with care transgressing home/work, family/state boundaries (also see Emmel and Hughes 2010; Tarrant 2010). As discussed in Chap. 2, and illuminated further here, care work is not restricted to families, but interacts with various personal and intimate spaces and relationships.

Reflecting on the ongoing care crisis in Canada (where there is a deficit of care particularly for children, the elderly and people with illnesses and disabilities), England (2010, p. 135) also notes how the home 'is the location of a set of contradictory discourses and practices [...] an apparently private, domestic place marked by intimacy'. In such circumstances 'the boundary between the supposedly private space of home and the public space of the state and the market gets blurred when non-family paid caregivers provide care' (England 2010, p. 146). So, 'in some instances, the care is provided by a family member or a friend; in other cases, it comes from a paid care worker' (England and Dyck 2011, p. 206). Caring roles can thus be various, overlapping and multidirectional, formal and informal, resulting in—as I will explore in more depth—different dependencies and obligations.

Much domestic care work, whether paid or unpaid, is disproportionately carried out by women (England 2010; England and Dyck 2011). As noted in Chap. 2, the politics of care become further realised when considering that care work is largely gendered, classed and racialised labour, and most care is received by privileged individuals 'in professional and managerial jobs' (England 2010, p. 134; Duffy 2011; McDowell 2012; Tronto 1993). By virtue of the close corporeality involved in everyday geographies of care work—as intimate, embodied and interpersonal—the politics of care become ever more pronounced (see England and Dyck 2011; Popke 2006; Power and Hall 2018; Twigg 2000).

Providing personal care has also been described as a form of 'body-work' (Twigg 2000), 'involv[ing] intimate work done directly on other people's bodies' (England and Dyck 2011, p. 206). Care work results in bodies interacting and bodily differences, boundaries and between-ness being confronted, traversed, even redefined. At the same time, caring and cared-for bodies are regularly 'defined through medical and policy discourses' (Dyck 2005, p. 238), and in relation to one another (Devault 1991; Longhurst et al. 2008; Massey 2004; Twigg 2000). This reshapes the politics of care according to popular and political ideologies.

It is important not to separate the conceptual, political and lived accounts of care, and remember that despite its continued marginalisation and devaluing, 'care work is work' (Mountz et al. 2015, p. 1238; Lawson 2007). Beneath the 'hidden, silenced character, the low occupational esteem in which it is held and its gendered nature' (Twigg 2000, p. 389; also see Dyck 2005), caring is often physically and emotionally strenuous (Held 1993; Hochschild 1983). And this gendered labour is arguably essential for societies to function:

> The sphere of reproduction supplies services directly concerned with the daily and inter-generational reproduction of people as human beings, especially through their care, socialisation and education. It includes unpaid work in families and communities, organised unpaid volunteer work, and paid work in public services like health and education that produce for use rather than for sale. It is in this sphere that the care essential for human well-being is created. (Pearson and Elson 2015, p. 10)

Everyday care as defined above is assembled across sectors, spaces and social groups, and scales up to shape political discourse and decision-making. Dyck (2005, p. 235) makes this same point, wherein 'the everyday activities of care work [...] are not simply a local matter. They are effects of the stretching of social, political and economic relations over space, constructed and negotiated at interlocking scales of bodies, homes, cities, regions, nations and the global.'

Politics of care therefore account for who cares and why, alongside what caring achieves, at multiple scales (Held 1993), from care as embodied gesture to care within fiscal policies. At the personal scale, care (giving and receiving) can take multiple forms. It can be expressed through actions, words or even silences. It can be direct, corporeal and interpersonal, or it can be indirect, mediated by space, other people or technologies. It can be deliberate or serendipitous. These are all part of the tapestries of everyday social infrastructures of care.

Growing significance of the politics of care can also be observed in the current context of austerity policies in the UK, Ireland and southern Europe (Hall 2016a; Power and Hall 2018). Past research, particularly in feminist political economy, highlights that women bear the brunt of economic crises and recession (Bradley 1986; Volger 1994). They are key recipients and beneficiaries of state welfare and providers of formal and informal care, as well as making up the majority of public sector workers where austerity cuts have also fallen hard (Hall et al. 2017; MacLeavy 2011; Pearson and Elson 2015). Recent research has identified the contemporary condition of austerity as a gendered burden in everyday care provisioning (Hall 2016a, 2017; Power and Hall 2018), and balanced alongside dual roles in paid and unpaid labour (Greer-Murphy 2017; Jupp 2017; MacLeavy 2011; McDowell 2017).

Within emerging critiques of the gendered politics of austerity, concerns have also been raised that, where state investments are made, the focus remains on physical infrastructure (transport, housing, military). This comes at the expense of investment in what Pearson and Elson (2015, p. 26) term 'social infrastructure': the provision of 'health [care], education, childcare, social housing and lifelong care which benefit all, not just the few' (although see Jarvis 2005 for discussion of the social implications of this physical infrastructure). Social infrastructures are as much relational and political, since the authors identify that in practice, to invest in social infrastructures requires the 'incorporation of reproductive and care work into economic analysis and economic policies' (p. 9). This echoes Smith's (2005, p. 15) proposal that a politics of care is 'steeped in principles which can be institutionalised across all spheres of social life'.

Extending this connection further, I posit that investment in social infrastructure is one way of realising a politics of care in times of austerity. This investment is also interpersonal and relational, since it centres social and political responsibilities and institutions. However, the retraction of public expenditure and a lack of investment in social infrastructure do not necessarily result in care-less social relations. As discussed in Chap. 2, and as Power and Hall (2018, p. 311) acknowledge, 'new spaces, relations, networks and practices of care and caring are emerging in difficult times, in unexpected and unconventional places'. Austerity may, then, present revised opportunities for care, interconnection and togetherness (Hall and Jayne 2016; Holmes 2018; Tarrant 2018).

Bringing feminist theories on the politics of care (Held 1993; Tronto 1993) and gendered labour (England and Dyck 2011; Twigg 2000), together with emerging ideas about social infrastructures (Pearson and Elson 2015), I now examine the colourful tapestries of care infrastructures through the lens of the everyday. Conversely, ideas around social infrastructures have tended to be levelled at institutional and national scales (MacLeavy 2011; Smith 2005), rather than working upwards from personal experiences (Dyck 2005; Lawson 2007). Daly and Lewis (2000, p. 287) briefly touch on care as social infrastructure, though they also see infrastructure as 'macro', consisting of cash and services, in contrast to 'micro' practices of performance, receipt and relations of care.

Drawing on both ethnographic field diaries, visual materials and spoken narratives from taped discussions, I address these criticisms by placing participants' lives and experiences at the centre of analysis (Gregson and Rose 1997; Hanisch 1970). Throughout I continue to apply the relational framework set out in Chap. 2, considering who provides and receives care, and the impacts of care on everyday social relationships. Starting with intergenerational and gendered care, I explore how everyday social infrastructures of care for children and older generations in particular are shaped by austerity cuts, which in turn have implications for the social relations with which they are interwoven.

Intergenerational and Gendered Infrastructures

Across the ethnography, and aligned with historical research in political economy (Bradley 1986; Volger 1994), dealing with the brunt of changes to services and personal finances as a result of austerity was observed as a distinctly gendered activity. Gendered care responsibilities, at home and amongst family and friends, were also routinely acknowledged and regularly discussed by participants. Childcare is an important form of gendered labour within social infrastructures and frequently arose in conversations regarding austerity (Jensen and Tyler 2012; McDowell et al. 2005; Pearson and Elson 2015). With the local council budget slashed, cuts to social security and child tax credits, a reduction in wages in real terms and high levels of unemployment, participants were being hit on multiple fronts (Hall 2016a; Langley 2008).

Informal, trusted networks of female friends and family provided the main framework of social infrastructures of childcare (McDowell et al. 2005; Millar and Ridge 2013), and these women were under increased pressure because of sharp cuts to social care budgets. As discussed in Chap. 2, since retiring just over a year before taking part in the research, Pauline had been drafted in to look after her grandchildren more and more often. When not babysitting, Pauline would often knit clothes for them, from hats and scarves to complicated cardigan and jumper patterns. These personal geographies of care also extended beyond her immediate family, to strangers and other species; 'an ex-colleague of mine's just expecting a baby so I've knitted for her, [and I've done some] hats with little flaps in for premature babies [in hospital]. And [knitted mice for] Cats Protection' (Pauline, taped discussion, August 2015). I explore these material intimacies further in Chap. 4.

Despite being a more regular feature in their family's life—particularly their younger son, his wife and their two sons, who lived in Argleton—Pauline and George described how they were not necessarily emotionally closer to them as a result. This was expressed as a sense of distance and lack of contact. 'We don't see the boys on a regular basis, or the grandkids', George said. Pauline likewise said, 'we speak to the partners more than we do the boys' (taped discussion, March 2015). At other times, Pauline complained about getting worrying health news 'by text message rather than a phone call' (field diary, March 2015), not being sent a Mother's Day card by one of her sons (field diary, March 2015) or her not featuring in any of the pictures taken on family days out (field diary, July 2015). She talked about buying a cake from her daughter-in-law and feeling guilty because she was paying only for the ingredients, but justified this because 'she gives them a lot of time with babysitting and helping out' (field diary, May 2015).

I witnessed their sons and daughters-in-law calling and texting them on a fairly regular basis. Pauline also saw one grandson almost every Wednesday at a playgroup session she organised. George saw one of his sons 'at weekends when we're at football together' (taped discussion,

March 2015). In providing childcare to assist with the changing work and leisure patterns of her son and daughter-in-law, Pauline had become an important part of their social infrastructures of care. However, neither she nor George saw this care as being reciprocated, whether with care or anything else (also see Bowlby 2011). It had not brought them any closer together in their intergenerational relations, a fact they put down to gender differences. Pauline said that 'when kids grow up they tend to be close to the woman's family anyway' (field diary, July 2015). That Pauline and George did not *feel* as though they saw their family much was as significant as whether they actually did. Physical proximity and familiarity does not equate to emotional closeness. Social infrastructures of care are shown here to be textured, multidirectional and open to interpretation. When examined in detail, tensions can be seen within the tapestry.

As recipients, participants also acknowledged that care work could be multifaceted, and that gendered care burdens were multiple and intergenerational. These relational qualities of care become particularly pronounced under austerity. Laura described her mum 'helping me out a lot with the kids, she works seventeen hours a week at [retail store] and my nana's 92, she helps out and looks after nana as well' (taped discussion, August 2014). This is a common story, what with simultaneous austerity cuts to child and social care, leaving 'sandwiched' generations such as Laura's mum and Pauline shouldering additional care burdens (Person and Elson 2015). Laura said she felt sorry for her mum, 'she's got enough going on and could do with a break' (field diary, July 2014). She explained that this gendered responsibility was also situated in wider familial and generational tensions, that Laura's uncles (her mum's brothers) are less than useful, and that 'she's the only one who looks after nana, because she's the only daughter' (field diary, July 2014). Tapestries of care are thus tightly interwoven with social identities, responsibilities and moralities. When these tapestries are explored with a close eye they reveal gendered and generational familial tensions.

Adding further texture to these everyday infrastructures of care, in relying on both her mum and mother-in-law for childcare, it was Laura and not partner Rich who carried the emotional load of arranging this care (see Hochschild 1983; Lawson 2007; Twigg 2000). Laura was in charge of organising the complex medley of diaries to ensure the children were cared for, as well as looking after other guests:

> Rich's mum was helping more than ever. In the past she would not do very much around the house when the kids were in bed, leaving Laura to feel as though they had "another person to take care of and another mouth to feed". But she's started helping out more, doing things like putting the washing out in the morning, helping to tidy up after a meal—doing more than helping with the kids. "Why do you think this is?", I asked. "'Probably because she could see how hard it's been for us to work and look after two young kids", Laura suggested. (field diary, May 2014)

The threads of care were overlapping and messy, because Rich's mum had 'stepped in while Laura's mum had been looking after nana' (field diary, July 2014). Care infrastructures tended to be complicated, involving lots of people and planning, as an additional form of gendered labour. Similarly, when Kerry had hospital appointments to attend or when she and husband Dan went away for a few days, she had to develop a strategy to make sure her four young sons were looked after. She arranged for her mum and sister to look after two sons each, and also dealt with arranging any associated tasks. She arranged where they would sleep, the times they would be picked up from school or nursery, the meals they would eat, including buying the food and having it delivered, too. This took up lots of time, energy and consideration; what Hochschild (1983) famously termed 'emotional labour'. I come back to this in Chap. 6 when discussing crises in everyday life.

For the families who participated in the ethnography, informal childcare was mostly provided in kind, although sometimes friends and family were paid to provide this. Continuing with the example of Kerry's everyday social infrastructures:

> As of June next year [I'll be an] unofficial child-minder for my sister's baby [...] [her husband] now does shifts, so he doesn't know what his shifts are until, like, a month in advance, so he wouldn't get a child-minder to fit around that. [...] She's going to pay me. [...] Anything would be better than nothing. (Kerry, taped discussion, April 2014)

Kerry was caring for multiple individuals here: not only her nephew, but also for her sister by-proxy. Her sister's husband had been out of work for a nearly a year and struggled to find steady employment (in the context of extreme job scarcity), leaving them with few savings. They had to balance forthcoming parental responsibilities with unpredictable shift patterns. This arrangement therefore enabled Kerry's sister and brother-in-law to continue their current employment without forking out for expensive childcare. The individualisation of childcare costs, as a trend that has been compounded by austerity cuts in the UK, can have significant impact on family finances and decision-making (also see McDowell 2012). At the same time, Kerry was considering her own children and the advantages of extra income, as well as practical positives: 'I still have to be going to school, doing the school run, so having another child in a buggy … it's easier, I put my shopping in the buggy' (taped discussion, April 2014). These everyday social infrastructures are 'enmeshed […] in human relationships' (Held 1993, p. 30), the result of interpersonal and intimate relations, as well as with material and financial resources. I explore the tensions that can arise from these and similar intimate monetary arrangements further in Chap. 4.

My findings revealed how women were also taking on more (often precarious) work, balanced with this familial and extra-familial care, in order to weather the storm of austerity. In the case above, Kerry took on cash-in-hand care work that might have jeopardised her state benefits (housing benefit and child tax credits, upon which she and Dan were reliant), when she already had her hands full with four young boys. Husband Dan would also find risky ways to make some extra cash. At the car garage where he worked he would often buy cars from clients, renovate them and sell them for a profit, although he had made a few losses. Kerry told me that 'Dan seems to think he has to do it so that they have enough money, a buffer to help when things get a bit tight' (field diary, March 2014).

These informal money-making strategies caused worry for Kerry. In one of our taped discussions 'she pointed to the dictaphone and shook her head when asked about the paid childcare for her sister, and only continued when I reassured her she would be anonymous' (field diary, April 2014). While constraints posed by local labour markets had a role to play here, these experiences of hardship were considered by participants to be largely due to changes made to welfare, and the broader impacts of austerity on living costs and work opportunities.

Moreover, dual burdens such as these have long been recognised as a gendered phenomenon (Lawson 2007; MacLeavy 2011; McDowell 2017), with austerity heightening them and adding extra care burdens to those already overstretched. Zoe was another such example. She was a mum to two young children, and a registered carer to her youngest child who had complex needs. In addition to working and studying part-time, she also engaged in informal paid work for her friends' catering business. Alongside her employment and training in social work, Laura had 'a casual bar job at the club down the road' to help with everyday living costs, 'because there's two of them [children] and our rent's more now than when we were renting a flat' (Laura, taped discussion, May 2014). The increase in rents at the same time as the rising costs of day-to-day living hit some participants hard (Hall 2016a; Langley 2008).

However, gendered intergenerational care work is not bound to home or kin-like relations (England 2010; England and Dyck 2011), and this becomes abundantly clear in the context of austerity. Care work in communities, towards strangers and acquaintances, was a similarly gendered responsibility. Women were providing all three key sources of social infrastructure described by Pearson and Elson (2015): unwaged, volunteer and paid care. School committees, toddler groups, after-school clubs, coffee mornings, craft clubs, survivor support groups, reading circles, just a few examples from my fieldwork, were often run by and for women as caregivers (also see Chap. 5).

Both Zoe and Pauline were involved in organising local social groups. Zoe ran a mother and toddler session, and Pauline co-organised both a morning playgroup and a coffee and chat afternoon. These activities were important strands in local care infrastructures for children and parents, and the coffee afternoon attracted a large number of older people living alone. Interestingly, these groups emerged from personal caring responsibilities. Zoe started the playgroup when her kids were young. She had been persuaded by the other mums to continue organising, even after her two children had begun school, because she was so good at it. Pauline helped to run the morning playgroup because her eldest grandson had once attended, so she continued until the younger one was of the right age to attend, too. These roles were entirely voluntary and carried out alongside other gendered care responsibilities. Moreover, the child-centred sessions were a response to the closure of locally funded activities (a local Sure Start centre and sessions at the local library) where demand for replacement services had therefore increased and so more hands were needed on deck for coordination and management. It was here that the impacts of austerity were sharply felt, due to a combination of public spending cuts for social and childcare, while personal and familial resources were also depleted.

In times of austerity, relational and gendered politics of care acquire new significance. In many of the examples above, the everyday care enacted can be understood as gendered experiences that are already under-resourced, and as pressures and responsibilities made even more acute in an era of austerity. In this sense, austerity operates as both a marker of a particular time period and a particular policy approach. Nevertheless, women were providing the social glue that held their families and communities together, attending to the rifts opened by a retreating, shrinking state.

Tangled, Knotty and Textured Infrastructures of Care

As already highlighted, everyday social infrastructures are knotty and interwoven, making complex forms and fabrics of care. In this section, I play closer attention to these complexities, unpicking some of the everyday reciprocities—givings and takings, and everything in between—that constitute and maintain social infrastructures. I want to build on the point that social infrastructures of care are not always multidirectional, that different types and intensities of care are present, and that they can create or amplify power imbalances (also see Bowlby 2011; Hall 2016a). Furthermore, I want to ensure that my findings reflect the gendered complexities of care; that while emotional and embodied labour may often fall to women in times of austerity (MacLeavy 2011; Pearson and Elson

2015), as described in the previous section, this is not an exclusive account (see Fodor 2006; Tarrant 2018). The example of financial advice (different to monetary lending) reveals how there are various gendered forms of care at work, disrupting notions of feminised care. Using rich ethnographic accounts, I will focus in particular on two examples—Kerry and Zoe—woven together with other examples.

As already described in Chap. 2 and in earlier sections of this chapter, Kerry was a key source of support for her sister, providing emotional and physical care, which ramped up when her sister became pregnant. Kerry would be in contact daily (if not hourly) with her sister to answer her many questions, and had been plugged for cash-in-hand childcare when her nephew was born (more on this in Chap. 4). She was also a stay-at-home mum, looking after four young boys. This meant her everyday rhythms were shaped by gendered care responsibilities (McDowell et al. 2005; Millar and Ridge 2013; Tronto 1993), maintaining everyday social infrastructures for her family and friends. Kerry explains the complexity of care in the extract below, taken from a taped discussion in December 2013.

Sarah: Who would you go to if you needed someone to talk to? Like if you needed, like, moral or emotional support?

Kerry: Probably my sister.

Sarah: Yeah? She'd like, be your first? And how about if you needed like, help with financial stuff?

Kerry: My mum! The Bank of Mum.

Sarah: You wouldn't go to your sister for that?

Kerry: No, my sister comes to me!

Sarah: Right. What, for advice about money?

Kerry: No, for money! Because her fella's not got a job, so she like "erm Kerry, can you lend me some money until pay-day?". I'm like "riiiiight". […] She normally … she seems to need money as I'm getting my money, coincides. She must get the wages the week after I get my [benefits] payments. But she does just pay it me back, whereas if I lend [Dan's sister] money I know that we wouldn't see it for God knows how long. She's like "yeah, I'll pay you back' and then would never pay it back because she's skint. Whereas my sister, she will pay it back when she says and she'll buy stuff on the Next [catalogue] and pay it off when she gets her wages.

Sarah: So she shares your Next account?

Kerry: She knows my details, so she'll always ask and say "can I get some leggings?" And I'm like "right", so she'll do it. [...]

Sarah: So you'd go to your sister for emotional support, your sister comes to you ... would she come to you if she needed emotional support, does it work both ways?

Kerry: I think so ... I think she's got more closer friends she could probably go to.

Sarah: And then, you go to your mum if you wanted financial support. Do you do what your sister does for you, like do you borrow money from your mum before pay-day and stuff?

Kerry: Not done it in absolutely years. But like I say, she'll be paying for the honeymoon until we get the money. That's only because my grandma died, so she's got all the money from when my grandma died. When I asked her, I asked after I knew she got the money, and like "will you be able to pay?", she went "well as you know, money's not an issue at the moment". I was like "thank you!"

Sarah: [...] And how about, like, if you wanted financial advice, like if you didn't actually want money but you wanted advice about maybe where to save money or borrow money? Is there anyone you'd go to?

Kerry: I don't know. Well, I text my boss, I text Garry who is my ex-boss because obviously he's high up [a bank manager], and I asked him a question about a mortgage the other day, saying "do you know if mortgage people will take in to consideration your benefits, or is it just your actual income?" and he left me an answer machine message saying "Hi Kerry, give us a call and I'll get one of the proper people to discuss this." [...] and I was like "no, I don't want these financial people talking to me. I just wanted an answer, because I don't want a mortgage at the moment". We were just talking about it in general!

Sarah: That was interesting though, that you've contacted him. I've only got one last question, I know you've got to go in a minute. Who would you go to if you needed help with everyday tasks and chores and stuff? Or like, picking the boys up or ...

Kerry: I tend to ask Dan's mum at the moment because she's got made redundant and she lives opposite the school. Like on Tuesday she's going to have Zack for me for a couple of hours.

This dialogue between me and Kerry covers a lot of ground so far as everyday social infrastructures are concerned, from emotional to monetary to practical support (including our wrapping the conversation up because she had to collect the boys from school). What she describes was largely confirmed by my own observations, too. When asked to unpick the different threads of these tapestries of care, Kerry identifies a number of trends, many of which were replicated across the ethnography.

Firstly, that she seeks care and provides care, of very different types and forms, from and to a range of family, friends and intimate others. Her everyday social infrastructures of care are especially varied and textured. Secondly, that this care is not always reciprocal. It is not imparted or received in a like-for-like fashion, and is sometimes not reciprocated at all. Some threads are looped or tied; others are left hanging. Thirdly, that gendered and generational entanglements are an important part of the picture. In particular they influence where and from whom care is sought, sticking largely to gendered norms and socialised responsibilities. By this, I mean that emotional care and embodied, practical care is largely provided and sought by female family members and friends. However, Kerry identifies how for financial advice she would approach an older male, her former boss who is a bank manager. She does not actively reflect on this gendered and generational (and so too political and relational) distinction. This is perhaps telling in itself; it is rendered so normal and naturalised that it is simply explained and not questioned.

One might wonder at this point whether Kerry's example is just a commonsensical instance of obtaining financial advice from somebody who works in the financial sector. However, this was something that was seen across the whole ethnography: a trend of seeking advice on financial matters—including where to bank, save or sort out issues with Inland Revenue or the Job Centre—from older, male and/or professional family, friends and intimate relations. But for most other sorts of emotional, embodied or practical support participants would approach a female friend, family member or intimate other. These examples of seeking trusted financial advice, and their impact on social relations, are of particular interest in the context of austerity when both personal and public finances are contracted (also see Hall 2016a).

To illustrate, I'll use a second extended example. Zoe's everyday routines, also discussed in Chap. 2 and earlier in this chapter, are reflective of her central role in maintaining personal and social infrastructures. As well as caring for her children, being the primary carer for her son Ryan who has a life-limiting illness, and running a local playgroup, Zoe was also studying at a local college and working at a school. The example of Zoe rolls together domestic labour, social care, community work and education (see Pearson and Elson 2015). Similar to the example of Kerry, Zoe and I also discussed the different threads that make up her everyday social infrastructures of care. The extract below, taken from a taped discussion in January 2014, reflects some of this conversation.

Zoe: My network of friends, they're brilliant and we all have each other's kids all the time. So we have swaps for teas, we'd run each other's kids here, there and everywhere. We see each other on weekends. If I was having a problem that I had to talk to somebody about, that would tend to be my friends. Crystal probably mostly. [...] If I was upset about something, if I'd had a falling out with Stuart or had a falling out with my mum or whatever. Or upset about something that happened at school, I would always go to my friends first. Unless it was something very serious. If I had anything, say, medical, I'd go to my mum. Medical, emotional kind of, to do with me. If it was just a bit of a whinge and I wanted a bit of a sounding off, I'd go to my friends. If it was something serious, I'd go to my mum.

Sarah: And how about help with ... I mean, you've mentioned that your dad gives you advice, but help with financial stuff. So say if you had a question about money matters, or ...

Zoe: Well, I'd discuss it with Stuart first. Stuart is quite good at those kind of things. There would be a temptation to ask my dad because he is very good at money stuff but he is also a massive worrier, so if it was something that we were worried about, that we didn't feel like we needed any extra pressure on somebody else worrying about it, we probably wouldn't go to my dad. [...] And maybe we would go to Stuart's parents before my parents on something like that, partly because he deals with the money and he's closer to his own parents. You tend to go to ... whoever deals with it goes to their own kind of respective set of parents. So anything to do with the kids or day to day living, probably go to my parents because it's me that deals with that kind of thing, whereas with the finances it may well be that we discuss that with Stuart's parents because he deals with that.

Sarah: [...] How about if I kind of flipped that on its head? Who comes to you and Stuart if they want ... who would speak to you if they wanted emotional support?

Zoe: My friends would tend to. My sister. She probably leans on me more emotionally than I would lean on her [...]. My mum to some extent as well. Sometimes my mum will tell me things or ask me about things. My friends definitely, I do tend to ... I probably have a lot more to do with my friends' lives, in some ways—this might sound a bit funny—than they do with mine. I think that's maybe got to do with the fact that I do have parents local, whereas my friends, a lot of my friends around here ... Argleton's a very funny place, it's a very transient place. People tend to not be born here, but move here as a result of jobs or whatever the reason. So a lot of people aren't brought up here or anywhere close. So I've got friends who are from very down south or very up north whose parents or in-laws or any other family support aren't close.

Here, like Kerry, Zoe picks up on how care comes in many different forms, and in being enmeshed within social relations is often interpersonal and collective (Barnett and Land 2007; Held 1993). Also, like Kerry, she recognises that such care is not always reciprocal: for example, her sister and friends are more reliant on her than she is on them (Bowlby 2011).

Zoe also picks up on threads of the discussion from Chap. 2 on the role of mundane mobilities and social and spatial proximities, when talking about how physical closeness to or distance from family can shape capacities for care. She explains how she seeks emotional and financial advice from different social relations, how she goes to female family and friends for emotional or practical help (as depicted in Fig. 3.1), and to her husband or dad for financial advice. That being the case, she does not characterise this gendered distinction as a problem. It is interesting, too, that Zoe discusses not wanting to overload her dad with worry. She considers and cares for him when she (hypothetically) requires financial advice, and prioritises his needs above her own.

Zoe and Kerry are not alone in identifying a male family member, friend or intimate relation to provide financial advice and support. Laura, for example, said that for emotional support or someone to talk to she goes to 'a friend, or to my mum', and that for financial advice, such as 'when we buy our own house, I have to go to my dad and go to a financial advisor, you know, mortgage broker' (taped discussion, November 2013). Pauline described how emotional and physical support came from her

Fig. 3.1 Zoe together with her network of friends (illustrated by Claire Stringer, from the *Everyday Austerity* zine by Sarah Marie Hall, see https://everydayausterity.wordpress.com/zine/)

friends, particularly two women from her reiki class. They met up often to practice their healing upon one another, after which they often feel 'loads better' (field diary, March 2015). For financial advice, Pauline and George would go to a professional. During the ethnography, they signed up to an over-50s retirement and pensions information event in their local church, led by a local man who works as a financial advisor (field diary, July 2015). Selma would approach her 'three friends, good friends' for emotional or practical help, all of whom are female, but for financial advice would go to her older, male cousin (taped discussion, May 2014). Finally, Sharon and Bill talked with me about their various tapestries of care, including going to 'each other' as well as friends and intimate others for emotional and practical support. But for financial advice, Bill explained, 'I'd probably talk to a financial adviser at the bank or something [...] or we'd ask [a friend] for advice, but Noel's probably the most, he's the one that keeps changing his bank accounts and his credit cards' (taped discussion, January 2014).

Findings about female family, friends and other intimates providing practical and emotional support, discussed earlier in this chapter and reiterated here, are not necessarily surprising given that feminist geographers have long shown that care-giving is often a gendered responsibility (see England 2010; Lawson 2007; McDowell et al. 2005), and that in times of austerity it is women who bear the brunt of the everyday financial, material and emotional impacts (see Bradley 1986; Hall 2016a; Volger 1994). What is interesting is the role of male family members in providing financial advice and support, such as where to bank, how to get the most from your savings, pension investments, and where to buy a house, that speak to a much broader gendering of everyday social infrastructures of care in austerity.

While it is not my aim to essentialise gendered care, these findings are significant for showing how ingrained and embedded gendered norms and knowledge claims are in our society, and how these can come to frame and shape the social relations and care infrastructures upon which they are predicated. There did emerge a distinct binary in terms of the types of knowledge and skills that participants considered themselves and others to possess, which in the main was arranged around markers of gender. This binary serves to reinforce traditional gendered and micro-spatial and micro-political divisions, with male family members positioned as knowledgeable, rational and calculative, as well as being ultimately in charge of the financial purse strings. This finding also provides an alternative analysis to writing on gender and poverty that finds women take charge of household budgets so as to avoid conflict and manage male feelings of gender crisis (see Fodor 2006). In this sense, my findings help to flesh out the wider picture of everyday social infrastructures of care in times of austerity, which can take many forms. When the underside of the tapestry of relationships in everyday austerity is exposed, a messiness of knots, tangles and threads is revealed.

Fieldwork as Care Work

Thirdly, and bringing together multiple threads discussed so far, is the matter of care work and body-work within academic fieldwork. In developing a rapport over months or even years of research, employing ethnographic tools of deep immersion and trust, fieldwork can become an interpersonal and relational space where care (of various kinds and intensities) is given and received. In this way, researchers can become intimate others, knotted within the everyday care infrastructures of participants' lives, and part of the very phenomenon one might be studying.

Such intimacy and care-full relations (see McEwan and Goodman 2010) between researchers and participants might be expressed in numerous ways and through different mediums. The role of body-work that fieldwork involves (if not requires) is one such example, being a conduit for and form of care work. Highly corporeal, embodied and sensual practices of *doing care with* participants—such as eating with them, listening to them or simply being with them—are often a means of developing connection and intimacy (see Popke 2006; Pottinger 2017). Mirroring Longhurst et al. (2008, p. 208), my fieldwork experiences revealed how 'the body is a primary tool through which all interactions and emotions filter in accessing research subjects and their geographies'.

My field diaries were filled with references to biscuits, cakes and sweet things. Sometimes these were items I had given to participants as a small, absorbable thank-you gesture for taking part, albeit the edible items I took along were rarely shared with me (see Chap. 5 for a discussion of the politics of payment). Perhaps also reciprocating my contributions to their lives, material and otherwise, participants' generosities, gendered practices and care-giving were expressed with things made or bought for my visits. Pauline, for instance, would regularly bake a cake if we were meeting at their home. I relished hearing the words 'I've been doing some baking' as I peeled off my coat and popped off my shoes, and would often walk into the kitchen or sitting room to find a cake or other baked goods there to greet me. Over a slice of cake I would always stress to Pauline that 'you really don't need to do this for my visits, you know', to which she would often respond that 'it's a good excuse to bake'. I was often sent home with a parcel of cake, or a pot of home-made chutney or jam (like the one pictured in Fig. 3.2), themselves the product of embodied care work, as well as a kind of compensation for my field visits and a recognition of the labour it involved (also see Pottinger 2017, 2018).

Whether giving through their time, resources or efforts, I was always extremely humbled by these care-filled exchanges. As I listened back to taped discussions, there would be plates clattering, food crunching, apologies of 'sorry, my mouth is full', and offers of a cuppa or a crumpet. One windy April afternoon I had nipped into the bakery on the way to meet Kerry, planning to buy her favourite, a custard tart, as my thank-you offering that day. 'The last one has just gone', the lady behind the counter told me, so I begrudgingly settled on some brownies instead. When I arrived at Kerry's house, I passed her the brownies apologetically, relaying the message that somebody had just pipped me to the last egg custard. Laughing, Kerry pointed to a white paper bag on the side—*she* had bought that last egg custard for us to share. And Selma would always make sure she had a selection of fruit in whenever I visited, displayed with pride on the dining table. Small, quiet ways of expressing care through typically classed and gendered care practices of food and feeding (Devault 1991; Longhurst et al. 2008; Popke 2006). I was touched that these women, who had very busy and often stressful lives, with lots of other people to care for and things to remember, would take out of their squeezed time, energy and resources for me. It is difficult, then, not to consider how being part of the research was tangled up within participants' everyday infrastructures of care in austerity, and their participation might even have added an extra burden (also see Chap. 5).

Moreover, I found myself documenting these exchanges (like in Fig. 3.2), and not always out of an ethnographic compulsion but also a personal urge to remember these intimate moments with people I had come to know well. I often photographed the food they made, and kept jars, recipes and home-made Christmas cards, as much as I mentioned them in my field diary. These exchanges were not, however, always physical or material. It is here that notions of everyday social infrastructures make an important and direct contribution to current literature regarding state infrastructure, and how such infrastructures have been eroded by austerity. For emotional and embodied care is especially significant in times of austerity; yes, material fabrics of shelter, equipment and technologies are necessary for care, but there are significant personal and

Fig. 3.2 A jar of rhubarb and ginger chutney made by Pauline and gifted to me (photograph taken by Sarah Marie Hall)

social investments that complete and embroider the tapestry of social reproduction, too. The emotional and physical labour that maintains social infrastructures of care, socialisation and education (Pearson and Elson 2015) is also distinctly gendered, classed and racialised. This means when investments to social care are cut, the impacts are not evenly spread (Hall et al. 2017).

Considering the care work and body-work of fieldwork helps to bring these gendered social infrastructures further into focus. Spending time with families day to day inevitably involved everyday practices of care and consideration which were also forms of body-work (Twigg 2000), like heating hands with hot cups of tea to save turning on the central heating at Laura's house; or helping Kerry make four lots of cheese sandwiches for the kids while she unloaded the washing machine, or entertaining youngest son Zack by playing with him in the park (see Fig. 3.3); or carrying half of the shopping bags back to Selma's flat after a weekly grocery shop. Other examples of bodily labour can be seen in the activities I engaged in to meet and mingle with people in their everyday lives, some

Fig. 3.3 Playing in the park with Zack (photograph taken by Kerry)

more strenuous than others. Aerobics classes in church halls, knitting groups in the local library and children's craft clubs in a local shop (if they were still running and had not closed down) (Hall 2017) were ways of creating a familiar, bodily presence. These spaces were part of the tapestry of everyday care infrastructures in austerity—woven into the fabric of these social spaces and communities (Conradson 2003; Held 1993), creating a space of togetherness, interaction and corporeal closeness.

Many of the activities I undertook during fieldwork also included multiple forms of body-work involving movement and dexterity, made possible by me being able-bodied and skilled in certain gendered practices. When attending toddler groups, tea mornings or women-only exercise classes, my identity and implicit body-work as a young female researcher granted access to these spaces and moments, and a sense of belonging (Askins 2014, 2015; Massey 2004; also see Chap. 5). I would be 'put to work' helping to tidy gardens, wash pots or feed pets. While I readily offered a helping hand, over time participants were more likely to ask than wait for an offer, recognising the body-work I might provide (also see England and Dyck 2011; Twigg 2000). It was assumed at community cooking classes or knitting groups that I possessed the necessary skills to join in. While this was often the case, I ended up questioning my own abilities and feeling very much 'on show'. I wondered if this was how my participants felt, too.

For instance, in the same afternoon spent with Pauline and George, I chopped vegetables with George in the kitchen, making veggie chilli for our lunch, and then sat with Pauline stuffing, sewing up and embellishing catnip-filled crocheted mice for the local Cats Protection charity. I was eager to please them both, wanting to lift their load by offering my help where possible, but this only made me jittery and nervous. I made a total mess of chopping up the onion for the chilli, to the point where George asked if I needed a hand. The eyes I sewed onto the crocheted mice were wonky, making the mice look deranged. I wrote in my field diary that I felt as though 'I had let them down … they were really getting into the swing of the ethnography, involving me in their everyday practices, and I was making an absolute pig's ear of everything I turned my hand to' (field diary, February 2015). At the time I could not interpret what my embarrassment about poor performance in these tasks meant.

With hindsight I see that I too was affected by socialised norms and expectations about gendered care work and embodied skills (see Hall 2016b for further discussion of gendered socialisation).

The trust placed in me as a researcher, doing my 'day job', particularly as a young woman, also illustrates the interconnectedness of gender, body-work and care. I was left literally holding the baby on many occasions, including one time when I met a young woman, who asked me to look after her youngest child for a few minutes in the middle of a shop while she nipped to the toilet. After visiting her house for the first time, Laura was in a mild panic having lost her house keys and needing to collect her eldest son from school. She asked me if I would mind waiting in the house while she did the school run, to ensure she would not be locked out. And when participants wanted a second opinion, like whether vegetables looked out of date, if a pair of shoes were too tight or if a text message read as passive aggressive, I was there to answer. In previous studies I have explored how 'families acknowledged feeling comfortable with my being in their home specifically because I was a young woman' (Hall 2014, p. 2180). Here, I want to extend this further by highlighting how being involved in the study with a female researcher contributed to participants' everyday social infrastructures of care.

By listening to, empathising and being with participants, in providing companionship or intimacy, practical help or assistance, as I have done, researchers can assume a caring disposition. There may be, as Hanisch (1970) identifies, therapeutic elements to these encounters. But so too are they political in what they reveal of researchers' academic labour and body-work. Participants with young children, such as Kerry, Selma and Laura, expressed being glad of the adult company when I visited. Rather than a drain on time, resources and energy, they described their participation as a boost to their confidence, an outlet for their frustrations and an opportunity for private conversations. I got the distinct impression that they felt like they could say things to me that they would not dare to say to their friends or family because they knew, as part of the consent process and my role as a researcher, it would never be revealed in connection with their identity.

Embodied fieldwork encounters therefore need to be understood as more than simply bodily contact, closeness or corporeality, but also as relational spaces and part of broader social infrastructures of care. At cooking clubs and cafes, attendees and I talked together about how our mothers and grandmothers had taught us to cut vegetables a certain way, and how washing an onion before chopping (to stop you crying) or using a lemon to clean the sink (as natural antibacterial) were tricks passed down generations. These fieldwork encounters were all bodily encounters, involving co-presence, the sharing of utensils and material spaces, smells and tastes, the enactment of reproductive and repetitive tasks, or a slight touch, nudge or the brush of an arm (also see Horton and Kraftl 2009; Longhurst et al. 2008). Embodiment and body-work can also be seen in the sharing of experiences, memories and socialised (often gendered) skills. And more than the physical, material and visceral body-work, bodies here are also vessels of memories and emotions, providing the capacity to make connections to others within these spaces, to create everyday, relational spaces of care (Hall 2017; Massey 2004). Researchers, then, can be important and intimate others, woven within the fabric of everyday social infrastructures, our bodies as instruments of research (Longhurst et al. 2008), and simultaneously of care-giving (and receiving) in austere times.

Conclusions

In their everyday crafting and practice, social infrastructures are tangled and messy. Tapestries of care are also shown to be tightly enmeshed with social identities, gendered responsibilities and normative moralities. This raises many questions about the politics of care in times of austerity; who the burden falls upon and why, and how this can impact on social relationships. This is both in terms of whether appropriate care is being provided to those most in need, and by whom, and of 'the field' as a space of labour and care, shaping social infrastructures in the course of our research.

Centring women's stories and narratives plucked from ethnographic accounts also reveals the deep interconnections between day-to-day experiences with the personal and relational gendered politics of care in times of austerity. Built largely on gendered, reproductive labour, these social infrastructures are also intensely political. This is not just because participants were directly responding to the impacts of austerity, but also because in doing so they sought to bring about interconnection, interdependence and collectivity (Barnett and Land 2007; Mountz et al. 2015; Smith 2005). These social infrastructures were shown to be differently gendered when financial, emotional and practical supports were contrasted. For while women were shown to be making contributions to unwaged, volunteer and paid care (see Pearson and Elson 2015), gendered norms around finance, money and knowledge emerged through reliance on male family, friends and intimate relations for financial advice.

I explore these themes and the tensions therein in the next three chapters, moving first to intimacy and austerity.

Bibliography

Anderson, B., & McFarlane, C. (2011). Assemblage and Geography. *Area, 43*(2), 124–127.

Askins, K. (2014). A Quiet Politics of Being Together: Miriam and Rose. *Area, 46*(4), 353–354.

Askins, K. (2015). Being Together: Everyday Geographies and the Quiet Politics of Belonging. *ACME: An International E-Journal for Critical Geographies, 14*(2), 470–478.

Barnett, C., & Land, D. (2007). Geographies of Generosity: Beyond the "Moral Turn". *Geoforum, 38*, 1065–1075.

Bowlby, S. (2011). Friendship, Co-presence and Care: Neglected Spaces. *Social & Cultural Geography, 12*(6), 605–622.

Bradley, H. (1986). Work, Home and the Restructuring of Jobs. In K. Purcell, S. Wood, A. Waton, & S. Allen (Eds.), *The Changing Experience of Employment: Restructuring and Recession* (pp. 95–113). London: Macmillan.

Braun, B. (2006). Environmental Issues: Global Natures in the Space of Assemblage. *Progress in Human Geography, 30*(5), 644–654.

Conradson, D. (2003). Geographies of Care: Spaces, Practices, Experiences. *Social & Cultural Geography, 4*(4), 451–454.

Daly, M., & Lewis, J. (2000). The Concept of Social Care and the Analysis of Contemporary Welfare States. *British Journal of Sociology, 51*(2), 281–298.

Devault, M. (1991). *Feeding the Family: The Social Organisation of Caring as Gendered Work*. London: The University of Chicago Press.

Duffy, M. (2011). *Making Care Count: A Century of Gender, Race, and Paid Care Work*. London: Rutgers University Press.

Dyck, I. (2005). Feminist Geography, the "Everyday", and Local-Global Relations: Hidden Spaces of Place-Making. *The Canadian Geographer, 49*, 233–245.

Ellegard, K., & De Pater, B. (1999). The Complex Tapestry of Everyday Life. *GeoJournal, 48*(3), 149–153.

Emmel, N., & Hughes, K. (2010). "Recession, It's All the Same to Us Son": The Longitudinal Experience (1999–2010) of Deprivation. *Twenty-First Century Society, 5*(2), 171–181.

England, K. V. L. (1994). Getting Personal: Reflexivity Positionality and Feminist Research. *The Professional Geographer, 46*, 80–89.

England, K. (2010). Home, Work and the Shifting Geographies of Care. *Ethics, Place & Environment, 13*(2), 131–150.

England, K., & Dyck, I. (2011). Managing the Body Work of Home Care. *Sociology of Health & Illness, 33*(2), 206–219.

Fisher, B., & Tronto, J. (1990). Toward a Feminist Theory of Caring. In E. Abel & M. Nelson (Eds.), *Circles of Care* (pp. 36–54). Albany: SUNY Press.

Fodor, E. (2006). A Different Type of Gender Gap: How Women and Men Experience Poverty. *East European Politics and Societies: And Cultures, 20*(1), 14–39.

Greer-Murphy, A. (2017). Austerity in the United Kingdom: The Intersections of Spatial and Gendered Inequalities. *Area, 49*(1), 122–124.

Gregson, N., & Rose, G. (1997). Contested and Negotiated Histories of Feminist Geographies. In Women and Geography Study Group (Ed.), *Feminist Geographies: Explorations of Diversity and Difference*. Harlow: Addison Wesley Longman.

Hall, S. M. (2014). Ethics of Ethnography with Families: A Geographical Perspective. *Environment and Planning A, 46*(9), 2175–2194.

Hall, S. M. (2016a). Everyday Family Experiences of the Financial Crisis: Getting by in the Recent Economic Recession. *Journal of Economic Geography, 16*(2), 305–330.

Hall, S. M. (2016b). Moral Geographies of Family: Articulating, Forming and Transmitting Moralities in Everyday Life. *Social & Cultural Geography, 17*(8), 1017–1039.

Hall, S. M. (2017). Personal, Relational and Intimate Geographies of Austerity: Ethical and Empirical Considerations. *Area, 49*(3), 303–310.

Hall, S. M., & Jayne, M. (2016). Make, Mend and Befriend: Geographies of Austerity, Crafting and Friendship in Contemporary Cultures of Dressmaking. *Gender, Place & Culture, 23*(2), 216–234.

Hall, S. M., McIntosh, K., Neitzert, E., Pottinger, L., Sandhu, K., Stephenson, M.-A., Reed, H., & Taylor, L. (2017). *Intersecting Inequalities: The Impact of Austerity on Black and Minority Ethnic Women in the UK*. London: Runnymede and Women's Budget Group. Retrieved from www.intersecting-inequalities.com.

Hanisch, C. (1970). The Personal Is Political. In S. Firestone & Koedt (Eds.), *Notes from the Second Year* (pp. 76–78). New York: Published by Editors.

Held, V. (1993). *Feminist Morality: Transforming Culture, Society and Politics*. Chicago, IL: University of Chicago Press.

Hochschild, A. R. (1983). *The Managed Heart: Commercialization of Human Feeling*. Berkeley, CA: University of California Press.

Holmes, H. (2018). New Spaces, Ordinary Practices: Circulating and Sharing Within Diverse Economies of Provisioning. *Geoforum, 88*, 134–147.

Horton, J., & Kraftl, P. (2009). Small Acts, Kind Words and "Not Too Much Fuss": Implicit Activisms. *Emotion, Space and Society, 2*(1), 14–23.

Jarvis, H. (2005). Moving to London Time. *Time & Society, 14*(1), 133–154.

Jensen, T., & Tyler, I. (2012). Austerity Parenting: New Economies of Parent-Citizenship. *Studies in the Maternal, 4*(2), 1–5.

Jones, M. (2009). Phase Space: Geography, Relational Thinking, and Beyond. *Progress in Human Geography, 33*(4), 487–506.

Jupp, E. (2017). Home Space, Gender and Activism: The Visible and the Invisible in Austere Times. *Critical Social Policy, 37*(3), 348–366.

Langley, P. (2008). *The Everyday Life of Global Finance: Saving and Borrowing in America*. Oxford: Oxford University Press.

Lawson, V. (2007). Geographies of Care and Responsibility. *Annals of the Association of American Geographers, 97*(1), 1–11.

Longhurst, R., Ho, E., & Johnston, L. (2008). Using "The Body" as an "Instrument of Research": Kimch'i and Pavlova. *Area, 40*(2), 208–217.

MacLeavy, J. (2011). A "New" Politics of Austerity, Workfare and Gender? The UK Coalition Government's Welfare Reform Proposals. *Cambridge Journal of Regions, Economy and Society, 4*, 355–367.

Massey, D. (2004). Geographies of Responsibility. *Geografiska Annaler B, 86*(1), 5–18.

McDowell, L. (2012). Post-Crisis, Post-Ford and Post-Gender? Youth Identities in an Era of Austerity. *Journal of Youth Studies, 15*(5), 573–590.

McDowell, L. (2017). Youth, Children and Families in Austere Times: Change, Politics and a New Gender Contract. *Area, 49*(3), 311–316.

McDowell, L., Ray, K., Perrons, D., Fagan, C., & Ward, K. (2005). Women's Paid Work and Moral Economies of Care. *Social & Cultural Geography, 6*, 219–235.

McEwan, C., & Goodman, M. (2010). Place Geography and the Ethics of Care: Introductory Remarks on the Geographies of Ethics, Responsibility and Care. *Ethics, Place and Environment, 13*(2), 103–112.

Millar, J., & Ridge, T. (2013). Lone Mothers and Paid Work: The "Family-Work Project". *International Review of Sociology, 23*(3), 564–577.

Mountz, A., Bonds, A., Mansfield, B., Loyd, J., Hyndman, J., Walton-Roberts, M., Basu, R., Whitson, R., Hawkins, R., Hamilton, T., & Curran, W. (2015). For Slow Scholarship: A Feminist Politics of Resistance Through Collective Action in the Neoliberal University. *ACME, 14*(4), 1235–1259.

Nelson, G. D. (2018). Mosaic and Tapestry: Metaphors as Geographical Concept Generators. *Progress in Human Geography*. https://doi.org/10.1177/0309132518788951.

Pearson, R., & Elson, D. (2015). Transcending the Impact of the Financial Crisis in the United Kingdom: Towards Plan F—A Feminist Economic Strategy. *Feminist Review, 109*, 8–30.

Popke, J. (2006). Geography and Ethics: Everyday Mediations Through Care and Consumption. *Progress in Human Geography, 30*(4), 504–512.

Pottinger, L. (2017). Planting the Seeds of a Quiet Activism. *Area, 49*(2), 215–222.

Pottinger, L. (2018). Growing, Guarding and Generous Exchange in an Analogue Sharing Economy. *Geoforum, 96*, 108–118.

Power, A., & Hall, E. (2018). Placing Care in Times of Austerity. *Social & Cultural Geography, 19*(3), 303–313.

Smith, S. (2005). States, Markets and an Ethic of Care. *Political Geography, 25*, 1–20.

Strong, S. (2018). Food Banks, Actually Existing Austerity and the Localisation of Responsibility. *Geoforum*. https://doi.org/10.1016/j.geoforum.2018.09.025.

Tarrant, A. (2010). Constructing a Social Geography of Grandparenthood: A New Focus for Intergenerationality. *Area, 42*(2), 190–197.

Tarrant, A. (2018). Care in an Age of Austerity: Men's Care Responsibilities in Low-Income Families. *Ethics & Social Welfare, 12*(1), 34–48.

Tronto, J. (1993). *Moral Boundaries: A Political Argument for an Ethic of Care*. London: Routledge.

Twigg, J. (2000). Carework as a Form of Bodywork. *Ageing and Society, 20*(4), 389–411.

Volger, C. M. (1994). Money in the Household. In M. Anderson, F. Bechhofer, & J. Gershuny (Eds.), *The Social and Political Economy of the Household* (pp. 225–262). Oxford: Oxford University Press.

4

Austere Intimacies and Intimate Austerities

To fully appreciate the tapestries of everyday life in austerity, we need to pay closer attention to a wider range of social relationalities and intimacies between and beyond friends and family. In Chap. 2, I fleshed out the conceptual framework for the project and this book: that through a focus on social relations and relational geographies, we might more fully comprehend the ways in which everyday austerity cuts through, across and between spaces. Intimacy can be found in an array of places, limited not by home, familiarity or proximity. Other intimate relations are a key part of complicated social infrastructures, practices, emotions and responsibilities that shape how everyday austerity is experienced and encountered. Taking family, friends and intimate relations as the core of significant everyday relationships, I continue to explore how austerity is a simultaneously economic and political as well as social, personal and *intimate* condition.

With what follows, I carry on scrutinising and critiquing current conceptualisations of everyday life in austerity. Having already established that everyday social relationships are made up of family, friends and other intimate relations, I set about exploring the intimacies that constitute these relationships: their forms, consistencies and reciprocities. Such

S. M. Hall, *Everyday Life in Austerity*, Palgrave Macmillan Studies in Family and Intimate Life, https://doi.org/10.1007/978-3-030-17094-3_4

intimacies can lead to further closeness and strengthened bonds, or to tensions and conflict. Both of these elements are significant within relational geographies of austerity. Situating social relationships as the focus, in this chapter, I work outwards to consider the difference that austerity makes for intimacy, and that intimacy makes for austerity. My aim is to illustrate how the hidden or less-discussed pockets of everyday intimacies in austerity can be uncovered when our focus is on relationships and relational space.

After introducing ideas about intimacy from a range of scholars across human geography, sociology, philosophy and social care, the chapter is then arranged into four parts. Based on my ethnographic findings, I start with intimate monetary arrangements, to explore how often-intimate practices of favours, labour and leisure are shaped by austerity and in turn shape the intimacies in which they are rooted. Momentary encounters are another way in which to think about the personal and wider social impacts of austerity and the reshaping of relational space. With a discussion of more-than-human intimacies, I consider the role of intimate interspecies relations in times of austerity, and what can be gained or lost from such physically and emotionally close encounters. Lastly, I look at material proximities, and how material givings, sharings and receivings can provide a conduit for social proximities which become particularly significant in times of austerity. To close, I highlight how, in adopting a relational approach, intimacy and austerity are shown to be contingent upon one another, creating, bending and shaping everyday relationships, for better or worse.

Intimacy Between/Beyond Kith and Kin

Previous chapters have argued that everyday life is a relational space, made up of various types of social relationships and intimacies, within which and across austerity takes place. To understand the difference that intimacy makes to austerity, and austerity to intimacy, involves first identifying the scope of intimacy and intimate relations. We must then ascertain what and who this involves, and what the outcomes of such intimacy might be. Writings on intimacy across the social sciences have typically adopted geographical terminologies and concepts, such as proximity and propinquity, closeness and distance (Hall 2014; Harker and Martin 2012; Oswin and Olund 2010). Here, intimacy is described as a physical, corporeal and material *and* an emotional, social and personal way of relating to others.

These intimate 'others' have been, for the most part, assumed to be known, familiar individuals. The notion of intimate relationships is typically applied to certain kinds of social relationships. Morgan (2009, p. 1), for instance, distinguishes between 'intimates and strangers', arguing that what comes 'between' are acquaintances. He, like many others writing on intimacy (also see Jamieson 1997), positions familiarity as a prerequisite to intimacy. Whether physically intimate, emotionally intimate or possessing intimate knowledge, in Morgan's (2009) conceptualisation of intimacy, these relationships are almost always interpersonal. In *The Transformation of Intimacy*, Giddens (1992) also propagates the notion that there exist 'pure relationships' of mutual disclosure and 'mutual liking' (Giddens 1992, p. 98), which forms the basis of intimacy and equitable relations. Again, intimacy is restricted to particular relationships, namely sexual and romantic engagements, in Giddens' view. While recognising that 'it is quite possible to have intensely intimate relationships which are not sexual and sexual relationships which are devoid of intimacy', Jamieson (1999, pp. 478–479) also highlights Giddens' 'optimism', or what can more cynically be described as a romanticism about intimacy, as having 'the potential for radical and positive social change through personal life'. As described in Chap. 2, intimacy can emerge from within loving and affectionate encounters, as it can from difficult and painful situations (also see Hall 2014). The capacity for austerity to shape these relationships, and for austere conditions to be shaped by intimacy, is therefore of interest.

Within geography, while most writings on intimacy have tended to focus on love, sexuality, romantic, familial and friendship relations (e.g. Bunnell et al. 2012; Holdsworth 2013; Morrison et al. 2012), there are examples of where the scope of intimacy and intimate relations has been widened. Valentine (2008a, p. 2101) also argues that 'the emotional ties, the meaning and quality of relationships' beyond family and friends are lesser understood, that 'the whole affective register of familial connections and practices, including erotic and non-erotic relations has been largely neglected'. However, family—as an institutional, heteronormative and patriarchal concept (Hall 2016b; Hubbard 2001)—often remains the underpinning concept against which other intimacies and intimate relations are compared. And, as described in the previous chapter, ideologies of family are strongly coupled with notions of gendered responsibility and care.

One area of everyday life that Valentine (2008a) and Morgan (2009) both identify in their interest on intimate relations is care work, which is also an area of significant interest in austerity due to spending cuts targeted at social care budgets (see Pearson and Elson 2015). Additional writings on (non-familial, non-friend) embodied intimacies have also considered the role of gendered care work and body-work as forms of labour that interconnect but are not synonymous with familial or friend relations (e.g. Askins 2015; Horton and Kraftl 2009; Twigg 2006). As Twigg (2006, p. 6) describes, 'social care is all about the spatial and temporal ordering of care, and its interaction with the management of the body'. These relations, this bodily management, are often tied up with service encounters and forms of labour steeped in transactional arrangements. They are also commonly marked by 'rules and regulations, uniforms, formal bodily stance, Taylorised task performance' (Twigg 2006, p. 8), and with implicit power binaries (see Cox and Narula 2003; Holmes 2015; Jayne and Leung 2014; Morgan 2009). But there are also possibilities for intimacies to develop here. Rose (1995, p. 82), for instance, in her autobiographical work on love, life and death, notes how she would learn the names of nurses 'immediately so that we may also exist for each other as single beings as well as impersonal functions'. Embodied intimacies can lead to emotional intimacies, not as friend or family. Nor is familiarity a prerequisite here. And yet these various types of social relationships can also 'intersect and blur' with other types of intimacies, 'including with familial relations' (Hall 2016c, p. 16).

As noted above and discussed in more detail in Chaps. 2 and 3, the example of care is particularly pertinent in the context of austerity. Valentine (2008a, p. 2106) also points this out:

the rolling back of the welfare state and financial insecurity that characterises contemporary neo-liberal economies mean that many people are increasingly dependent on family or other intimate relations for material and moral support.

It is by considering intimate relations between and beyond family and friendship that the multiscalar and relational geographies of everyday austerity really come to the fore. Furthermore, a relational analysis highlights how care is emplaced within both home and economy, led by policies as much as everyday practices (also see England 2010; England and Dyck 2011). Others writing on the relationship between the state and the body also identify intimacy and intimate knowledge as an outcome of state intervention in bodily and personal practice, albeit an intimacy that may not necessarily be encouraged or enjoyed (also see Jackson 2016; Oswin and Olund 2010).

In the opening lines of *Feminism, The State and Social Policy*, Charles (2000, p. 5) makes the point that the state has 'the power to change policies which affect women and to give women certain rights'; the state has the power to give with one hand and remove with the other. For Twigg (2006, p. 3), however, such 'power has no definable centre, so its sites are scattered, and this helps to refocus analysis away from the classic arenas of the State or overt political conflict towards the micro-politics of daily life and of the body'. This aligns very much with my own ideas explored within this book, including gendered politics, responsibilities and moralities discussed in previous and later chapters.

Paying attention to these various and plural interdependencies also creates a space for talking about the surfaces of intimacy, where feelings, bodies, identities and responsibilities meet. By this, I adopt Sara Ahmed's ideas about emotions and relationships as creating 'surfaces and boundaries', from which intimacies can be built (Ahmed 2004, p. 10; Hall 2014; Twigg 2006). Power, difference and inequality are brought into being through intimate encounters, as the surfaces and boundaries upon which relationships can be made and unmade (also see Wilson 2017). In this vein, Twigg (2006, p. 7) uses the example of hospitals as 'places of raw feeling—fear, disgust, humiliation and abandonment—and these feelings are experienced in the body'. Intimacy is, then, also political (Oswin and Olund 2010); 'the possibility of intimacy means the promise of democracy' (Giddens 1992, p. 188).

Concerning the politics of intimacy, in *Love's Work*, Gillian Rose makes a number of acute observations about personal life, intimacy and love, and the power relationships that emerge in the spaces between. She writes about how

> in personal life, people have absolute power over each other, whereas in professional life, beyond the terms of the contract, people have authority, the power to make one another comply in ways which may be perceived as legitimate or illegitimate. In personal life, regardless of any covenant, one party may initiate a unilateral and fundamental change in the terms of relating without renegotiating them, and further, refusing to even acknowledge the change. (Rose 1995, p. 60)

While one might dispute whether the personal and professional exist in such a neat binary (also see Hall 2009), claims about power, negotiation, change and decision are pertinent to everyday austerity. Different ways of relating to other people can shift social contracts, reshaping everyday experiences, and opening or closing doors of opportunity. What happens, then, when the terms of our intimate relationships are dramatically altered, alongside the economic, social, political and personal contexts in which they are rooted? How does austerity rework these intimacies and relational boundaries, and what are the results?

We might not only consider what everyday intimacies look like in austerity but go beyond thick description to also examine how, and through whom or what these social relationships are mediated. The most obvious mediator of intimate relations is money. Economic activity and intimacy, as Viviana Zelizer (2005, p. 1) explains in *The Purchase of Intimacy*, is a territory that many people consider as particularly incompatible and antagonistic, and that 'economic activity—especially the use of money—degrades intimate relationships, while interpersonal intimacy makes economic activity inefficient'. However, 'people often mingle economic activity with intimacy' (ibid.), and not always with unpleasant results. As she goes on to explain, 'people lead connected lives and [...] plenty of economic activity goes into creating, defining, and sustaining social ties'

(Zelizer 2005, p. 2). The context of austerity can further unsettle some of these tensions between money and intimacy, because

> in everyday life, people invest intense effort and constant worry in finding the right match between economic relations and intimate ties; shared responsibility for housework, spending of household income, care for children and old people, gifts that send the right message, provision of adequate housing for loved ones, and much more. (Zelizer 2005, p. 3)

What is less clear here, however, is how intimate monetary encounters also go beyond familial and friendship intimacies, to those where no prior relations have been established, and what this might mean in conditions of everyday austerity.

In fact, in much academic writing around intimacy, there also seems to be very little that is spontaneous, emerging or unexpected about 'other' intimate relationships and their resultant intimacies. This is because they are taken for granted and assumed to be *already intimate*. They also seem to me rather static and fixed, whereas in my previous work, I have argued that different forms of intimacy and intimate relations 'can coexist and can change over time' (Hall 2014, p. 2177). Are all familial and friend relationships intimate? How and why does intimacy change, and under what conditions? In what ways does intimacy shape how austerity is experienced in everyday life? Moreover, where does this leave unsustained, passing and fleeting encounters (see Jackson et al. 2017; Morgan 2009; Valentine 2008b; Wilson 2017)? Do these not also have the possibility of being intimate and to lead to additional intimacies (see Hall and Jayne 2016; Holloway 1998; Jupp 2013a)? And what happens when we unpick ideas of intimacy, to look at family, friendship and intimate relations as intertwined and interdependent in everyday austerity?

Recent research on intimacy and encounters has also identified how 'there remains a fetishisation on the stranger-as-figure with regard to the everyday', which has the effect of 'deny[ing] the positionality of strange and stranger as experience and as more than the body of the other' (Jackson et al. 2017, p. 7). There also tends to be a temptation in writings on intimate encounters to explore how encounters themselves are intimate, defined according to proximity or propinquity (see

Valentine et al. 2015). Less often do authors consider the possibilities within or the aftermath of the encounter, the emotional lingerings, that can behold intimacy. Valentine (2008b, p. 325) refers to this as 'meaningful contact', albeit Wilson (2017, p. 460) contends that 'to identify something as meaningful is to simultaneously create value'. Morgan's (2009, p. 48) writing on the spaces between intimates and strangers highlights this very point that 'acquaintanceship has to be worked at'. Morgan's (2009) use of terminology here is, however, telling. In dichotomising between intimates and strangers, but defining intimacy as comprising physical/embodied intimacy, emotional intimacy or intimate knowledge (also see Chap. 2), he asserts that strangers cannot be intimate. I refute this point below. Nonetheless, this working through of relationships is interesting and can lead to intimacies, as well as a sense of self and others (i.e. relationality). Applying Jackson et al.'s (2017, p. 7) thesis, an appreciation of momentary encounters can provide us with greater understanding of 'geographical or socio-spatial positioning(s) in the world', such as in the context of austerity.

Reading literature about 'intimate others' and spending time with people in their everyday lives has also given me pause for thought about how this 'otherness' is constituted, beyond being distinct from family and friendship. 'Intimate others' are commonly described within the literature as being family or friends (including lovers), or at least people who sit on a 'social horizon' (Morgan 2009, p. 1; Valentine 2008a; Valentine et al. 2015). In the main, these intimate relationships are also between people, whereas interspecies relationships rarely enter into broader discussions about intimacy. When animal-human or more-than-human intimacies are described, they tend to sit within the framework of familial relationships. Charles and Davies (2008, 9.6), for instance, describe how their participants identified animals (as pets) as playing 'an active part in social relationships […] regarded as fictive kin and also as companions and friends', with similar findings from Fox (2006), Power (2008) and Tipper (2011). In these examples, the focus of the research was on families and kinship, and living with animals as pets as a form of 'emotional and spatial intimacy' (Power 2008, p. 536). There are, of course, instances of 'animal-human relations in non-pet contexts' (Nast 2006, p. 897; Wilson 2017), though in these instances, intimacy is not on the agenda.

In this chapter, I add to these discussions by considering the role of animal-human intimacies in the context of austerity.

Extending further these ideas of the more-than-human, the place of material objects within and for producing and sustaining intimate relationships is another area of burgeoning interest within the social sciences (Holmes 2018b; Lewis 2018). Previous work on materiality and intimacy has often focused on commodification and the process of consuming things. Bridge and Smith (2003, p. 258) argue that 'expressing this intimacy with things is hard to do. It involves thinking about encounters with objects not as place-bound intimacies, but as local articulations of material flows that are more extensive in time and space.' Considering intimacy in this way does remove a preoccupation with place-based intimacies, such as in the home or domestic space (also see Dyck 2005; Smith and Stenning 2006; Tarrant 2010), but this is not a statement I wholly agree with. In light of recent research, such as by Burrell (2017), Holmes (2018b) and Lewis (2018), it is apparent that the sending, giving, circulating and sharing of things within relationships (friend, family and communities) constitute a mundane and regularised element of everyday lives. Rather than intimacy through material things being 'hard to do', it is actually normalised. However, here again intimacy is often limited to known relations, within already-existing relationships, which I argue can be expanded to incorporate a fuller spectrum of intimate relations. Seeing materials as points of connection and encounter with people, memories and emotions (see Wilson 2017), and as intimate objects engaged with through proximities, touch and affinities (see Holmes 2018b), I also explore materials as conduits and points of potentiality for intimacy and intimate relations in austerity.

In what now follows I explore these four outlined themes in turn: intimate monetary arrangements, momentary encounters, more-than-human intimacies and material proximities. In doing so, I detail the impacts that austerity can have on intimate relationships (austere intimacies) and how intimate relationships can serve to highlight the most personal and intimate experiences of austerity (intimate austerities). Throughout I adopt a relational approach, considering intimacy within and beyond kinship and friendship.

Intimate Monetary Arrangements

The exchange of money within intimate relationships is not a new phenomenon, nor is it unusual for intimate relationships to form from relations involving monetary transactions. As Zelizer (2005) argues, intimate practices are often bound up with monetary practices, sometimes in complicated but taken-for-granted ways. As we saw in the last chapter, everyday practices of caring, sharing and love operate as gendered moral economies (also see Hall 2016b), while also intersecting with moneyed economies. However, these intimacies are of increased interest in times of austerity when personal and public purse strings are tightened. What happens to intimate monetary arrangements and intimate relations in the context of austerity? I want to show how the giving of favours, cash-in-hand work, leisure activities and hobbyist interests not only are shaped by austerity but also have implications for the personal, intimate and social relationships in which they are rooted.

In particular, intimate monetary arrangements were found to be largely bound up with care-giving practices (including self-care—see Hall 2016b), which can alter the spatiality of intimate relationships. As Kim England (2010, p. 146) explains, 'the boundary between the supposedly private space of home and the public space of the state and the market gets blurred when non-family paid caregivers provide care, which in turn destabilises the meanings of home'—and, I might add, family. However, definitions and boundaries of family, friendship and intimacy are open to change in the context of austerity policies that reduce funding for social care, cut benefits and decimate public services. These gendered care burdens are then often placed on kith and kin, perhaps in combination with intimate others, and may well involve moneyed transactions. However, these intimacies are not always positive; rather they can elicit tense, awkward encounters. This, as I show, can shape, break and complicate intimate relations.

Two main 'stories' emerged from my ethnographic observations and discussions on this subject: that of participants either giving or receiving money within intimate relations, and often for intimate practices, although reciprocities in this regard were not always present. Participation in both, simultaneously, was quite usual, though to adequately communicate these findings, I am required to strip back layers of complexity to get to the detail of the intimate arrangements. This can have the effect of perhaps oversimplifying these examples, when in fact they are marked by the busyness, messiness and fuzziness of everyday practices and relationships.

During the fieldwork, I saw and heard many examples of intimate relationships being reshaped by monetary arrangements. A result of this was an exposing of the inner workings of the social relationships in question. One of the most striking examples of this came from Kerry. She had worked in nurseries and as an au pair for a number of years before she had her own children. In fact, this accounted for the majority of her paid work experience. Whenever she spoke about the possibility of going back to work, it always involved paid and unpaid childcare in one capacity or another.

In August 2014, just less than a year into her involvement in the research, Kerry started to look after her friend's child. This arrangement came about rather quickly; the friend had recently moved back to the UK from New Zealand. Having remembered Kerry had experience of childminding, as well as having her own children, she approached Kerry with the proposition. Kerry jumped at the chance. Earlier that year changes to tax credits, housing benefits and tax codes meant that she and Dan would now be £80 short a month. Prior to this (a few days before Christmas 2013), they received a letter about their entitlements, explaining they had been overpaid by £150 in the preceding months and would have £15 deducted from the next ten payments. On top of this, Kerry was required to confirm the date of their rent payment and, upon asking her landlord for a copy of the contract as evidence, he then decided to issue a new contract and increase the rent by £25 per month. Combined, the financial strain of having £120 less a month was a worry for Kerry and Dan.

The suggestion of childminding made by her friend was an opportunity that Kerry could not pass up, as it would help mitigate the damage caused by these benefits cuts and increased rental charges. However, it was a very short-lived arrangement. They had settled on £20 per day for three days a week. As Kerry was quick to point out, this is much cheaper than any other childminding options. It meant Kerry could pocket the cash without having to declare it, and they agreed that the £20 would be paid if childcare was cancelled with short notice. Kerry looked after her friend's son over the course of a week, but then at the start of the second week, her friend broke their agreement by cancelling at the last minute and not paying for that day. It happened a couple more times, and then her friend stopped asking her to childmind. Kerry was disappointed by this. She had been relying on the extra income, and had enjoyed reconnecting with an old friend. Their friendship soured, and the last I heard Kerry and her friend were no longer in touch.

Around the same time (as noted in Chap. 3), Kerry had set the ball rolling for an arrangement to look after her sister's child full time so that her sister and brother-in-law could return to work. At first Kerry was of the view that, in terms of payment, 'anything would be better than nothing' (taped discussion, April 2014). However, tensions soon started to emerge when it came to working out the finer details. Kerry later explained that

> She's going to pay me. We've said, originally, just for the food, but then a little something wouldn't go amiss … she said "the little something's up to you, dot dot dot" in her messages. So I went, "okay, yes, thank you". "It'll be … obviously less than I'd be paying nursery, but it'll be something". And that's how she left it! She's not told me how much. (taped discussion, September 2014)

Their communications about the arrangement seemed awkward, fragmented across text messages, emails and brief conversations in person. I even noted in my field diary that I was 'getting the feeling Kerry was becoming increasingly frustrated with the situation', as well as a concern that she was 'investing a lot in this arrangement going ahead' (field diary, March 2014). Payment for this informal, familial childcare added new dimensions to this sibling relationship, tied up with personal conditions of austerity and a distinct need for the extra cash, given the difference it would make to Kerry and Dan's monthly income.

It also seemed that the intricacies of their relationship and the power dynamics fuelled by monetary exchange were part of the tensions emerging. Kerry knew she was offering her sister a service for a price she would not be able to get anywhere else. A nursery or a childminder would be 'too expensive … it wouldn't be worth her going back to work' (taped discussion, April 2014). She was also jeopardising her benefits by taking cash-in-hand payments and not declaring it, similar to Zoe working for her friend cash-in-hand, as discussed in the previous chapter (also see Chap. 5). Kerry would be receiving 'just fifty pounds a week. So it only works out a tenner a day' (taped discussion, October 2014), and was already mentally allocating this extra money to future expenses:

Kerry: If she gives me money in June … no, when will I get him? June, July … no … yeah, it is June. So I can book a holiday in July then.
Sarah: You're going on holiday in June, aren't you?
Kerry: Yeah, so I'm not getting him until I'm back. So the money will be then [for] birthdays in September. (taped discussion, October 2014)

It took a number of unsubtle hints to get the point where Kerry and her sister discussed the actual amount she would receive, using the previous example of her friend's child:

I said to my sister, I said "oh, we'll be getting more from [friend's child] having him less days and hours than I would be getting from her". But I suppose it's family' (ibid.). Given the obvious similarities with the situation with her friend, I asked about being paid in the event of cancellations. Kerry had 'not actually worked this out […] I'm going to say yeah. I don't know, but then if she's given me enough notice, if she gives me a month's notice […] I don't really know, we haven't really finalised it all. (ibid.)

With the arrangement being up in the air, Kerry also seemed to be mentally playing out other things that could go wrong. Further annoyances about her sister came out as a result:

> I know she's going to be a pain, have organic this and organic that. Like now, she don't care because me and my children eat turkey dinosaurs and smiley faces, but I know for a fact it won't be good enough for her little "Gertrude". (taped discussion, September 2014)

Here, the layers of intimacy within the sisters' monetary arrangement become clearer: this was about the care of a child, and tensions about the gendered responsibilities and corporeal practices wrapped up in such care came bubbling to the surface. Kerry's qualities not only as a childminder but also a mother were bound up in this intimate monetary arrangement—intimate because of both who (family) and what (care work) it involved. Kerry's comments revealed her concerns about being judged for feeding and caring her children (also see Devault 1991), and an assumption that her current meal offerings wouldn't be 'good enough' for 'Gertrude' (a name Kerry uses to emphasise the snobbery she associates with her sister). Kerry's caring responsibilities were significantly altered in the context of austerity policies, both as they affected her and her kinship and friendship networks. Intimate familial and friendship relations were shifted by the introduction of moneyed arrangements concerning intimate bodily practices, arrangements that were designed to counteract multiple impacts of austerity.

While Kerry was in receipt of money for care-based labour in the context of intimate relationships, Laura was on the other side of the fence. She was, in a transactional sense, the 'customer' in a similarly fuzzy relationship. During her time as a participant, she paid for her friend and neighbour, Sophie, to look after her two young children on the days that her mum and mother-in-law could not. I witnessed the development of this arrangement, from hearing about Sophie as a 'friendly neighbour' to the evolvement of a formalised understanding about regular childcare for Isaac and Lucas, and the changes this made to everyday intimate relationships and practices.

Laura, as described in Chap. 2, started participating in the research while she was on maternity leave. I was privy to much of the planning and preparation about her return to work. The tapestry of childcare was one she and Rich, her partner, began to weave well in advance. They were clearly concerned about making sure things were in order so their children would be properly looked after, and that childcare was affordable so as not to negate Laura returning to employment. The first I heard about Sophie was when Laura was still on maternity leave and we were discussing how she spends the afternoons with the boys, when Lucas is out of nursery and she has two of them to entertain. She described how Lucas often feels cooped up if he is indoors all day and the heating bills shoot up in winter, but that it was just as expensive to sign him up for activities every week. To get around this, she would often take the boys to visit her friends, especially 'if it's friends that've got children, like I've got a lot of friends who've got kids Lucas's age, so we tend to see them in the afternoons. [...] There's a girl next door but one [Sophie], and she's a child-minder and she's got a little boy as well, so we'll probably go over there this afternoon for an hour' (taped discussion, November 2013).

It soon transpired that Sophie was due to look after Lucas and Isaac two days a week, and Laura's mum one day a week, covering the three days of Laura being at work. What started out as a friendly acquaintanceship then transitioned into them visiting each other's homes with their children, and into a formal childcare arrangement. Laura seemed comfortable with this, later telling me 'I'm not worried about Lucas at all, she'll pick Lucas up from school and have him for the afternoons and then in school holidays she'll have him for full days. He knows her so well and I'm not worried.' This was the first mention of a formal arrangement. Before this I knew Sophie as being her neighbour and friend. So I asked, 'Is it Sophie, the neighbour? Is she going to do, like, mates rates for childminding or..?' 'No', Laura replied, 'but I get a little sibling discount, she has two of them so I get a little bit' (taped discussion, May 2014). Prior friendship, familiarity and intimacy meant that Laura trusted Sophie with care of the boys.

However, Laura struggled to articulate this as a formal agreement, even though it involved set weekly payments and an agreement to pay in the event of a cancellation. She always discussed it as simply an extension of their friendship: 'it's probably a bit more of an informal arrangement. I mean, she obviously is a registered child-minder, but it's more like ... I mean, obviously we pay her, she's registered. But it's a bit more ... do you know what I mean?' (taped discussion, May 2014). Paying for her friend for childcare seemed to alter the definition of the childcare, rather than their friendship. Their already-established friendship gave rise to additional intimacies and close, personal familiarities. Laura told me 'she's got a key to this house. And I've got a key to her house. So like, yesterday, I'd forgotten to put Lucas's shorts in the bag and it ended up being a really nice day so she just let herself in and got the shorts' (ibid.). Having a key to each another's houses, living in close proximity and being able to access private spaces and personal items indicate an enrichment of an intimate friendship already in place. Sophie seemed to be going above and beyond her role as a childminder, utilising her intimate knowledge and access as a friend and neighbour.

In the case of Kerry and Laura, family and friendship relations were already present before intimate monetary arrangements were initiated, which might explain some of the tensions and awkwardness that these examples evoked. However, there were instances of paid-for intimate bodily encounters, intimate forms of labour (also see McDowell 2012; Twigg 2006), as providing the beginnings for future familiarity and personal relationships. Sharon, for example, had developed a schedule of alternative healing therapies to accompany her medical treatment for breast cancer. These activities were described as a large but necessary expense and meant that Sharon was left with very little at the end of the month: 'I spend so much on health stuff [...] my treatments, my pilates classes, my sports therapy, my osteopathy. It costs me money. So that's where I would save' (January 2014, taped discussion). These practices and the people who provided them were very much a source of physical and emotional support for Sharon. It involved bodily touching, physical closeness and the requirement for another person to be working upon her body (also see Holmes 2015; Jayne and Leung 2014; Twigg 2006). They were intimate without necessarily being personal; it was only later that Sharon developed friendships with some of these people.

However, the reciprocity of intimacy was not always clear in Sharon's articulation of their friendships. Yes, physical intimacy had to be shared because of bodily surfaces being touched and traversed in her treatments. However, emotional intimacy appeared to be somewhat one way. It was not an intimate relationship of equal parts (if this is ever truly possible). For instance, Sharon described going to her sports therapist, Reiki teacher and osteopath for advice about her sister, Pat. They had exchanged some heated words and as a result Sharon felt 'very low'. At this point, she told her Reiki teacher, and he gave her advice on how to deal with her sister's 'bad energy':

> "Pretend to be a crystal", he told her, "and literally reflect back her bad energy". Sharon checked this with her osteopath, in whom she had also confided about the fall out, and she suggested similarly tactics. "It's all in the mind", the osteopath said. (field diary, November 2013)

Her osteopath was an individual that stuck out. Sharon would talk about her regularly and admitted to her being a key source of support in her life. When Sharon received her diagnosis that her breast cancer had returned, 'she was one of the first people I told outside the family [...] I actually took her for the second consultation with my surgeon' (taped discussion, January 2014).

While Sharon seemed to share lots of intimate details with her osteopath, and described her as also being a friend, I found it telling how she spoke about her. She mostly referred to her as 'my osteopath', and it was only after ten months of knowing Sharon that I learned her first name. Furthermore, their interactions were often founded on therapeutic practices and discussions, mostly in the space of the clinic: intimate encounters that were facilitated by monetary exchange for a particular service. Sharon would often relay health advice provided by her osteopath. From the outset, it appeared to me that while their relationship may have been intimate, it was not necessarily an even relationship or the same type of friendship for both individuals. Her role in Sharon's life was so crucial that she paid for the osteopathic therapy above saving money each month. It made me question what the personal and social effect would be if Sharon were no longer able to afford these appointments.

The disintegration of intimate relationships as a result of saving money was again something I observed in the ethnography, not least where public services like Sure Start centres, library reading groups and community coffee mornings were cut (more on this in the next section, and also in Chap. 5), but also in the case of personal financial frugality. When I first met Zoe in October 2013, she had been paying for a cleaner for four hours on a Thursday morning every fortnight. This brought some much-needed support with the housework to Zoe, who was a carer for her son as well as working part time and studying at a local college. Her partner Stuart worked more than full time hours, and Zoe openly admitted that he 'has no idea where the hoover is or how to use it' (field diary, August 2014).

However, the cleaner was more than someone with 'intimate knowledge' (Morgan 2009) of her house and personal habits, privy as domestic workers are to such information (see Cox and Narula 2003; Pratt 1997). She was also a confidante, someone who Zoe spoke with about family and personal issues, though Zoe did not necessarily think of her as a friend. Much like Sharon's references to 'the osteopath', I never learnt 'the cleaner's' name. When their cleaner needed to return to Bulgaria for a few months to look after her elderly parents, Stuart suggested they reassess whether they could afford to keep her on. Zoe found herself 'just about coping with the cleaning' (field diary, December 2013) and was disappointed when they eventually let her go. She was valuable practical support and a friendly ear to whom Zoe had become quite emotionally attached. This example also reminds me of Cox and Narula's (2003) work on false kinship and domestic workers, whereby Zoe and her cleaner seemed to develop false friendship relations. It was a monetary arrangement that entailed the sharing of intimate personal details, but without it developing into anything more sustained for either party.

Through these examples, intimate relationships of varying types are shown to provide the basis for intimate monetary arrangements, the giving and receiving of money for intimate practices such as care work, domestic work and body-work. In austerity, people become reliant on but are not always able to continue to afford these practices, services and arrangements. This means that the viability of maintaining their associated social relationships also comes under question. There are gendered implications to this, too. Many of the intimacies described here relate to intimate feminised labour, bound by neither family nor household. The accounts provided also show how intimacy does not always have to be reciprocal. Intimacy and intimate relations can be one-way processes of varying positive and negative consequences for the people involved. I want to continue this theme of intimacy and familiarity by considering the role of momentary encounters as a source of intimacy in times of austerity.

Momentary Encounters

In Chap. 2, I explored how the parameters of everyday social relationships reach much further than family and friends, but include a whole host of intimate others that play an important role in daily life. Taking this premise, my ethnographic observations revealed that a consideration of intimacy in austerity needs to also account for momentary encounters. Momentary in that they are passing, fleeting, they are not necessarily sustained or repeated. They happen by chance, are rarely planned and involve strangers who, in the process of the encounter, may become less strange (see Jackson et al. 2017; Morgan 2009). These encounters offer intimacy in the sharing of personal details, emotionally or physically proximate space, glancing looks, the flash of a smile, temporary bonds and comfort in the moment. They may be remembered, they may be forgotten. They can resonate or be missed, even dismissed, and they might offer a platform for familiarity, and for further intimate social relations to develop. They might be painful, or funny, and these sentiments are not always reciprocal or shared between those involved in or witnessing the encounter.

My ethnographies diaries are full of notes about momentary encounters, too many to cover here in fact. After all, these encounters are integral to ethnographic research, observing the everyday as it happens and in detail (Herbert 2000). Momentary encounters are part and parcel of everyday life, whether it is on the street, on public transport or in institutional spaces such as schools or libraries (Valentine 2008b; Wilson 2017). They are not always profound, but they do not need to be in order to have significance. I will give some examples of such encounters, and how they feed into both personal and social conditions of austerity. All of these are taken from field diary entries. Momentary encounters, by their very nature, were not necessarily something participants chose to raise in conversation with me, or were even always conscious of, but were often observed in the moment as they happened.

Shared experiences of hardship were, in this research, one of the ways in which momentary encounters came into being. Engagement in passing conversations, not only for myself and participants, but also in recruitment settings, was a key interface for these intimate encounters. They were not provoked by a particular individual, though I cannot of course always be sure that my presence did not instigate or trigger these discussions. Sometimes they did not involve me directly but happened within earshot. My sense was that they came about from polite, passing conversations that could become intimate depending on the topic and the setting.

On a visit to the local park on a grey skied afternoon in March 2014, Kerry struck up conversation with a woman whose son was playing with Zack (also see Jupp 2013a; Holloway 1998). They exchanged the names of their children, spoke about how old they were, when they started walking and talking, and discussed what school they were going to. A lot of personal information was being passed back and forth, with connections emerging between people and places in Argleton. Kerry seemed excited. All the meanwhile the boys were chasing one another, whizzing down the slide either together or in quick succession, chuckling together as though they were old friends. When the woman answered that her son was going to school in Rochdale (a different, more remote part of Greater Manchester), because her husband had a new job there and they could not afford his commute, Kerry looked disappointed. She clearly had hoped to make a new friend off the back of this briefly intimate encounter.

While Chap. 3 focused on family, friendship and more sustained intimate relations, momentary encounters can also provide a space for support and can be surprisingly revealing and intimate. I was struck by one encounter I witnessed when out shopping with Laura. She was in a rush that day, and was practically running around the shops to get everything she needed so we would be back home in good time. As we sped around one store, Laura pushing the pram at record speed, a woman put her arm out to Laura (almost like waving down a bus) to ask where the baby changing rooms were. Her baby was crying, and the woman looked exhausted, her eyes glazed with tears. Laura seemed to shift gears entirely and told the woman she too was going upstairs and would show her where to go. As we slowly walked together into the lifts, I held back to let them talk, feeling wary of intruding on this intimate moment;

> Laura asked if her baby was a newborn, and how old she was. "Yes", the woman replied, "and I had no idea how hard it would be". Her face started to crumple a little, and Laura learned into the pram, said hello to the baby, and turned to the woman. "It gets easier, I promise", she told her. The woman nodded and smiled at Laura, who pointed her in the way of the changing rooms and parted with the words "good luck". (field diary, December 2013)

Confined together in the lift, this momentary encounter was marked by physical proximity and emotional closeness, the sharing of intimate experiences and feelings, with a passing stranger. Laura's careful words of advice seemed to be pitch perfect, just what was needed in that moment. She drew on her own life experience and memories to soothe and reassure the woman in a way that not everyone—myself included—would have been able to do.

Momentary encounters where physical space and intimate details were shared were not always fulfilling and constructive. Selma talked about an upsetting visit to the Job Centre when she had a meeting with a new employment advisor. This was commonly described in my fieldwork, by a number of participants, as a space of awkward, even hostile intimate encounters (also see Chap. 5). Selma recalled having gotten upset in front of her, saying how hard she found it living on such small amounts of money. The employment advisor's response, Selma told me, 'was to say "oh you are very lucky". Selma felt like she was being sarcastic, telling me "how can she understand how hard it is for me, she's got a job!"'(field diary, May 2014). This encounter stayed with Selma, in part I think because it made her feel especially vulnerable in what was already an emotionally charged situation. She was exposed, sharing personal feelings and intimate details, and her distress was met not with compassion but a distinct lack of care or concern. Intimate encounters in austerity can be braced by strong negative emotions, which in this example elicited feelings of loneliness and shame, rather than solidarity or collectivity (also see Stenning and Hall 2018).

In momentary encounters, because of their fleeting nature, misinterpretations and misreadings are also likely (also see Morgan 2009; Valentine 2008b). The community cooking club and cafe mentioned in Chap. 3 had a regular customer who came in every week for her lunch.

No sustained relationships had been developed; nobody knew the woman's name or spoke to her beyond taking her food order and thanking her when money was swapped for neatly wrapped meals. In many ways, the impersonality and swiftness of her visits maintained the temporary, passing nature of these encounters. The cafe manager told me 'we've always assumed she was homeless'; they had created a backstory for the woman based upon these fleeting exchanges. As it turns out, she was not homeless. While waiting for her food one day she initiated polite conversation with me, explaining that she lived nearby with her partner, and was picking up food as a weekly treat for when she was looking after her grandchildren (field diary, September 2014).

Nevertheless, the fictional life attributed to this woman was part of a broader narrative about the role of the community cafe in a time of austerity. It was a place where some of the most vulnerable people could go to stay warm and dry, to eat a healthy meal on a budget and sometimes to engage in conversation. As Heidi, the lead organiser of the cafe, put it, 'these are the sorts of people that we should be helping and who need our help'. The irony here is that community centres such as this have experienced severe disinvestment since the rollout of local government spending cuts (also see Brewster 2014; Jupp 2013a). There are strong political undercurrents to these momentary encounters that are worthy of further exploration. I will come back to this matter, and some of the examples discussed here, later in Chap. 5. Fleeting or temporary moments of intimacy are necessary for thinking though the personal and wider social impacts of austerity, particularly in the reshaping of relational space. I will continue on this track of considering less-discussed intimacies below by looking at relationships with more-than-human worlds.

More-Than-Human Intimacies

Intimacies between and beyond kinship and friendship are well known to extend to more-than-human relationalities, including between people and animals. As noted earlier in this chapter, a wealth of literature acknowledges the close relationships between people and pets. Animals have long been considered part of family life and 'objects of human affection and love' (Nast 2006; p. 894; also see Charles and Davies 2008; Power 2008). It is unsurprising that these intimacies were also part of the rhythms, routines and practices of everyday life in austerity, of getting by day-to-day. For those participants living with animals, their pets were described as being family members who offered comfort, security and felt connections.

For Pauline and George, their cat Xena was an esteemed family member. She was always either sitting with us or was winding around our ankles when we met at their home, reminding us of her presence. She was a focus of discussion when conversations ran dry, she purred in the background of taped conversations, and when she nested on the sofa next to me during one of my visits, I felt like I had finally been accepted as a regular visitor. Xena was company for George when he hurt his back and was housebound for a few days, and sat beside Pauline when she was knitting from the armchair. She prompted sometimes difficult discussions about memories and family relationships, such as Pauline describing how her mum 'has a very bad memory, sometimes she can't remember Pauline, but she does remember that growing up all their cats were called Eddie and the dogs were called Bruce' (field diary, May 2015). The intimate relationship Pauline and George developed with Xena opened up other caring relations and practices. They adopted Xena through a local Cat's Protection charity, what they described as 'one of our charities' (George, taped discussion, March 2015), and so now commit their time and energies into helping this organisation and the cats living there (more on this in the next section).

Similarly, the very first time I met Sharon and Bill, they told me that 'a pet is really a part of the family' (field diary, October 2013). Throughout their participation, they spoke often, and with heavy hearts, about their pet dog Kiki who passed away in 2005. On my first visit to their home, I noted in my field diary that there were 'framed pictures of dogs propped up on surfaces or mounted on various walls in the house, a pottery dog in the hallway and Sharon's car has a dog toy in the window. All that seemed to be missing was a dog' (field diary, November 2013). Being former dog owners continued to shape their everyday routines, too: 'every Saturday we go for a walk, come hail, rain or shine we will walk because for seven years we had a dog, we used to walk her, so we still do it' (Sharon, taped discussion, August 2014).

While the connections to everyday austerity might not be immediately clear, over my time with Sharon and Bill, I came to see how these routines were a significant part of getting by, and part of everyday coping mechanisms for Sharon who had recently undergone treatment for breast cancer. It provided a way for Sharon, in my view, to structure the parts of her life that she could still exert control over, and she seemed to take comfort in having planned activities to look forward to.

> Sharon and Bill have a Saturday morning routine that runs like a well-oiled machine. They wake early, have a cooked breakfast, and leave the house at 9.30 am sharp. They drive first to the newsagents to pick up their Saturday paper and pet the dog that lives there. Then they park up in town (they have to do this early otherwise there are no spaces left), and go to the market to buy their meat, vegetables and flowers, talking to all the trading staff who know them well. Then they go for a walk, feeding the horses (with carrots bought at the market), and onto the pub where they sit and do the crossword. (field diary, March 2015)

Although home-based, more-than-human relations are an everyday space for animal-human relations (see Charles and Davies 2008; Power 2008), other sites might also be important for interspecies intimacies. Meeting the dog at the newsagents and feeding the horses were key points in the Saturday routine, and it was Sharon in particular who sought out these animal intimacies. In fact, when asked to take pictures of how they get by (as part of the photo elicitation exercise described in Chap. 1), Bill took this photograph (Fig. 4.1) of Sharon feeding the horses during their Saturday morning walk. Sharon was also an avid horse rider, taking it up after Kiki died. She took a lot of comfort from spending time with horses and dogs, and described how horse riding 'itself is a therapy' (taped discussion, January 2014). She often spoke of how she had 'found it so beneficial, psychologically but physically as well. It made me stronger' (taped discussion, January 2014).

These furry encounters seemed to offer Sharon an embodied connection to the world around her, a sort of tactile mindfulness, a physical grounding, of being in the moment. Here, intimacy was described as both a form of corporeal closeness and 'emotional satisfaction' (Charles

Fig. 4.1 Sharon feeding the horses during a Saturday morning walk (photograph taken by Bill)

and Davies 2008, 3.1), or as Sharon put it, 'no matter how bad I'm feeling or how much pain, if I go round horses, I love it. And it heals me' (taped discussion, August 2014). These more-than-human intimacies also traversed family relations. Regular encounters with these intimate others—horses, horse trainers and other riders—were significant within Sharon's everyday social infrastructures of care and support.

Sharon wasn't the only one to actively seek out more-than-human encounters, though participants might have very different reasons for doing so. I described earlier in this chapter how Laura would often take her two children out in the afternoons, as a way to save money and prevent them all going stir crazy locked together in the house. She explained that as well as visiting friends, they might also do other cost-free activities:

> It's very rare that we'll stay in all day. Lucas likes … they do these things at the craft shop, where they do craft sessions from one 'til three. Yeah, and then go to the pet shop because Lucas likes going into the pet shop. (taped discussion, November 2013)

Other participants also discussed going to the pet shop to see the animals, visiting farms or going to the park where people were walking their dogs, all as ways of seeking out animal encounters. These forms of intimacy were often considered restorative. The animals brought joy and pleasure, comfort and companionship.

However, not all encounters with non-human species were enjoyable. They could also be unwanted, as well as a reminder of uncomfortable living conditions. This was certainly the case for Selma and Mya, whose close encounters with non-domestic critters served as an example of the difficulties of living alongside others, when intimacies are unpleasant (Morgan 2009; Wilson 2017). As briefly described in Chap. 2, Selma and her daughter Mya lived together in social housing, which had plain and very sparse decor. Mya mentioned to her mum that she didn't like her room, that her friends from school didn't want to visit because her house was 'horrible and cold'. Selma was upset because she couldn't afford anything better. Her eyes filled with tears as she recounted this to me (field diary, May 2014). She contacted a family member to ask for a loan of £30, but when she explained what she needed it for, he gave her £50 and said he didn't want it back. Selma used the money to buy paint, butterfly stencils and a bookshelf, and decorated the room herself, surprising Mya when she returned from school one day (as depicted in Fig. 4.2). However, decorating the room and moving the furniture around had the unfortunate effect of disturbing a mouse. On Mya's first night in her room, she

Fig. 4.2 Selma painting Mya's bedroom (illustrated by Claire Stringer, from the *Everyday Austerity* zine by Sarah Marie Hall, see https://everydayausterity.wordpress.com/zine/)

saw the mouse scuttling across the carpet and under the chest of drawers and was 'terrified'. She had been sleeping in Selma's bed ever since.

More-than-human intimacies can be incredibly rewarding and fulfilling, offering physically, bodily and emotionally close connections. However, unwanted intimacies with animals, such as rodents or what are considered to be pests, can also be a form of more-than-human intimacy. This physical proximity is too close for comfort; living with other species can sometimes be distressing. This was worsened by the fact that Selma was living in a property owned by someone else. She felt vulnerable to their whim as to whether or not they might fix the problem. In a time of austerity, more people might be forced to live in unfit housing and endure these unwanted intimacies (also see Hall and Holmes 2017).

Material Proximities

Although social connections and intimate relations in times of austerity remain my focus here, it is important to also consider the role of materiality. Materials can provide a conduit for social proximities, enabling contact and interaction, a form of fibrous interconnectivity. While monetary arrangements, momentary encounters and more-than-human intimacies typically encircle intimate relationships and bodily care practices, material proximities provide another example of intimate relations in austerity. Material givings, sharings and receivings can involve closeness, touching and embodiment, through proximate bodily surfaces and through things once worn, played with or part of personal memories.

I expand upon current literature regarding material intimacy and intimacy through materiality, namely the ways in which material objects have been found to facilitate and substantiate the practice of kinship and community (see Burrell 2017; Holmes 2018b; Lewis 2018). While some of the examples I draw upon below involve kith and kin relations, there are other intimacies at work. More specifically, intimate relations can emerge as a result of material proximities. The circulation of goods in order to save or make money in times of austerity can provide opportunities to meet new people and form new social relationships (also see Holmes 2018a). These items can also represent intimacies in and of themselves. Materialities are as much a part of the fabric of intimacy in austerity as the other examples provided in this chapter.

I'll start with the example of Selma and Mya, as a means of thinking about materiality and intimacy in pre-existing social relationships. Selma had struggled to find paid work to fit around looking after Mya. This meant they were completely financially dependent on social security. Day-to-day living was a financial and emotional struggle. Holidays, savings, shopping trips and keeping up with the latest fashion trends were just not possible. Their state-provided income could barely stretch to feed them both and heat their flat. On occasions when we met outside of the house, Selma would sometimes be inappropriately dressed for the weather, turned out in a hoodless jacket in the rain or wearing flimsy pumps in cold temperatures. She had only bought one thing for herself in the last five years, a faux designer handbag from the market when her old one fell apart.

Selma had a cousin who lived in London, who she and Mya would visit once every few months. He would pay for the train fare, and sometimes would even drive them back up north. Selma made it clear just how reliant she was on him: 'I would not be able to live without his help', she told me (field diary, March 2014). This ranged from small trinkets and furnishings for the flat (and the money for decorating Mya's bedroom), to £30 to buy Mya some new school shoes, to paying for a mobile phone contract each month. However, the mobile phone provided more than just communicative capacity and a sense of propinquity, as described in Chap. 2. Selma treasured its material properties as well as the intimate proximities it afforded. She and Mya would often sit together for hours at a time flicking through photos and videos either taken or sent to them by family and friends, including photographs of old, hard-copy photographs. The phone was itself a material reminder, a physical object and container of digital memories to be viewed and reviewed. It was part of 'doing' family (Holmes 2018b; Morgan 2011) both for Selma and Mya in their intergenerational, shared practices and in maintaining kinship at a distance. In times of hardship, mundane material things have the capacity to provide comfort and a sense of intimate proximity.

Continuing ideas of proximity and distance, the ethnographic findings revealed how material items are not always shared or gifted to known oth-

Fig. 4.3 A knitted doll for a charity raffle made by Pauline (photograph taken by Sarah Marie Hall)

ers. The politics of material intimacies are reshaped by and in austerity. Pauline regularly knitted clothes, accessories, dolls and toys (like the ones photographed in Figs. 4.3 and 4.4). Clothes would typically be for family members (as noted in Chap. 3), some of whom were especially frugal and appreciative of such gifts. However, at any one time she might have been making a hat for her sister-in-law and a cardigan for her grandson, whilst 'knitting premature baby cardigans ... hats for kiddies in Nepal ... [and] trauma teddies' as part of Mother's Union campaigns (taped discussion, March 2015). Whether for family, friends or unknown others, these tasks were all invested with the same quality of materials and careful craftwork.

Charitable offerings, such as those noted above, as well as knitted dolls for the local school raffle and crocheted mice stuffed with catnip for the local Cat's Protection charity were a way of expressing care and concern

Fig. 4.4 A cardigan knitted by Pauline for her grandson (photograph taken by Sarah Marie Hall)

for local and global issues. Pauline had never considered selling these items for money, preferring that they 'benefit a person who buys it, and the charity that it's gone to' (taped discussion, March 2015). Often these charities were lacking in funding, or were offering home-made goods to vulnerable communities, and so this was also entwined with notions of personal and social austerity. Moreover, the making and mending skills Pauline had acquired initially developed out of necessity, from knitting school jumpers for her sons with the primary purpose of saving money (field diary, August 2015). That her crafting knowledge and the material creations were being put to another purpose, and for different people, also speaks to the idea of intimate material proximities. Pauline's knitting skills were being shared and employed across time and for different purposes, ultimately benefiting unknown but nevertheless cared-for strangers via material proximities. And I was embroidered within these exchanges; when Pauline bought one too few buttons for a cardigan she was knitting for her grandson, I raided my own collection for the closest match I could find.

Selling old wares was a necessity for some, and increasingly so as a result of public spending cuts. A number of participants were observed making use of a local online sales forum—'Borough Deals'—for clothes, accessories and (sometimes) household items. It was this example that first alerted me to the possibilities of material intimacies in austerity, both concerning the materials themselves as intimate objects, and of the capacity of material exchanges to lead to intimate social relations. The forum, Zoe told me,

> was a closed group where people joined to sell things, often kids clothes and toys but sometimes adult clothes and shoes. They post a picture with the amount they wanted beneath and there's an etiquette that you sell your item to the first person who posts a message saying they want it. People often write "collection only", and then would send a personal message with their address and a good time to collect. (field diary, August 2014)

'Borough Deals' was well known in Argleton, and a go-to for some participants. It allowed them to sell items in bulk without having to pay any charges for advertising, unlike eBay. For example, when decorating Isobel's bedroom, Zoe had cleared out all the toys she no longer played with, and she also found lots of fancy dress costumes. She asked Isobel if she still wanted them (she didn't) and then sold them on the site as a bulk buy for £20 (field diary, August 2014).

Laura was also an avid user of the forum, mainly for selling things 'like, toys, clothes, books. You know … basically, any old bric-a-brac.' When asked, 'and what do you think will happen with the stuff that … the money that you get from it?', she told me, 'I'm going to stick it in my wedding fund, I'm going to get it changed into two-pound coins and stick it in the wedding fund' (taped discussion, May 2014). Laura had a distinct strategy of selling Lucas and Isaac's old clothes, shoes and toys to help fill up her and Rich's wedding fund. The fund was made up specifically of two-pound coins, because Laura might be given a few of these a week, and when saved they can add up quickly. Material exchanges, for hand-held, tangible coins as cash, were then also a conduit for the resourcing of intimate, familial practices (also see Hall 2016a).

Moreover, when I witnessed Laura selling some of these items, they were not always—contrary to her claims—'any old bric-a-brac'. On one of my visits, for example, the heating was blasting out, drying a white furry snowsuit on the radiator by the front door. Laura was frantically tidying the hallway, because the buyer was going to pick it up that morning—she'd sold it for £4 on the forum. As she spoke, she stopped to stroking the outfit, once worn by Isaac but was now too small for him. She talked about how cute he looked in it, encased in a ball of fur and how cuddly he felt when he wore it. For Laura, this outfit was clearly part of fond memories of Isaac growing up, but was also tangibly comforting. It was an item worn and fitted to Isaac's body, and its materiality was also intimate in its once-close corporeality. Having a stranger come into her home, to collect the item, adds further layers to the intimacies created by such material exchanges.

Furthermore, these practices were part of a wider tapestry of material proximities and circulation practices. For while Laura was selling on a local online site, she would also sell items on car boot sales and be given her Mum's hand-me-downs, who luckily was 'very cool with loads of nice clothes' (field diary, May 2014). A family member's house removals business was also a source of second-hand items, 'all sorts, from toys to furniture, clothes and antiques; but she mainly gets the kids stuff' (field diary, July 2014). Laura also enthusiastically described a book she recently purchased second-hand, 'Austerity Bites', by Mary O'Hara, which she felt 'everyone should read' (field diary, July 2014). She would regularly ask me 'had I read it yet?', until one day she asked if I wanted to buy her copy. Describing it as a 'win-win' situation for us both, she said she wanted the book to be read by someone who would appreciate it (field diary, November 2014). The passing on of material items can therefore also be a way of maintaining already-established intimacy through shared knowledges, memories and personal politics (Burrell 2017; Holmes 2018b; Lewis 2018). More than this, they can be a significant way of getting hold of more money for those in cash-strapped situations. Laura would regularly make £100 at a time selling a glut of items on the forum, and 'within a year she had made about £400 from selling on Borough Deals alone' (field diary, October 2014).

I would sometimes accompany Kerry, another keen forum user, to drop off or meet up with buyers of the items she was selling. On one occasion we went to meet a woman who was buying a pair of Dan's trainers. Kerry preferred not for people to come to her house for collection, because it meant they would know where she lived. It was a foggy, drizzly day and the woman we were meeting was late. Kerry kept chuntering 'I hate late people' and 'I hate being kept waiting'. When the woman finally arrived and gave £5 for the shoes, Kerry whispered to me as we walked away 'I'll remember her, I'll remember not to sell to her again' (field diary, November 2014). These material exchanges could, therefore, also lead to uncomfortable intimate proximities.

Realising how useful online selling sites were for like-minded people living nearby, Kerry and a friend decided to set up another Facebook selling site for her local area—'Argleton Bargains'—as an arena to sell second-hand children's clothes and toys. While this would allow her to de-clutter and make a bit of money in the process, she also liked that it would be accessible to others 'even if you are not friends', allowing her to meet new people living nearby (taped discussion, April 2014). She thought of the site as a helpful resource for other mums looking to buy affordable children's clothes. Kerry and her friend would be the online administrators of the group, so allowing people to join and ensuring appropriate behaviour of users.

Before long, people beyond Kerry's social circle were advertising, selling and buying goods on the Argleton Bargains forum. She would often update me on how many more people had joined, and would look on their Facebook profiles. A few times we were out in Argleton and she was recognised by someone who had joined the group, another time she pointed out another lady she recognised from her Facebook picture. These encounters were also momentary, led by potential material proximities from selling online, as a practice that had become a way for some of my participants to make money out of 'dormant things' (also see Woodward 2015), of getting by in austere times. It was also form of social connection being made through these material exchanges. For Kerry, despite her negative previous experience with some buyers, this was one of the incentives for creating the group: to meet new, like-minded people.

The intimate encounters created by material proximities, in the sharing or circulation of things, were not always positive. Zoe spoke of how 'she'd seen a few scraps on the forum, where people haven't sold to the first person who posted, or where people started offering a lower price, or bartering by asking sellers what they would take' (field diary, August 2014). Depending on the context, hand-me-downs and gifted second-hand items can also be a source of embarrassment. Selma, for example, found it demeaning that all her and Mya's clothes had to be second-hand: 'I find it hard that I can't have new things' (field diary, March 2014). Despite only being eight years old, Mya was acutely aware of the stigma around having second-hand clothing. Selma's cousin would often give her clothes for Mya, since he had a daughter just two years older than Mya. Once they'd been washed, ironed and folded, Selma would present them to Mya, exclaiming 'look, new clothes!' However, as she got older, she started to remember having seen her cousin's daughter wearing them and would say 'this is secondhand, I don't want it' (taped discussion, May 2014).

Selma's discomfort with second-hand clothes was down to a mixture of factors. There was her sensitivity about her lack of money and resources, bound up with gendered moral responsibilities. And there was the sometimes off-putting material and sensory properties of second-hand items. She explained: 'they smell, they have to be washed, sometimes more than once' (field diary, March 2014). Here, the proximity of second-hand clothing to other people's bodies renders their material intimacy problematic.

While material things are often passed within already-existing intimate relations, such items can also provide opportunities for people to meet or reconnect, facilitating and sustaining social proximity and intimacy. These material proximities can be welcomed or unwanted, and may have the capacity to lead to sustained connections, or to tension and discomfort. The materials being shared, gifted, sold, bought and circulated can themselves also be intimate, whether as a conduit to care or because of their corporeal connections, sensory features and material memories. Material proximities may therefore be emergent, a conductor or a starting point for intimacies to flourish.

Conclusion

With this chapter I have explored a multitude of ways in which intimacies may change, bend or retreat in times of austerity. Austerity and intimacy were shown to be contingent and interdependent, shaping relational spaces. By this I mean that austerity policies and a personal condition of austerity can have significant impacts on intimate relationships, or what I refer to as 'austere intimacies'. Taking a closer look at intimate relationships, between and beyond family and friends, revealed just how intimate and personal austerity can be—otherwise termed 'intimate austerities'. Intimacy and austerity are entwined in the proximities, propinquities, distances and tensions that can result from monetary, momentary, more-than-human and material relations. And within these relationships intimacy can blossom or sour. Tensions and awkwardness are as common as rapport and comfort.

Intimacy is as much about what it involves—bodies, care, labour, emotions—as who it involves. They are inextricable from one another, because intimate relationships in austerity are maintained, forged or fragmented through intimate, embodied and proximate practices. When we take relationships as our starting point, surprising aspects of everyday life in austerity can be revealed. In the next chapter, I take this relational approach further to consider personal and relational politics at a time of austerity, as a space for tension as much as conviviality.

Bibliography

Ahmed, S. (2004). *The Cultural Politics of Emotion*. Edinburgh: Edinburgh University Press.

Askins, K. (2015). Being Together: Everyday Geographies and the Quiet Politics of Belonging. *ACME: An International E-Journal for Critical Geographies, 14*(2), 470–478.

Brewster, L. (2014). The Public Library as Therapeutic Landscape: A Qualitative Case Study. *Health & Place, 26*, 94–99.

Bridge, G., & Smith, A. (2003). Intimate Encounters: Culture—Economy—Commodity. *Environment and Planning D: Society and Space, 21*, 257–268.

Bunnell, T., Yea, S., Peake, L., Skelton, T., & Smith, M. (2012). Geographies of Friendships. *Progress in Human Geography, 36*(4), 490–507.

Burrell, K. (2017). The Recalcitrance of Distance: Exploring the Infrastructures of Sending in Migrants' Lives. *Mobilities, 12*(6), 813–826.

Charles, N. (2000). *Feminism, the State and Social Policy*. Basingstoke: Palgrave.

Charles, N., & Davies, C. A. (2008). My Family and Other Animals. *Sociological Research Online, 13*(5), 4.

Cox, R., & Narula, R. (2003). Playing Happy Families: Rules and Relationships in Au Pair Employing Households in London, England. *Gender Place and Culture, 10*, 333–344.

Devault, M. (1991). *Feeding the Family: The Social Organisation of Caring as Gendered Work*. London: The University of Chicago Press.

Dyck, I. (2005). Feminist Geography, the "Everyday", and Local-Global Relations: Hidden Spaces of Place-Making. *The Canadian Geographer, 49*, 233–245.

England, K. (2010). Home, Work and the Shifting Geographies of Care. *Ethics, Place & Environment, 13*(2), 131–150.

England, K., & Dyck, I. (2011). Managing the Body Work of Home Care. *Sociology of Health & Illness, 33*(2), 206–219.

Fox, E. (2006). Animal Behaviours, Post-Human Lives: Everyday Negotiations of the Animal-Human Divide in Pet-Keeping. *Social and Cultural Geography, 7*(4), 525–537.

Giddens, A. (1992). *The Transformation of Intimacy: Sexuality, Love and Eroticism in Modern Societies*. Cambridge: Polity.

Hall, S. M. (2009). "Private Life" and "Work Life": Difficulties and Dilemmas When Making and Maintaining Friendships with Ethnographic Participants. *Area, 41*, 263–272.

Hall, S. M. (2014). Ethics of Ethnography with Families: A Geographical Perspective. *Environment and Planning A, 46*(9), 2175–2194.

Hall, S. M. (2016a). Everyday Family Experiences of the Financial Crisis: Getting by in the Recent Economic Recession. *Journal of Economic Geography, 16*(2), 305–330.

Hall, S. M. (2016b). Moral Geographies of Family: Articulating, Forming and Transmitting Moralities in Everyday Life. *Social & Cultural Geography, 17*(8), 1017–1039.

Hall, S. M. (2016c). Family Relations in Times of Austerity: Reflections from the UK. In S. Punch, R. Vanderbeck, & T. Skelton (Eds.), *Geographies of Children and Young People: Families, Intergenerationality and Peer Group Relations*. Berlin: Springer.

Hall, S. M., & Holmes, H. (2017). Making Do and Getting By? Beyond a Romantic Politics of Austerity and Crisis. *Discover Society*, p. 44. Retrieved from https://discoversociety.org/2017/05/02/making-do-and-getting-by-beyond-a-romantic-politics-of-austerity-and-crisis/.
Hall, S. M., & Jayne, M. (2016). Make, Mend and Befriend: Geographies of Austerity, Crafting and Friendship in Contemporary Cultures of Dressmaking. *Gender, Place & Culture, 23*(2), 216–234.
Harker, C., & Martin, L. L. (2012). Familial Relations: Spaces, Subjects, and Politics. *Environment and Planning A, 44*(4), 768–775.
Herbert, S. (2000). For Ethnography. *Progress in Human Geography, 24*, 550–568.
Holdsworth, C. (2013). *Family and Intimate Mobilities*. Basingstoke: Palgrave Macmillan.
Holloway, S. L. (1998). Local Childcare Cultures: Moral Geographies of Mothering and the Social Organisation of Pre-school Education. *Gender, Place & Culture, 5*, 29–53.
Holmes, H. (2015). Transient Craft: Reclaiming the Contemporary Craft Worker. *Work, Employment and Society, 29*(3), 479–495.
Holmes, H. (2018a). New Spaces, Ordinary Practices: Circulating and Sharing Within Diverse Economies of Provisioning. *Geoforum, 88*, 134–147.
Holmes, H. (2018b). Material Affinities: "Doing" Family Through the Practices of Passing On. *Sociology, 53*(1), 174–191.
Horton, J., & Kraftl, P. (2009). Small Acts, Kind Words and "Not Too Much Fuss": Implicit Activisms. *Emotion, Space and Society, 2*(1), 14–23.
Hubbard, P. (2001). Sex Zones: Intimacy, Citizenship and Public Space. *Sexualities, 4*(1), 51–71.
Jackson, L. (2016). Intimate Citizenship? Rethinking the Politics and Experience of Citizenship as Emotional in Wales and Singapore. *Gender, Place & Culture, 23*(6), 817–833.
Jackson, L., Harris, C., & Valentine, G. (2017). Rethinking Concepts of the Strange and the Stranger. *Social & Cultural Geography, 18*(1), 1–15.
Jamieson, L. (1997). *Intimacy: Personal Relationships in Modern Societies*. Cambridge: Polity Press.
Jamieson, L. (1999). Intimacy Transformed? A Critical Look at the 'Pure Relationship'. *Sociology, 33*(3), 477–494.
Jayne, M., & Leung, H. H. (2014). Embodying Chinese Urbanism: Towards a Research Agenda. *Area, 46*(3), 256–267.
Jupp, E. (2013a). Enacting Parenting Policy? The Hybrid Spaces of Sure Start Children's Centres. *Children's Geographies, 11*(2), 173–187.

Lewis, C. (2018). Making Community Through the Exchange of Material Things. *Journal of Material Culture, 23*(3), 295–311.

McDowell, L. (2012). Post-Crisis, Post-Ford and Post-Gender? Youth Identities in an Era of Austerity. *Journal of Youth Studies, 15*(5), 573–590.

Morgan, D. (2009). *Acquaintances: The Space Between Intimates And Strangers: The Space Between Intimates and Strangers*. Maidenhead: McGraw-Hill Education (UK).

Morgan, D. (2011). *Rethinking Family Practices*. Basingstoke: Palgrave Macmillan.

Morrison, C., Johnston, L., & Longhurst, R. (2012). Critical Geographies of Love as Spatial, Relational and Political. *Progress in Human Geography, 37*(4), 505–521.

Nast, H. J. (2006). Critical Pet Studies? *Antipode, 38*(5), 894–906.

Oswin, N., & Olund, E. (2010). Governing Intimacy. *Environment and Planning D: Society and Space, 28*(1), 60–67.

Pearson, R., & Elson, D. (2015). Transcending the Impact of the Financial Crisis in the United Kingdom: Towards Plan F—A Feminist Economic Strategy. *Feminist Review, 109*, 8–30.

Power, E. (2008). Furry Families: Making a Human-Dog Family Through Home. *Social & Cultural Geography, 9*(5), 535–555.

Pratt, G. (1997). Stereotypes and Ambivalence: The Construction of Domestic Workers in Vancouver, British Columbia. *Gender, Place and Culture, 4*(2), 159–178.

Rose, G. (1995). *Love's Work*. New York: New York Review Books.

Smith, A., & Stenning, A. (2006). Beyond Household Economies: Articulations and Spaces of Economic Practice in Post-Socialism. *Progress in Human Geography, 30*(2), 190–213.

Stenning, A., & Hall, S. M. (2018). Loneliness and the Politics of Austerity. *Discover Society*, p. 62. Retrieved from https://discoversociety.org/2018/11/06/on-the-frontline-loneliness-and-the-politics-of-austerity/.

Tarrant, A. (2010). Constructing a Social Geography of Grandparenthood: A New Focus for Intergenerationality. *Area, 42*(2), 190–197.

Tipper, B. (2011). "A Dog Who I Know Quite Well": Everyday Relationships Between Children and Animals. *Children's Geographies, 9*(2), 145–165.

Twigg, J. (2006). *The Body in Health and Social Care*. Basingstoke: Palgrave Macmillan.

Valentine, G. (2008a). The Ties that Bind: Towards Geographies of Intimacy. *Geography Compass, 2*(6), 2097–2110.

Valentine, G. (2008b). Living with Difference: Reflections on Geographies of Encounter. *Progress in Human Geography, 32*(3), 323–337.

Valentine, G., Piekut, A., & Harris, C. (2015). Intimate Encounters: The Negotiation of Difference Within the Family and Its Implications for Social Relations in Public Space. *The Geographical Journal, 181*(3), 280–294.

Wilson, H. F. (2017). On Geography and Encounter: Bodies, Borders, and Difference. *Progress in Human Geography, 41*(4), 45–471.

Woodward, S. (2015). The Hidden Lives of Domestic Things: Accumulations in Cupboards, Lofts and Shelves. In E. Casey & Y. Taylor (Eds.), *Intimacies, Critical Consumption and Diverse Economies* (pp. 216–231). Basingstoke: Palgrave Macmillan.

Zelizer, V. (2005). *The Purchase of Intimacy*. Princeton, NJ: Princeton University Press.

5

The Personal Is Political (and Relational)

In her essay 'The Personal Is Political' (1970), Carol Hanisch argues that women's groups who meet to discuss personal stories of oppression and discrimination should be understood not just as a form of therapy but as a politically significant act. She explains:

> I think we must listen to what so-called apolitical women have to say—not so we can do a better job of organising them but because together we are a mass movement. [...] there are things in the consciousness of "apolitical" women (I find them very political) that are as valid as any political consciousness we think we have. (Hanisch 1970, p. 78)

These personal and relational politics form the core focus of this chapter. The phrase—'the personal is political'—has since become something of a feminist mantra, sewn into banners, printed on badges, cited in speeches and echoed in paper titles (see Braithwaite 2002; Cahill 2007; Domosh 1997; Morris 1992). It was written on the cusp of an awakening and an honest reflection from within feminist organisations and groups about the diversity of experience. Critical and Feminist Race scholars

S. M. Hall, *Everyday Life in Austerity*, Palgrave Macmillan Studies in Family and Intimate Life, https://doi.org/10.1007/978-3-030-17094-3_5

especially, such as Kimberlè Crenshaw and Angela Davis, were making much-needed interventions, pointing out that there is no single understanding of being a 'woman', no simple categorisation, but that gender has to be understood according to socio-spatial contexts of culture, class, race, sexuality, disability and so forth (see hooks 1981). To homogenise these experiences—to give them one voice, one narrative—was to erase difference and associated inequalities, including within the feminist movement itself. For Hanisch (1970), seeing the political potential of all women, regardless of background, was also key to ensuring that experiences, needs and injustices are given the recognition and validity they deserve.

With this chapter I explore the relational politics of austerity. I return to and refresh Hanisch's essay and ideas about personal politics, connecting them with long-standing concepts in human geography regarding relationalities and care ethics, alongside burgeoning work on quiet politics and activisms. With this body of literature I conceptualise how the personal and relational affects of austerity are inherently and deeply political, expanding upon discussions in earlier chapters about everyday social infrastructures and intimacies. Placing personal and political geographies at the heart of enquiry, this chapter offers new ways of thinking about austerity in everyday life, particularly in terms of social unevenness and everyday politics and the potential of relational space. I also aim to connect disparate feminist literatures on everyday politics and care ethics, grounding them in spatial and relational contexts.

As in preceding chapters, I present ideas from across geographical and feminist literatures, continuing to craft a relational approach in which to situate my ethnographic findings. After describing work on personal-political geographies, the findings are arranged into three themes: quiet politics of austerity, micro-aggressions and the everyday politics of difference, and the politics of presence. Ultimately, the chapter makes the case for deeper understandings of the personal, political and relational geographies of austerity, and why they remain as important as ever.

Personal-Political Geographies

The idea of the personal as political is now almost ubiquitous in human geography, for according to Oswin and Olund (2010, p. 60) 'intimacy is personal. It is also, therefore, political'. For Pain and Staeheli (2014, p. 344), the false dichotomy of 'personal/political', like global/local or familial/state, is a customary boundary that politicised understandings of intimacy can help dissolve. Personal politics are then not only about scale—that which is close, tangible and identifiable—but also the relational possibilities of the political (Massey 2004). The crux of Hanisch's (1970) argument, with which I opened this chapter, lies in broadening understandings of and approaches to 'politics'. As clarified in a recently appended preface to Hanisch's original piece: '"political" was used here in the broad sense of the word as having to do with power relationships, not the narrow sense of electoral politics' (Hanisch 2006, p. 76). The standpoint that 'the personal is political' has inspired a multitude of geographical writings, from work on geopolitics, difference and corporeality, to discussions on reflexive, auto-ethnographic and participatory praxis.

One of the earliest examples in human geography of engagement with this feminist mantra comes from Domosh (1997). Consideration of the personal, she explains, has the capacity to rescale political economies, encouraging us to 'think about the complexities of analysing everyday encounters where different forms of power are enacted' (Domosh 1997, p. 81). Writing of the affective nature of bell hooks' writing, particularly her ability to 'relate large-scale political issues to [...] personal life and personal stories', Domosh (1997, p. 81) argues that in sharing experiences with others and making politics personal, points of social connection and relationality emerge, that 'the stories broke down some of the distances between myself and bell hooks—her stories were, after all, similar to some of mine'. To use Massey's (2004) terminology, infusing the personal into political storytelling becomes a form of space-making and relationship-building, and works to reconfigure social distances and interpersonal differences (Hall 2017).

Here, like in Hanisch's thesis, the personal is grounded in sharing stories and giving voice to hidden or silenced experiences, connecting everyday practices to show the 'bigger' or 'broader' political picture (also see Dyck 2005; Kraftl and Horton 2007). It is also about a sense of place (Massey 1991), of being in the world and articulating how this feels, both physically (in terms of corporeality and embodiment) and emotionally (Domosh 1997; Hyndman 2004). But while bodies and emotions have long been centred in feminist philosophies, the 'personal' remains 'part of an emotional lexicon' typically considered 'inappropriate to critical geopolitics' (Hyndman 2004, p. 318). The personal, it would seem, is not always considered political.

Emerging geographical writing on 'quiet politics' (Askins 2014, 2015; Hankins 2017), 'quiet activism' (Hackney 2013; Pottinger 2017) and the everyday-ness of political practice operates very closely to these earlier writings. Such work is similarly rooted in the notion that political actions need not always be noisy and disruptive, and that despite the tendency of academics to prioritise the 'dramatic, iconic, glamorous and heroic', political acts can also be quiet and unassuming, grounded in 'banal, day-to-day practices' (Horton and Kraftl 2009, p. 16; Bayat 2000; Staeheli et al. 2012). Hankins (2017, p. 3), echoing these sentiments, contends that such acts are 'quiet in so far as we are not talking about picket lines or placards. Quiet in that we are talking about decision-making, which is inaudible but can have important consequences.'

Examples of recent research on quiet politics and activisms include seed-saving (Pottinger 2017), urban yarn bombing (Mann 2015) and hobbycrafts (Hackney 2013), 'as small, everyday, embodied acts, often of making and creating, that can be either implicitly or explicitly political in nature' (Pottinger 2017, p. 251). Askins' (2015, p. 475) work on befriending encounters between refugees and residents in north east England likewise reveals the value of these 'everyday activities in quotidian spaces which are part of a broader continuum of movements for change'. Bayat's (2000, p. 545) notion of 'quiet encroachment' also marks an important contribution here, describing 'the silent, protracted but pervasive advancement of the ordinary people on the propertied and powerful in order to survive and improve their lives'. The personal and relational become inextricable, given that such 'quiet politics [are] enacted in initiating *interpersonal* relationships, while simultaneously caught up with/in wider geopolitics, and interwoven through scale' (Askins 2014, p. 353—emphasis added).

There are a few instances where such ideas have been applied to the context of austerity in the UK, which also provides the contextual backdrop to the research reported in this book. From in-depth interviews with carers and parents at a Sure Start centre in the East Midlands, UK, Horton and Kraftl (2009) identify what they refer to this as 'implicit activisms'. Small acts and kind words are, they posit, examples of everyday political practices commonly unnoticed, overlooked or dismissed in traditional understandings of political activism. They argue that 'such everyday, affective bonds and acts ultimately constituted political activism and commitment, albeit of a kind which seeks to proceed [...] with "not too much fuss"' (Horton and Kraftl 2009, p. 15). In related work by one of the same authors, it is suggested that the 'anticipatory politics' of austerity might at times be more damaging than the actual spending cuts, and that to understand this process 'research exploring other (smaller, less obvious) kinds of anticipatory political action in other (local, everyday, perhaps less noticeable) politicised spaces' is needed (Horton 2016, p. 352).

Jupp (2017), also studying community activism in low-income areas, builds on Howard's (2014) notion of 'affective activisms'. She draws attention to political acts 'based on relationships and community building at a micro, everyday level of the home and household, consisting, for example, of sharing childcare arrangements and organising meals together' Jupp (2017, p. 353). In particular, Jupp (2017, p. 353) identifies gendered dimensions to the marginalisation of everyday activisms, which 'are often overlooked in both academic and other commentaries because of their low-key and apparently non-confrontational nature, consisting of embodied practices based on care, intergenerational exchange, everyday coping and support in home spaces and beyond'.

Geographers' engagement with 'the personal is political' has also been led by empirical technique, such as Valentine (1998) who makes the case for using personal stories and reflexive methods to situate and analyse political acts. As she explains:

> The authority of personal experience was a central tenant of 1970s British and North American Feminism, epitomised by the mantra of the time:

> "the personal is political". It produced a significant amount of personal testimony in the social sciences, although feminist geographers have until recently been notably more circumspect about baring their souls in academic writing than have feminist writers in sociology and anthropology or those in literary and cultural criticism, where there is a tradition of this form of writing. (Valentine 1998, p. 305)

Valentine draws on her own experience of harassment to tell a very personal story of homophobia, sexism and discrimination, laying bare for the reader a shocking mosaic of poisonous letters, disturbing memories and silent phone calls. Picking through these materials, supported by auto-ethnographic accounts and vignettes, she unveils the provocative politics of stigma, shame and othering operating within everyday (academic) life that serve to oppress and govern certain social group practices and identities. The scope of auto-ethnography in this regard has, nonetheless, been questioned by geographers, given that 'claiming the personal is political set into motion a path for white, North American women to raise their consciousness about their own (oppressed, exploited, marginalised) positions in society' (Moss 2001, p. 7). These two issues are particularly illuminating for the discussions in this chapter: the potentially violent, hostile nature of personal politics, and the epistemological matter of how personal politics are told and who they are told by.

Following the first point, it is worth stressing, as I have in previous chapters, that personal politics should not be presumed to be always positive. A romantic take on quiet politics can mask everyday micro-aggressions and confrontations with difference. While the majority of emerging work on quiet politics is conceptualised on positive and affirming encounters and experiences, micro-politics tinged with exclusion, hostility or antagonism are another form of quiet and subtle politics. Clayton et al. (2016, p. 68) refer to micro-aggressions as 'less overt forms of discrimination', which while not necessary extreme, violent or categorised as serious, can be 'everyday and pervasive' (p. 65). Commenting on micro-aggressions within academia, Mullings et al. (2016, p. 166) highlight the need to better understand 'micro-scale and subtle relationships that are capable of much harm, and the often unrecognised groups within our communities that suffer, often silently, and sometimes from multiple and overlapping forms of distress'. They also make reference to a newsletter article by Mona Domosh, during her time as President of the *Association for American Geographers*, in which she explains how

> overt acts of sexism, racism and homophobia in Geography are far less apparent than they used to be, but not so their subtle, small, everyday enactments, what Chester Pierce called microaggressions, that serve to keep people in their place [...]. The words that recognise and speak back to these microaggressions are difficult to conjure; a rebuke does little good since the insult wasn't "intended", while a complaint raises the specter of the "sensitive and difficult person". What some have called death by a thousand paper cuts keeps cutting; perpetrators not recognising the damage they cause, the victims still and again left silent. (Domosh 2015)

There is a growing body of geographical research concerned with everyday politics of difference and how micro-aggressive actions and words can serve to reinforce social differences (also see Pugh 2018; Torres 2018). Within this work, as can be seen in Domosh's above description, quiet politics are articulated as being two-fold, referring to the means by which the politics of difference are enforced (quietly, subtly), *and* the effect they can have on recipients (quieting, silencing).

Joshi et al. (2015) make similar observations in their work on whiteness and invisible micro-aggressions. Arguing that micro-aggressions are embodied and visceral, they illustrate how 'microaggressions affect people of colour in unique and often traumatising ways' (p. 300), which can 'elicit a visceral reaction from most people who experience them' (p. 305). However, the quietness of these politics is also acknowledged, because 'by design' micro-aggressions 'are difficult to pinpoint' (p. 317) and can lead to the silencing and internalisation of visceral reactions. There is an inherent geography here, with micro-aggressions operating at the 'micro-scale, embodied, intimate' (Torres 2018, p. 16; also see Derickson 2016). It is at the scale of the body that micro-aggressions are expressed, and micro-aggressions can themselves be 'the embodiment of broader narratives and structural inequalities that occur at many other scales' (Skop 2015, p. 433; Joshi et al. 2015).

Krumer-Nevo (2017, p. 6) similarly identifies how micro-aggressions 'may include inconspicuous, apparently innocuous behaviours, such as a facial expression of disgust, or a bodily expression of distancing or withdrawal', and Skop (2015, p. 433) notes how through micro-aggression 'the body becomes a vessel for destructive narratives that centre on power and privilege'. This also relates to Sara Ahmed's (2004) writing on the cultural politics of emotion and relationships as surfaces and boundaries, as mentioned in Chap. 4. Emotions, Ahmed (2004, p. 8) reminds us, 'are relational'. Likewise, micro-aggressions are enacted at the bodily scale, between bodies, to inflict and impress emotional harm (also see Hall 2014).

Continuing the theme of power and privilege, I now want to unpick the second thread from the earlier Valentine quote, regarding whose voices are amplified in research of an auto-ethnographic nature. Similar praxes of power have been widely noted by feminist scholars working with reflexive methods (see Lumsden 2009), of how 'researcher, researched and research make each other' (Rose 1997, p. 316). England (1994, p. 81), for instance, asks whether

> in our rush to be more inclusive and conceptualize difference and diversity, might we be guilty of appropriating the voices of "others"? How do we deal with this when planning and conducting our research? And can we incorporate the voices of "others" without colonizing them in a manner that reinforces patterns of domination?

Writing about and through personal accounts, then, brings to the surface political and social tensions around the power dynamics between researchers and subjects, requiring academics to face head-on the politics of fieldwork.

Participatory methods are often hailed as examples of where the personal and political not only meet, but are enveloped within the very processes of research, as 'one answer to recent calls for more relevant, morally aware and nonhierarchical practice of social geography which engages with inequality to a greater degree' (Pain 2004, p. 652). By placing empirical focus on self and subjectivity, Cahill (2007, p. 273) argues that 'similar to the feminist practice of "consciousness raising" [...] political understandings are developed through an analysis of personal experiences'. However, the capacity of participatory research to enrol political and personal concerns is 'not unproblematic', Askins (2015, p. 471) explains, 'given its explicitly political approaches to co-producing research and knowledges, [and] the ethical complexities of working alongside participants'. In my own earlier work, I have also touched on how fieldwork can be a space of personal and relational concerns, the meeting of researcher and participant 'worlds' (Hall 2009; Longhurst et al. 2008). As described in Chap. 3, it can also be a space of gendered labour and responsibility (Hall 2017).

Hanisch ultimately calls for the unmasking of emotional labour involved in the behind-the-scenes work of doing politics, of being present and vocal and of being a woman in a patriarchal society, including social institutions. While 'feminism and poststructuralism have opened up geography to voices other than those of white, Western, middle-class, heterosexual men' (England 1994, p. 80), this masking of gendered labour is nevertheless mirrored in academic practice. Despite 'multiply voiced histories', 'homogenising representations of the geographical tradition which all too frequently erase feminist knowledges from their script' (Gregson and Rose 1997, p. 41). For Domosh (1998, p. 278), 'integral to feminist analyses have been the unmasking of biases that have directed fields of study, a reshaping of the contours of acceptable objects and subjects of study, and new ways of interpreting traditional material'. The value (or lack thereof) attributed to gendered labour was mirrored in the subjects deemed worth of geographical study.

Related to this, and as already approached in Chap. 1, is the matter of citation. Ahmed (2017, p. 15) claims that 'citation is feminist memory [...] how we acknowledge our debt to those who came before', and that current citation practices reify the masking and devaluing of gendered labour. She calls for feminist scholars to cite one another rather than reproducing 'citational privilege' (Ahmed 2017, p. 150), what she considered a form of feminist activism. Ironically, while Hanisch's (1970) essay has seeped into an academic consciousness of writing on the personal and political, the majority of writings dealing with these ideas (within and beyond geography), even those quoting the phrase directly, fail to cite the original source (e.g. Ahmed 2017; Cahill 2007; Domosh

1997; Moss 2001; Valentine 1998). In doing so, the very processes against which feminist writers have been collectively rallying—marginalisation, subordination, silencing—are inadvertently perpetuated and replicated.

As an attempt of redress, I have opened my discussion with Hanisch's essay, working outwards and sidewards to bring together those writers having similar yet somewhat disparate discussions. I now continue this task, by presenting ethnographic findings that display a spectrum of everyday life in austerity as personal, political and relational.

Quiet Politics of Austerity

In recent years, human geographers have started to explore diverse forms of activisms and politics, arguing for recognition of implicit activisms (Horton and Kraftl 2009), small acts and kind words (Askins 2015; Hackney 2013; Pottinger 2017). In the ethnographic research that forms the empirical basis of my study, I found that these quieter politics of austerity—a smile, a nod, a mutter of encouragement, a brief conversation over a counter—were all significant ways of building relationality, a politics of togetherness, at a time of social and personal hardship (Askins 2014). As such, I argue that these quieter moments of social and personal life in austerity should not be dismissed as ineffective or trivial. They can 'have important consequences' for relational connections (Hankins 2017, p. 3), and relational spaces within and between family, friends and intimate others.

At a coffee and cake morning held in a local primary school in Argleton, parents of new children to the school gathered to meet for the first time. I was struck by the 'pockets of conversation springing up around the table; to my left a group of women were talking about how high their electricity bills were, that they'd had to use a heater over the recent cold spell; to my right a discussion about the local housing shortage, finding somewhere to live in the catchment area, and the perils of renting from a private landlord' (field diary, October 2014). At a Sure Start children's centre I visited, I noted in my field diary that 'two women waiting to speak to a member of staff spoke across the room about finding affordable childcare, which somehow then moved onto a conversation about their rent arrears' (field diary, September 2014).

These gatherings provided spaces for people—often women—to talk about pressing but often very personal issues relating to their home life, relationships and income. In doing so, the spaces themselves became charged with intimacy and relationality, even though they were often public and populated with other people (including me) in earshot. This could sometimes enrich ongoing social relationships. At a playgroup session, I met two women 'who had come here together, but had themselves only met two weeks ago at another toddler group. They'd stayed in touch because they "just clicked". As they spoke, one woman was feeding the other one's daughter; they seemed so familiar, I thought they must have been friends for years' (field diary, March 2014). This example also echoes the discussion from the previous chapter regarding momentary encounters and relational spaces of austerity.

In these and similar spaces, counsel and care were readily exchanged, connecting everyday concerns to broader socio-economic change (see Askins 2015). At the coffee morning mentioned above, when discussing electricity bills, one of the other women at the gathering suggested contacting their energy supplier to try and come off a prepayment metre, explaining how they were paying more for their electricity than if they paid by direct debit. The talk about rent arrears ended with advice about how to negotiate repayment with a social housing provider. These were nuggets of information that might make a meaningful difference to someone's situation (Valentine 2008b). Such quietly political acts and conversations are crucial when austerity cuts mean those already struggling find themselves in the firing line of changes to welfare benefits, and at the mercy of rising everyday costs.

At other times, quiet politics were more implicit (Horton and Kraftl 2009), observable by actions rather than words. The cooking club and cafe mentioned in Chaps. 3 and 4, for instance, was run almost entirely by mostly female volunteers, in a community centre that had seen most of its local authority funding for adult and social community services stripped away in recent years. Here, members of the community were invited to engage in collective cooking and informal teaching on thrifty and healthy food preparation, encouraging social interconnection and commensality (Holmes 2018a; Howard 2014; Jupp 2017). The labours of this love were then sold in the cafe: stews and soups for a pound, cake for 50p.

As she chalked the day's menu on the sandwich board (mains: chicken stew with dumplings or mushroom soup with bread; pudding: plum cake), lead organiser Heidi explained that the cafe had been 'quiet over the summer', but was starting to pick up again now the kids had gone back to school. Parents and grandparents might now be able to spare some time to come to the class, and eating at the cafe was cheaper if they came alone. These activities were set up to educate, advise and feed some of the most vulnerable members of the community, but the cafe attracted a wide range of customers. Across four visits over a few months, I saw groups of elderly women, middle-aged couples, office workers, lone diners and young families all come to the cafe. Most sat inside to eat, with a few taking food away. On one of these occasions, nobody had turned up for the cooking class. We held on for a few minutes just in case, but the two volunteers and Heidi suggested we start following the recipe. People might drop in, and in any case, the food was needed to sell in the cafe. They did not appear annoyed or disappointed about the poor turnout, but they were set on ensuring that the cafe fulfilled its purpose. '[I]f there weren't people to teach, there'd be people to feed' (field diary, September 2014).

I took a photograph of the space that day (as featured in Fig. 5.1), capturing some of this quietness, but also the political possibilities of the cafe. I had instinctively taken it only after the cooking class was finished and the room was set up. This was partly for practical reasons (taking photos is difficult while rolling dumplings), and due to ethical concerns (to retain the anonymity of participants). With hindsight, however, I realise I was also capturing the anticipation that I felt in waiting for people to arrive. I felt proud of the food we had cooked together, and wondered how people might answer the small photocopied feedback forms asking 'how was your meal of the day?' My anticipation, along with the material stillness of tables and chairs (poised ready for cross-table conversations), worked to further establish the cafe as a 'less obvious' (Horton 2016, p. 352) politicised space, part of a broader resistance to austerity cuts both at home and in the community (see Askins 2015; Jupp 2017).

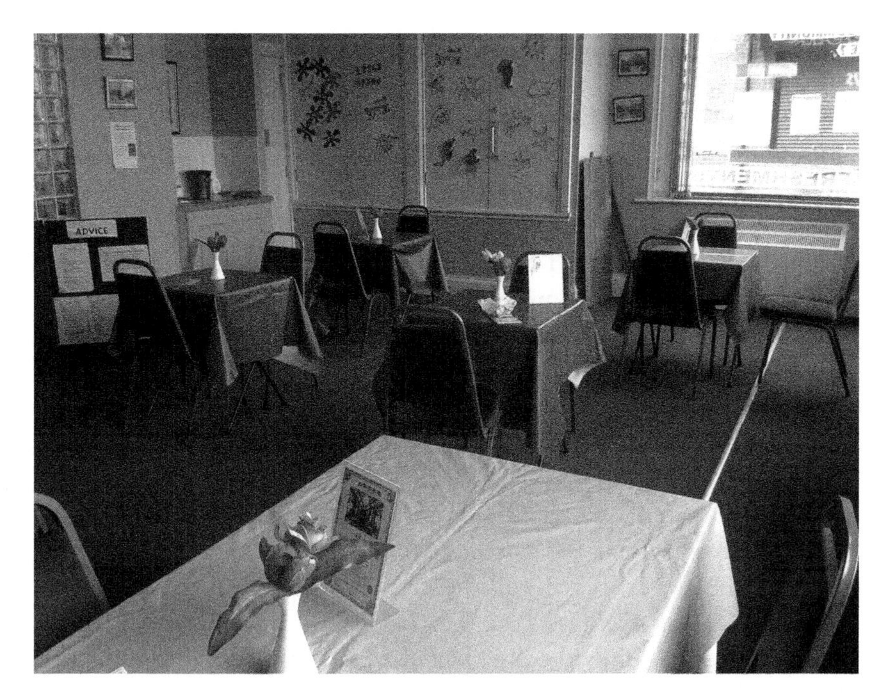

Fig. 5.1 A community cafe in Argleton awaiting customers (photograph taken by Sarah Marie Hall)

Similarly, at the other side of town, a South Asian women's group (also run almost entirely by volunteers) met on a weekly basis in a community hall attached to a church, which also provided modest financial support. Skills and advice, cultures and languages, sofas and kitchen counters were shared here, creating a relational space of similarity and difference between women from a range of generational, religious, ethnic, caste and class backgrounds. When local council funding for the community hall was cut, the women organised a 'celebratory' event, accompanied by a 'bring a plate' buffet, piled with all sorts of colourful regional dishes, sweet and savoury (field diary, February 2014). There was talk of the women applying for their own funding as a separate organisation, though these suggestions came from staff and volunteers at the community hall, rather than within the group. Refusing to let the cuts curtail their meetings, the women took a quieter, more low-key tack. They spoke about relocating the meetings to their own homes, organised on a rota (also see Jupp 2017). External funding was thought unnecessary in order for them to be together in the same place. The things they brought to the table, edible or otherwise, were considered a small but worthy expense. They were not giving up, just getting on, moving forwards, in different, subtler ways.

Over the ethnography, I bore witness to many instances of these and similar quiet activisms, some even more 'microgeographical' in terms of the people and spaces involved (Horton 2016), though no less political. What these examples have in common is that they are all centred around social interconnection and interpersonal relations, creating political and commonly gendered spaces of care, hope and activism (also see Horton 2016; Jupp 2017). Brought together by similar experiences, geographical proximity or material objects, presenting opportunities for sharing things, skills and stories (Hall and Jayne 2016; Holmes 2018a), these findings illustrate a quieter politics of togetherness, close corporeality and conviviality (also see Askins 2014; Pottinger 2017). Also revealed are the often hidden politics of embodied, gendered labour and social reproduction (Dyck 2005; Twigg 2000). Activities such as cooking, crafts and consumption provided the basis for interaction, creating spaces of relationality at a time of austerity. However, this is certainly not to say that all such encounters and everyday politics of austerity are positive or convivial. Tensions and difference are likewise part of everyday quiet politics, such as in the form of micro-aggressions.

Micro-aggressions and Everyday Politics of Difference

While the ethnographic examples presented in the section above were for the most part encouraging and fulfilling encounters, politics of the personal can also be tinged with negativity, even violence (see Askins 2014; Valentine 2008b). Within much of the literature on quiet politics, equally subtle but tense incidents (both momentary and sustained) tend to be overlooked. During the ethnography, examples of quietly fraught politics were sometimes apparent, and sometimes not. Part of their quietness, the passivity of the aggression, is that such words and actions can be dismissed or denied, and can lead to silencing (Domosh 2015; Joshi et al. 2015). Sometimes participants wanted to name and talk these everyday subtle forms of aggression, or micro-aggressions, recognising how the impacts could reverberate. As such, it was common for these micro-aggressions and everyday politics of difference to be felt personally and relationally, sometimes causing lasting emotional harm. A form of personal and political storytelling (Hall 2017), recounting these micro-aggressions might also therefore be described as reconfiguring relational space.

I start here with a scenario described in Chap. 4, of Selma's visit to the Job Centre. While previously analysed as a momentary encounter, it is arguably also an instance of micro-aggression. When Selma confessed to struggling for money, the employment advisor told her, in a sarcastic voice, that she is 'very lucky' to be receiving benefits. In that moment, Selma felt ashamed and embarrassed, and I wrote in my field diary that 'this incident had clearly upset Selma, she shook her head almost in disbelief as she talked, and muttered something about how the advisor clearly wasn't a very nice person' (field diary, May 2014). I heard many similar stories during the ethnography, of people being ignored or spoken to rudely in these and other institutional settings. During a discussion at a community toddler group I attended, 'one woman described being asked to leave, having the door closed in her face just for asking at the job centre for help improving her CV. Her eyes filling with tears as she recounted the memory' (field diary, April 2014). It was common for quiet politics of micro-aggression to be identifiable by small acts (Horton and Kraftl 2009), but rather than hugs, gestures or kind words, hostile embodied and visceral gestures were enacted (also see Joshi et al. 2015; Krumer-Nevo 2017). For some people, these micro-aggressions could build up, eventually becoming a routine part of everyday life, reminding participants of their social differences and exclusions. I'll stay with the example of Selma.

As a woman of colour receiving welfare payments, Selma often felt that she was a target of micro-aggressions, stigma and racism. These everyday politics of difference were, as identified within the aforementioned literature (see Domosh 2015; Joshi et al. 2015; Mullings et al. 2016; Skop 2015), played out in often subtle and dismissible ways. Selma often paid for her shopping in cash because she felt more on top of her finances that way, able to keep track of daily outgoings. Early on in her participation, we went to the local supermarket where Selma collected a small basket of items: milk, juice, eggs, salad, bread and yoghurt. At the till,

> she took out her wallet and plucked the coins out one at a time, setting them down on the ledge in front of the cashier. The store was not particularly busy, the person behind us in the queue did not appear to be in a rush, and yet the cashier stared sullenly at Selma, rolling her eyes as the silver pieces made a neat mound at her eye level. (field diary, March 2014)

I was not sure if Selma had noticed. I certainly did, but I did not feel any good could come of pointing it out to her. While I might be reading too much into the situation, it seemed that Selma's accent and her paying in cash marked her out as different and may have provoked this gesture of micro-aggression from the cashier.

Other acts of micro-aggression, as a different form of quiet politics in austerity, were also observed during my time with Selma. One instance that particularly stands out in my memory is when Selma and I went to the Post Office to post a letter. I flicked through greetings cards on a turning display while Selma joined the queue for a stamp. As the line of people slowly snaked around the barriers, the air was punctuated by automated calls for people to go to 'till seven .... till one .... till three'. We had been there maybe five minutes when 'an elderly white man came through the doors and went to join the queue but stopped in his tracks, huffing and puffing, looking around in an animated fashion, before loudly grumbling "it must be giro day"'(field diary, March 2014). In the UK, 'giro' is the word informally used for state benefits, though specifically refers to the slip of paper formerly received in the post which could then be cashed in at the Post Office. By referring to it as 'giro day', coupled by the noises and physical gestures, the man was being derogatory about the people in the queue, including Selma, suggesting they were all there to claim their benefits. Selma later told me that 'she felt like people were looking at her and whispering after the man's comments'. It made her feel uncomfortable, different. Such innocuous acts as to pay for shopping with cash or to be standing in a post office queue could provoke small acts of micro-aggression, depending on how the people in that situation (or rather, their bodies) are read and culturally constructed. Bodies are the surfaces upon which such micro-aggressions and differences are played out (also see Ahmed 2004).

In the context of austerity, stigmatising politics have grown, particularly around welfare provision and those who receive it. These ideas have arguably been catalysed by discourse of blame and shame that pervaded media and political rhetoric around the financial crisis (see Elwood and Lawson 2013; Hall 2015). As described in the introduction, austerity can work to expose, exacerbate and exploit such socio-economic differences and unevenness. Other participants in receipt of welfare noted similar micro-aggressions in their daily interactions, and in the most seemingly innocuous of conversations. During one of my visits to her house, Kerry mentioned

> she'd been speaking to one of the other mums at nursery who had two sons only 11 months apart. She mentioned to the woman that there was a similar age gap between two of her boys, but then she had "two more of them". Kerry said the woman just replied "oh", followed by silence, which she felt was judgemental, because she has four children close in age and she doesn't work. (field diary, April 2014)

Here the silence works as a form of micro-aggression, a very literal quiet politics, making Kerry feel awkward and incongruous. Sharon likewise lamented her colleagues' lack of concern or care at the housing company she worked for, how they would disregard complaints from tenants about inadequate facilities, expecting them to go away if they ignored them' (field diary, August 2014).

The quietness and subtlety of politics of difference can also depend on how a message is received; not only mediated through bodily gestures and words, but also through institutional practices. The school was one key example of this, where a number of participants, including Laura, spoke about how

> there's always something the kids need for school, always something new to pay for or bring in; a tombola, no uniform day, raising money for disaster victims, children in need, bringing in a jam jar. I asked if the other mums felt the same. "I'm not sure", Laura told me, "I don't talk to them about it, and nobody seems to complain. I don't want my kid to be the only one without, though". (field diary, November 2013)

Zoe noted similar tensions at the school her children attended, warning that the 'parents and teachers association needed to be careful about how they pitched the different events they organised, and not make them too expensive so as to be exclusive' (field diary, May 2014). While a less obvious form of micro-aggression, the example of regular financial contributions served to highlight wealth disparities within the community, illuminating differences between parents and their children and effectively silencing their experiences through these routinised, normalised practices (see Domosh 2015; Joshi et al. 2015).

Micro-aggressions and politics of difference could also be seen in my own research encounters. There were many times when I felt very much out-of-place (Domosh 2015; Massey 1991). One example still sticks in my memory as a sharp reminder of the axes of power and privilege in social and personal encounters. I had been spending time around a community centre that was a regular meeting place and hub for varied social activities, including free ESOL (English as a Second Language) classes run by volunteers. Annie, the centre manager, recommended I go along to an advanced women-only ESOL class, as a friendly group that she expected would like to meet me. However, the visit did not go as planned.

> Annie said she'd passed a note to Julia, the co-ordinator of the ESOL class, earlier that morning. In it she'd explained her support of my research, and mentioned I'd be popping along to introduce myself to the group later on. I arrived early at the room to meet Julia beforehand. She greeted me with an up-and-down look and a subtle nod. The reception was frosty at best. I introduced myself with a handshake, and sat on the seat opposite her. Before I managed to speak, she instructed that she "wasn't going to let me meet to the class, that it simply wasn't appropriate" and it might jeopardise the trust she had built with the women. When I tried to speak, she held her

hand up, palm towards my face, and barked "I am not going to let you near my women". (field diary, March 2014)

After the encounter above, I felt hurt and belittled, not only by Julia's words but also her hostile bodily gestures, taking the decision quite personally. I was angry that the women in the class had not been able to make up their own minds about whether they wanted to meet me. Annie rang me later that day, having heard what had happened, and apologised profusely. She did not understand Julia's rationale for stopping me meeting the group and explained 'it was not the co-ordinator's place to make such decisions' (field diary, March 2014).

Looking back, the encounter was more complicated than it first appeared, a reminder of the aforementioned quote from Domosh (1997, p. 81) about 'the complexities of analysing everyday encounters where different forms of power are enacted'. This relates to concerns about speaking for others (England 1994; Hanisch 1970; Held 1993; Moss 2001)—not only by the ESOL co-ordinator but also the centre manager to whom I defaulted permission, and in the ethnographic fieldwork which is ultimately told through my eyes. Power and place are here entangled—between researcher, gatekeeper and participants, staff, volunteer and academic—and in the intersecting dimensions of gender, race and class. Through the body-work of fieldwork, political and social relations can thus be re-examined. Fieldwork is rich with intensely personal encounters with the potential to lead to exclusion and marginalisation, disenfranchising and possession. These can exist alongside belonging, care and connectedness; fieldwork is a relational space (also see Chap. 3).

Politics of Presence

Fieldwork is also a space as where social differences, distances, similarities and proximities are tried and tested (Hall 2017), a space of relational politics built on the co-presence of the researcher. Prolonged presence during fieldwork in and on the context of austerity can have the effect of further politicising people's everyday lives when they might not think they are affected or relevant to the phenomenon being studied. I found that during recruitment I needed to be with potential participants to explain fully what the project was about. This was because 'with the language on the leaflet, "getting by in recessions and austerity", I had assumed that everyone would know what these terms meant, but it also implied that if this was not part of their everyday lives, then they were not relevant to the study—which was not the case' (field diary, September 2013). In this sense, the fieldwork represented a quiet, relational politics unto itself; by raising questions about where the research was situated, who might be recruited and what participants' involvement might reveal to themselves about their own lives.

In fact, participants regularly expressed that they did not think their lives were all that interesting, and were quite bemused that I might think of them as such. I documented these remarks, reminding myself that key theorists on the everyday, as described in Chap. 1, regularly stress how everyday life is often dismissed for being so very ordinary. For instance, at one of our earlier meetings, Pauline and George 'said they understood why I want to spend time with people for my research, but that they don't think they are actually that interesting' (field diary, September 2014). Kerry apologised a number of times early on in the research, including once by text message, that she 'had nothing to do' and I might not find it useful to see her that day (field diary, January 2014), as though her life was not research-worthy. Laura also apologised 'for being quiet the other week, saying she was just really tired and wasn't feeling herself' (field diary, July 2014). Similarly, Zoe asked me, earnestly, 'are these sessions useful to you?' (field diary, January 2014). A researcher taking an interest in their everyday lives in this way was clearly an unusual experience for participants. But it was also arguably a subtle, low-key way (see Horton and Kraftl 2009; Jupp 2017) to raise their confidence in their own importance and place in the world (Massey 2004): that their everyday lives mattered, and the stories and experiences they shared with me were significant and heard (see Domosh 1997).

I found it interesting that as my presence in participants' lives continued over time, silences between us might grow, being not (at least from my perspective) spaces filled with hostility, awkwardness or aggression, but with comfort, companionship and trust. As I got to know participants more, I would be invited over to their house 'when things were a bit quieter' (Kerry, field diary, December 2013), we would 'sit next to one another on the bus, in comfortable silence' (Selma, field diary, September 2014), or 'sit quietly together in the living room, watching the birds in the garden and listening to the wall clock tick' (Pauline and George, field diary, March 2015). Comfort can also be found within such silences and stillness. One of my favourite stories from the research, that seems to encapsulate the political potential of silence, comes from a conversation with Kerry about her secret sofa button:

Kerry: at seven o'clock sometimes, say it's been a bad day, I sit here in silence because one of us tidies up and one of us reads stories, so if Dan does them [the boys] the story I put the telly on mute and sit back and recline the sofa. No one knows they recline, none of the kids. And I just sit in silence.
Sarah: Do they not know?
Kerry: No. They play with the handles, I'm like "do not pull the handles". And I just sit there in silence, Dan goes "what you doing?" and I go "shush. Don't want noise". And I just sit there … just quiet, calm. (Kerry, taped discussion, December 2013)

For Kerry, the quiet and calm that came from the boys being put to bed marked out personal, precious time when she was no longer having to be 'mum', and all the stresses and responsibilities that accompany that role. Taking pleasure in quiet moments, like putting her feet up in the reclining chair, and having a window into these quiet acts as a researcher, therefore works to illustrate the subtle, relational politics offered by physical presence, social connection and close corporeality (see Askins 2015; Domosh 1997; Horton and Kraftl 2009).

It might also be argued that there is a quiet politics, a strategic slowness and subtlety, within ethnography as method, of getting to know people over time, investing in relational connections, building rapport, trust, conviviality. Having said this, certain practices could also become more politically charged by having a researcher present to bear witness. In my research, these politics were also heightened by the socio-economic context of austerity. Ways of getting by, like working for cash in hand, not declaring all earnings, working while claiming benefits or shoplifting, are an important part of the story of everyday austerity. At the same time, these acts are made visible (or, in some cases, openly discussed) due to prolonged, trusted co-presence as an ethnographer, and the relational politics of being together (also see Askins 2015). A researcher's presence can also offer an insight into otherwise unnoticed quietly political acts. Like when I commented on a beautiful vase of flowers on the window ledge in Laura's kitchen, only to find out they had been gifted to her as a 'thank you' for helping set up a neighbours children's party (field diary, October 2014). Or when I was waiting at the school gates with Kerry and heard her youngest son shout 'Grandma Jean!' at a lady walking towards us: 'it turns out Grandma Jean was one of the other kid's grandmothers, but Zack was always excited to see her because she would play with him while he waited for his brothers' (field diary, April 2014). Each of these examples helped provide a better understand of everyday austerity and the impacts on social relationships for these participants, but were only brought to my attention by being co-present.

Moreover, hugs, handshakes, pats on the shoulder and pecks on the cheek were all forms of close corporeality, quiet acts of relationality shared with and often initiated by my participants. In Chap. 3, I explained how during ethnography, researchers have the potential to become intimate others and might end up knotted within the everyday care infrastructures of participants' lives. While body-work and co-presence can lead to enrolment in networks of support and care, there are other means by which physical presence can envelop researchers into the very phenomenon they are studying, and which can be highly political, such as through payment. While I have written more extensively on this elsewhere (see Hall 2017), it is an issue worth summarising here for its pertinence to the politics of presence.

As is common in long-term ethnography, participants were not paid to take part in the research, but gratitude was instead expressed through small offerings. These offerings took many forms (such as a pint of milk, a bar of chocolate or paying the bus fare to town) and came with a personal touch. Participants were asked if they needed anything picking up when I came to their house, and I remembered which flowers and biscuits they liked most. However, there was also a politics to the choice of recompensing participants and expressing gratitude in this way, born largely out of a concern about paying participants in cash (which can jeopardise claims to state benefits). In this way, the quiet politics of payment also speak to the broader socio-economic context of austerity and the pressures placed on those for whom welfare is a means of getting by. What I found, however, was that these offerings developed their own relational politics. Flowers were sometimes gifted to other people, biscuits kept aside for a later treat, or opened up for other guests, and chocolate bars packed into school lunch boxes. Through these practices, I was anchored further still into everyday social infrastructures and intimate relations of my participants. These commonplace practices of giving and receiving were, moreover, quiet political acts (see Horton and Kraftl 2009), subtly reminding participants of my presence in their lives, and of my continuous gratitude for their involvement and investment in the research.

Conclusions

Bringing together long-standing feminist discussions about the personal and political with emerging literatures on quiet politics and activisms helps to shine light on often hidden, silenced, unnoticed and marginalised experiences of everyday life in austerity. Quiet, subtle politics, those without too much fuss or disturbance (Horton and Kraftl 2009; Pottinger 2017), are described in this chapter as essential for understanding everyday relationships in austerity. Whether in spaces of community, microaggressions or presence through fieldwork, personal acts are simultaneously political (Hanisch 1970), but they are also relational.

Interconnection, togetherness and co-presence are a means of getting by within austerity, and for some can be a way of speaking back to it. Everyday politics of austerity can be built on collectivity and connectivity (Barnett and Land 2007; Massey 2004), offering space for social distances and interpersonal differences to be reworked. Furthermore, hostility, aggression and antagonism can expose personal-political tensions in austerity, at the same time as being inherently relational for where they rely on understandings of social difference. Relationality thus becomes both a personal and political tool in austerity. In the next chapter, I take these discussions of everyday austerity in another direction, considering shared and relational lives, temporality and conjuncture in the context of austerity as a very personal crisis.

Bibliography

Ahmed, S. (2004). *The Cultural Politics of Emotion*. Edinburgh: Edinburgh University Press.

Ahmed, S. (2017). *Living a Feminist Life*. Croydon: Duke University Press.

Askins, K. (2014). A Quiet Politics of Being Together: Miriam and Rose. *Area, 46*(4), 353–354.

Askins, K. (2015). Being Together: Everyday Geographies and the Quiet Politics of Belonging. *ACME: An International E-Journal for Critical Geographies, 14*(2), 470–478.

Barnett, C., & Land, D. (2007). Geographies of Generosity: Beyond the "Moral Turn". *Geoforum, 38*, 1065–1075.

Bayat, A. (2000). From "Dangerous Classes" to "Quiet Rebels": Politics of the Urban Subaltern in the Global South. *International Sociology, 15*(3), 533–557.

Braithwaite, A. (2002). The Personal, the Political, Third Wave and Postfeminisms. *Feminist Theory, 3*(3), 335–344.

Cahill, C. (2007). The Personal is Political: Developing New Subjectivities Through Participatory Action Research. *Gender, Place & Culture, 14*(3), 267–292.

Clayton, J., Donovan, C., & Macdonald, S. J. (2016). A Critical Portrait of Hate Crime/Incident Reporting in North East England: The Value of Statistical Data and the Politics of Recording in an Age of Austerity. *Geoforum, 75*, 64–74.

Derickson, K. D. (2016). Urban Geography II: Urban Geography in the Age of Ferguson. *Progress in Human Geography, 41*(2), 230–244.

Domosh, M. (1997). Geography and Gender: The Personal and the Political. *Progress in Human Geography, 21*(1), 81–87.

Domosh, M. (1998). Geography and Gender: Home, Again? *Progress in Human Geography, 22*(2), 276–282.

Domosh, M. (2015). How We Hurt Each Other Every Day and What We Might Do About It. *Association of American Geographers Newsletter*. Retrieved

December 14, 2018, from http://news.aag.org/2015/05/how-we-hurt-each-other-every-day/.

Dyck, I. (2005). Feminist Geography, the "Everyday", and Local-Global Relations: Hidden Spaces of Place-Making. *The Canadian Geographer, 49*, 233–245.

Elwood, S., & Lawson, V. (2013). Whose Crisis? Spatial Imaginaries of Class, Poverty, and Vulnerability. *Environment and Planning A, 45*, 103–108.

England, K. V. L. (1994). Getting Personal: Reflexivity Positionality and Feminist Research. *The Professional Geographer, 46*, 80–89.

Gregson, N., & Rose, G. (1997). Contested and Negotiated Histories of Feminist Geographies. In Women and Geography Study Group (Ed.), *Feminist Geographies: Explorations of Diversity and Difference*. Harlow: Addison Wesley Longman.

Hackney, F. (2013). Quiet Activism and the New Amateur: The Power of Home and Hobby Crafts. *Design and Culture, 5*, 169–193.

Hall, S. M. (2009). "Private Life" and "Work Life": Difficulties and Dilemmas When Making and Maintaining Friendships with Ethnographic Participants. *Area, 41*, 263–272.

Hall, S. M. (2014). Ethics of Ethnography with Families: A Geographical Perspective. *Environment and Planning A, 46*(9), 2175–2194.

Hall, S. M. (2015). Everyday Ethics of Consumption in the Austere City. *Geography Compass, 9*(3), 140–151.

Hall, S. M. (2017). Personal, Relational and Intimate Geographies of Austerity: Ethical and Empirical Considerations. *Area, 49*(3), 303–310.

Hall, S. M., & Jayne, M. (2016). Make, Mend and Befriend: Geographies of Austerity, Crafting and Friendship in Contemporary Cultures of Dressmaking. *Gender, Place & Culture, 23*(2), 216–234.

Hanisch, C. (1970). The Personal Is Political. In S. Firestone & Koedt (Eds.), *Notes from the Second Year* (pp. 76–78). New York: Published by Editors.

Hanisch, C. (2006). *The Personal Is Political: The Women's Liberation Movement Classic with a New Explanatory Introduction*. Retrieved April 10, 2018, from http://www.carolhanisch.org/CHwritings/PIP.html.

Hankins, K. (2017). Creative Democracy and the Quiet Politics of the Everyday. *Urban Geography*. https://doi.org/10.1080/02723638.2016.1272197.

Held, V. (1993). *Feminist Morality: Transforming Culture, Society and Politics*. Chicago, IL: University of Chicago Press.

Holmes, H. (2018a). New Spaces, Ordinary Practices: Circulating and Sharing Within Diverse Economies of Provisioning. *Geoforum, 88*, 134–147.

hooks, b. (1981). *Ain't I a Woman? Black Women and Feminism*. Boston: South End Press.

Horton, J. (2016). Anticipating Service Withdrawal: Young People in Spaces of Neoliberalisation, Austerity and Economic Crisis. *Transactions of the Institute of British Geographers, 41*(4), 349–362.

Horton, J., & Kraftl, P. (2009). Small Acts, Kind Words and "Not Too Much Fuss": Implicit Activisms. *Emotion, Space and Society, 2*(1), 14–23.

Howard, A. L. (2014). *More than Shelter: Activism and Community in San Francisco Public Housing*. Minneapolis, MN: University of Minnesota Press.

Hyndman, J. (2004). Mind the Gap: Bridging Feminist and Political Geography Through Geopolitics. *Political Geography, 23*(3), 307–322.

Joshi, S., McCutcheon, P., & Sweet, E. (2015). Visceral Geographies of Whiteness and Invisible Microaggressions. *ACME: An International E-Journal for Critical Geographies, 14*(1), 298–323.

Jupp, E. (2017). Home Space, Gender and Activism: The Visible and the Invisible in Austere Times. *Critical Social Policy, 37*(3), 348–366.

Kraftl, P., & Horton, J. (2007). "The Health Event": Everyday, Affective Politics of Participation. *Geoforum, 38*(5), 1012–1027.

Krumer-Nevo, M. (2017). Poverty and the Political: Wresting the Political Out of and Into Social Work Theory, Research and Practice. *European Journal of Social Work, 20*(6), 811–822.

Longhurst, R., Ho, E., & Johnston, L. (2008). Using "The Body" as an "Instrument of Research": Kimch'i and Pavlova. *Area, 40*(2), 208–217.

Lumsden, K. (2009). "Don't Ask a Woman to Do Another Woman's Job": Gendered Interactions and the Emotional Ethnographer. *Sociology, 43*(3), 497–513.

Mann, J. (2015). Towards a Politics of Whimsy: Yarn Bombing the City. *Area, 47*(1), 65–72.

Massey, D. (1991, June). A Global Sense of Place. *Marxism Today*, pp. 24–29.

Massey, D. (2004). Geographies of Responsibility. *Geografiska Annaler B, 86*(1), 5–18.

Morris, J. (1992). Personal and Political: A Feminist Perspective on Researching Physical Disability. *Disability, Handicap & Society, 7*(2), 157–166.

Moss, P. (2001). Writing One's Life. In P. Moss (Ed.), *Placing Autobiography in Geography* (pp. 1–21). Syracuse, NY: Syracuse University Press.

Mullings, B., Peake, L., & Parizeau, K. (2016). Cultivating an Ethic of Wellness in Geography. *The Canadian Geographer, 60*(2), 161–167.

Oswin, N., & Olund, E. (2010). Governing Intimacy. *Environment and Planning D: Society and Space, 28*(1), 60–67.

Pain, R. (2004). Social Geography: Participatory Research. *Progress in Human Geography, 28*(5), 652–663.

Pain, R., & Staeheli, L. (2014). Introduction: Intimacy Geo-politics and Violence. *Area, 46*(4), 344–347.

Pottinger, L. (2017). Planting the Seeds of a Quiet Activism. *Area, 49*(2), 215–222.

Pugh, R. (2018). Who Speaks for Economic Geography? *Environment and Planning A: Economy and Society, 50*(7), 1525–1531.

Rose, G. (1997). Situating Knowledges: Positionality, Reflexivities and Other Tactics. *Progress in Human Geography, 21*, 305–320.

Skop, E. (2015). Conceptualizing Scale in the Science of Broadening Participation of Underrepresented Groups in Higher Education. *The Professional Geographer, 67*(3), 427–437.

Staeheli, L., Ehrkamp, P., Leitner, H., & Nagel, C. (2012). Dreaming the Ordinary: Daily Life and the Complex Geographies of Citizenship. *Progress in Human Geography, 36*(5), 628–644.

Torres, R. M. (2018). A Crisis of Rights and Responsibility: Feminist Geopolitical Perspectives on Latin American Refugees and Migrants. *Gender, Place & Culture*. https://doi.org/10.1080/0966369X.2017.1414036.

Twigg, J. (2000). Carework as a Form of Bodywork. *Ageing and Society, 20*(4), 389–411.

Valentine, G. (1998). "Sticks and Stone May Break My Bones": A Personal Geography of Harassment. *Antipode, 30*(4), 305–332.

Valentine, G. (2008b). Living with Difference: Reflections on Geographies of Encounter. *Progress in Human Geography, 32*(3), 323–337.

6

A Very Personal Crisis: Family Fragilities and Everyday Conjunctures in Austerity

With this chapter, I explore the ways in which austerity and economic crises manifest as personal crises, shaping lifecourses, and ideas thereof, into the future. Where the previous chapter gave focus to the everyday politics of austerity, here I adopt a temporal perspective to relational geographies of austerity, using concepts of crisis, conjuncture and fragility. As noted in Chap. 1, the UK and a number of European countries implemented a series of fiscally austere policies following the Global Financial Crisis (GFC) and economic recession of 2008–2010. Although their ostensible purpose was to stabilise the national economy, these policies have arguably drawn out the economic crisis (Christophers 2015), meaning ideas and experiences of austerity, recession and the GFC are often intertwined. Throughout this chapter, I therefore refer to austerity and economic crises as interwoven, both with one another and within everyday life.

By bringing literatures on the geographies of crisis to speak to research in the wider social sciences (particularly sociological and anthropological contributions) regarding personal lives, vital events and the lifecourse, I show how austerity is woven into the temporalities of everyday life, knotted together with memories, experiences and imaginaries. Setting

S. M. Hall, *Everyday Life in Austerity*, Palgrave Macmillan Studies in Family and Intimate Life, https://doi.org/10.1007/978-3-030-17094-3_6

austerity in the language of crisis also reveals connections to the concept of conjuncture, which has been deployed in work on both economic and familial crises to describe spatial-temporal disruption but not brought together before in this way (see Elwood and Lawson 2013; Hall and Massey 2010; Johnson-Hanks 2002). I also place this work in conversation with theories of the family, namely Judith Stacey's (1990) notion of inherent 'structural fragility' of the modern family system, to illustrate how economic crises play out in everyday life and are felt—as per the title of the chapter—as a very personal crisis.

With this chapter I have two key aims. Firstly, to provide a meaningful contribution to emerging writing across the social sciences on crisis and austerity at the personal scale, wherein 'researchers have begun exploring geographical political-economic transformations of the crisis period at the institutional as well as individual/social level' (Christophers 2015, p. 208; van Lanen 2017). Secondly, I aim to develop new ways of understanding austerity and economic crisis as personal and relational. I do this by (1) deploying concepts of crisis and conjuncture to think about how austerity and economic crises are simultaneously personal crises, and (2) exploring how crisis temporalities shape personal and shared lives, biographies and futures. The chapter is structured as follows. First, I outline key literatures on crisis, conjuncture and everyday life, and on personal and familial crisis, identifying common trends within and across economic and social theory. Drawing on the ethnographic research in Argleton, I then evidence how crises are woven within and punctuate everyday life, as well as how austerity and economic crisis can lead to a sense of a 'life crisis'. In this way, austerity and economic crises are shown to have additional relational, spatial and temporal dimensions, to be *differently* geographical than is currently recognised within the extant literature.

Crisis, Conjuncture and Everyday Life

Crises are characterised by a jarring or disruption of time, momentum and change: the fracturing, fragility, rupturing and instability of the current, or an anticipated, situation. The times over which crises occur, and the pace at which they occur, are nevertheless marked into lived/social time, taking place in 'real time'. For Wendy Larner (2011, p. 319), the language of crisis is pervasive within contemporary geographical writings, emerging as a form of 'apocalyptic talk of environmental, economic and social crises ... [which] now dominates political-economic commentary'. According to French and Leyshon (2010, p. 2549), 'crises are about change [...] opportunities to impose new ideas and practices'. If, then, crises are about change, they are also about impermanence.

Hall and Massey (2010), in their conversation on *Interpreting the Crisis*, deploy the concept of conjuncture to deconstruct ideas about the temporality of crises. They describe how 'a conjuncture is a period during which the different social, political, economic and ideological contradictions that are at work in society come together to give it a specific and distinctive shape' (Hall and Massey 2010, p. 57): that conjunctures are the confluence of events, the culmination of circumstance that alter the status quo. As they elaborate:

> A conjuncture can be long or short: it's not defined by time or by simple things like a change of regime—though these have their own effects ... history moves from one conjuncture to another rather than being an evolutionary flow. And what drives it forward is usually a crisis, when the contradictions that are always at play in any historical moment are condensed [...] Crises are moments of potential change, but the nature of their resolution is not given. (Hall and Massey 2010, p. 57)

Here, crises and conjunctures are described like partners in crime, dancing together to punctuate, condense and intensify time—specifically lived time and memories of time ('history')—rather than being defined *by* time. Crises are like a catalyst for moving or altering conjunctures, creating a sense of 'time horizons', tempos and rhythms (Larner 2011, p. 319). Furthermore, the conjunctural nature of crisis is illustrated in the way crises disrupt and rupture the present state, offering new possibilities and continuities (Larner 2011; Wagner-Pacifici 2017). Predetermined outcomes would, therefore, suggest a non-crisis, because the magnitude of crisis is arguably shaped by unknown consequences and responses.

There are reminders here of Donna Haraway's (1997, 2008) work on 'response-abilities'—points of attachment, instability and fractures, and how dealing with change is ultimately a relational task. Haraway (2008, p. 71) elucidates this link between response, responsibility and relationality, arguing that 'response, of course, grows with the capacity to respond, that is, responsibility. Such a capacity can be shaped only in and for multidirectional relationships, in which always more than one responsive entity is in the process of becoming.' These ideas about the becomings, beings and answerings back to crisis similarly echo debates about events, emergencies and decisions, for where the temporality, connectedness and relationality of significant moments are considered. Wagner-Pacifici (2017, p. 1) proposes that events are 'rupturing moments' of 'unknowing and reknowing', 'located in time and space [...] somewhat dislocated and disorientated'. She goes on to explain that

> historical events provoke an enormous sense of uncertainty. The world seems out of whack, and everyday routines are, at the least, disrupted. People often experience a vertiginous sense that a new reality or era may be in the making, but it is one that does not yet have a clear shape and trajectory, or determined consequences. (Wagner-Pacifici 2017, p. 1)

I explore in this chapter how austerity and economic crises are one such event that can provoke a 'sense of uncertainty', throwing everyday lives, routines, relationships and imaginaries 'out of whack'. This then calls into question what, or whom, is in crisis.

Related to this, geographical conceptions of crisis have most often veered towards, and been dominated by, financial crisis—also referred to as 'a very geographical crisis' (French et al. 2009). Writings on '*the* crisis' are typically about the GFC of 2008–2010 (e.g. Christophers 2015; French et al. 2009; Hall and Massey 2010), despite acknowledgement that 'how a crisis is named has deep implications for how policy is framed and blame is meted out' (Elwood and Lawson 2013, p. 103; Sidaway 2008). The connectivity and knottiness of crises is also an emerging feature of writing about geographies of crisis. While 'we see this moment as a big economic crisis, it is also a philosophical and political crisis in some ways' (Hall and Massey 2010, p. 59). Part of the reason for this, as Elwood and Lawson (2013, p. 103) claim, is because 'the geographies of crisis [...] are always also social, cultural, discursive, and symbolic'. They are, at the same time, intensely personal.

Indeed, the personalising of crisis is not a recent phenomenon, but has long been part of discourses of change and upheaval. For example, environmental crises are commonly discussed according to kinship, consanguinity and future generations (see Shirani et al. 2013). Similarly, the recent adoption of the term 'snowflake' in the USA, and increasingly in the UK, is an instance in which political or moral crises—such declining mental health amongst young people, or demands for trans rights—are framed according to personal identities, of younger generations being emotionally unstable, lacking resilience and unable to cope with challenge or conflict. Christophers (2015, p. 210) makes a salient point when remarking that 'instead of discussing crisis in bald, abstract terms we should *always* ask (but rarely do): a crisis of what and *for whom*?'

Recent and emerging writings regarding financial crisis and austerity also make the case for deeper understandings of impacts at the personal scale, with individuals, families and households simultaneously affected in multiple ways (Elwood and Lawson 2013; García-Lamarca and Kaika 2017). These 'subjective experiences' and personal responses to financial crisis and austerity (van Lanen 2017, p. 1605) have been conceptualised according to theories of austerity urbanism, indebtedness, responsibilisation and financialisation (e.g. Di Feliciantonio 2016; Fields 2017; García-Lamarca and Kaika 2017), to name but a few. Within this literature, austerity is also generally acknowledged as exacerbating everyday social differences and inequalities (Christophers 2018; Di Feliciantonio 2016; Fields 2017; van Lanen 2017). Austerity is argued to expose stigmatising discourses that 'situate some people and places as sympathetic and deserving of help and others not' (Elwood and Lawson 2013, p. 104). Collectively, this work reveals the variety of ways in which austerity and economic crisis 'play out' and are responded to in everyday life.

For instance, van Lanen's (2017, p. 1607) study of disadvantaged urban youth in Ireland found austerity 'directly and indirectly narrows the lifeworld' for this group. In research based in the North of England, Pimlott-Wilson (2017, p. 288) found significant emotional burdens and negotiations for young people who 'acknowledge their own responsibility as future adult citizens'. Further research on generational inequality by Christophers (2018), Hochstenbach (2018) and MacLeavy and Manley (2018, p. 1438) reveals the intergenerational transmission of inequality, 'embedded over time' and across the lifecourse, leading to socio-economic polarisations. Likewise, according to Fields (2017, p. 589), changes to housing markets in New York leading up to and following the GFC 'reshaped tenant's social, emotional and embodied experiences of home', which in related work is argued to 'play against other problems such as marital strain or personal illness and perpetuating financial struggle and other crises' (Fields et al. 2010, p. 660). Similarly, García-Lamarca and Kaika (2017, pp. 322–323) situate 'mortgages as a disciplinary tool', 'that forges an intimate connection between everyday life, global practices of financial speculation and the creation of urban futures' (see also Di Feliciantonio 2016). In sum, austerity and economic crises are herein shown to be deeply affective, intimate and personal.

As Sidaway (2008, p. 197) questions, 'when the result is homelessness and more families without decent or secure shelter, should we not just call this a moral or a human crisis?' Larner (2011, p. 319) calls for 'an appropriate point of comparison' to understand current geographies of crisis; what about *personal* comparators, considering crises alongside other life events and relational equivalents? Responding to García-Lamarca and Kaika's (2017, p. 324) call for 'fresh conceptualisation', I expand upon these debates in this chapter by exploring how economic crisis and austerity constitute personal crises, by considering the temporalities of crisis, how they are lived through, and the impacts of crises on personal and shared lives.

Everyday personal lives are always couched in social, political and economic contexts, not only as a 'backdrop' (Christophers 2015, p. 206), but as they are felt, lived and experienced. An example of this comes from Judith Stacey's work on *Brave New Families*, a tracing of the connections between financial and familial crises. In what she calls an 'accidental ethnography', Stacey (1990, p. 27) maps out the extended kinship networks of two working-class women in Silicon Valley, USA. While more commonly cited for reworking and pluralising 'the family' from an institution to 'families' as social relationships (see Hall 2016b), Stacey also provides an insightful account of where economic and personal insecurities meet, mingle and collide.

More specifically, Stacey (1990, p. 9) coined the term 'structural fragility' in reference to 'the modern family system, particularly its premise of enduring voluntary commitment'. For while the 'cultural significance of the modern family grew, the productive and reproductive work performed within its domain contracted'. Changes in marriage, habitation, social attitudes to women's work and to childbearing, she posits, meant 'feminism received much of the blame for family and social crises' in the transition from industrial to post-industrial American urban society (ibid., p. 13). Writing at once of both 'family and social crisis', Stacey (1990, p. 13) forefronts the interrelationality of crises as they are lived. In the post-industrial society that Stacey describes, 'many women, perhaps the majority, found their economic conditions worsening'. Notions of the post-modern and post-industrial, she adds, themselves 'provoke uneasiness, because they imply the end and beginning of something, simultaneously' (ibid., p. 17). Again, the temporal dimensions of economic crises become entwined with personal and relational provocations.

Contemporary family arrangements are 'diverse, fluid and unresolved' (Stacey 1990, pp. 17–18), and in this realm of possibility and uncertainty, moments of financial and economic crisis can be revealing of fragilities within familial relations, 'when the belief in a logical progression of stages breaks down'. A crisis of family—the institutional, linear, progressive staging of personal relationships and kinship—is at the same time an economic crisis:

> out of the ashes and residue of the modern family, [people] have drawn on diverse, often incongruous resources, fashioning these resources into new gender and kinship strategies to cope with postindustrial challenges, burdens and opportunities. (Stacey 1990, p. 16)

Aligning familial and economic crises in this way rescales the focus of analysis, presenting points of everyday conjuncture, even disjuncture, between social norms, responsibilities and expectations. This comingling of familial and economic crisis has been noted in empirical work across the social sciences, particularly relating to intergenerationality and the lifecourse (Hopkins and Pain 2007). For instance, Edwards and Weller's (2010, p. 134) longitudinal study of British young people's trajectories into adulthood, coinciding with the recent recession, describes participants juggling unemployment with desires of wanting a family 'in the future'. MacLeavy and Manley (2018, p. 1436) also note how 'the problem of inequality can become greater when viewed from an intergenerational standpoint', whereby the transmission of inequalities means 'future trajectories' and lifecourse possibilities are constantly reshaped by past and present experiences (Hochstenbach 2018). Similarly, Pimlott-Wilson (2017, p. 293) identifies 'the enduring role of employment in establishing a successful and fulfilling adult future on the part of young people', with complex emotions 'arising from a failure to align with dominant constructions of neoliberal success in the future'.

Such discussions are also reminiscent of Gillis' (1996, p. xv) notion of the families we live with and by; how we represent 'ourselves to ourselves as we would like to think we are'. Imagined notions of family (as well as broader relational concepts such as generationality) are also rooted in literature on economic crisis, wherein

> Economic crisis *disrupts* not just social and spatial narratives of poverty, class, prosperity and vulnerability, but also *temporal imaginaries*. [...] The effects of these *ruptures in anticipated life trajectories* are engendering new social objects of concern such as 'the Boomerang Generation'—young people who return home to live with their parents, often remaining well into adulthood. (Elwood and Lawson 2013, p. 105—emphasis added)

This notion of 'temporal imaginaries' connects key ideas in this chapter, around the rhythms, traces and remnants of crises (i.e. crisis temporalities), as well as how crises shape temporality, spaces and experiences (i.e. crises in everyday life). The way in which crises are experienced, performed and anticipated also shapes how they are manifest in personal and shared lives and imaginaries. And yet, as Smart (2007) stresses, the imaginary aspects of personal life are just as important as the realised (also see Hall and Holdsworth 2016).

Lived experiences of crisis and austerity might therefore also be understood as moments of what Johnson-Hanks (2002, p. 871) calls 'vital conjunctures': 'a socially structured zone of possibility that emerges around specific periods of potential transformation in a life or lives [...] a temporary configuration of possible change, a duration of uncertainty and potential'. First developed in the context of research with women in southern Cameroon, the concept has since been deployed in a range of socio-economic contexts, including by geographers (see Evans 2014). Johnson-Hanks (2002, p. 865) describes how 'most vital events—such as marriages, motherhood and migration—are negotiable and contested, fraught with uncertainty, innovation and ambivalence'.

The 'vital' part is in fact taken from demographic concepts of 'vital events', key points such as birth, death and marriage, and is increasingly being applied within family and lifecourse geographies (Bailey 2009; Evans 2014; Hopkins and Pain 2007). Such moments are not simply institutional structures, but also everyday conjunctures. The vitality of the conjuncture, the change that might be unleashed, is also significant, since 'vital conjunctures are particularly critical durations when more than usual is in play, when the futures at stake are significant' (Johnson-Hanks 2002, p. 871). Here, the term is used 'to emphasize the dual character of vital conjunctures: at once manifestations of reoccurring systematicness *and* contexts of unique possibility and future orientation' (Johnson-Hanks 2002, p. 872).

Conjunctures, Johnson-Hanks (2002, p. 872) further argues, 'have duration. Whereas events are outcomes in themselves, conjunctures have multiple outcomes over different time frames', including crises. This is not to say vital conjunctures offer a linear, processional framing of everyday life. Rather 'vital conjunctures are experiential knots during which potential futures are under debate and up for grabs' (Johnson-Hanks 2002, p. 872). Vital conjunctures are then both cause and outcome; they are instigators of change whilst simultaneously representing the fallout of change. However (and crucially), they can also be shared, relational, diverging and intersecting with the conjunctures of others, whether familial, generational or societal.

Writings on geographies of the lifecourse are central here, particularly for where it is recognised that biographies are characterised by 'biological ruptures and discontinuities, rather than the assumed predictability of life cycles' (Hörschelmann 2011, p. 378). Indeed, 'vital life events are rarely coherent, clear in direction or fixed in outcome' (Johnson-Hanks' 2002, p. 865). Furthermore, with the move towards relational thinking in lifecourse geographies comes an acknowledgement that 'individuals and groups organize their lives in relation to others, society and its institutions', and that with interpersonal, intergenerational interactions comes disruption and 'temporal contingencies' (Bailey 2009, pp. 409–410; Hopkins and Pain 2007; Hörschelmann 2011). In this sense, through a focus on the temporalities of crisis and conjuncture as they are lived and experienced within everyday relationships, greater insight might be afforded into how biographies and lifecourses are both personal and shared.

While current experiences of austerity have the potential to significantly alter personal and shared biographies, memories of previous experiences of austerity might also be important for understanding practices and relationships in the present, as reference points that shape future personal lives. In austere times, questions are therefore raised about how people image themselves, the spaces and times in which they situate their lives. Considering the temporalities of crisis and austerity, such as through personal and shared crises and future lifecourses, offers new ways for thinking through crises as they are lived and experienced. It also simultaneously makes a political statement about crisis-prone and austere times, crystallised around the voices and experiences of those affected.

Crises as Part of Everyday Life

There is a rich and growing body of research that shows how austerity can have the effect of deepening and worsening financial situations. Many families and communities are being hit hard because they were struggling beforehand. Austerity can therefore expose already-existing tensions and vulnerabilities, working as a conjuncture, a tipping point, causing disruption and rupturing. However, this entrenching effect might not only be felt for those living in financial precarity—crises do not necessarily discriminate quite so easily—but can be felt in a whole range of personal situations.

Part of the reason for this is that crises punctuate and are woven within everyday life. Participants often mention how everyday life is difficult. It is hard to always be prepared, to have a contingency plan for every eventuality. Crises were described as constantly looming, always at the edge of possibility (Haraway 2008; Stacey 1990). Selma explained how she found it difficult to save any money, stating bluntly, 'life is hard [...] I have no have money, it's very very hard' (taped discussion, May 2014). As described in Chap. 2, Selma and her daughter Mya lived at a distance from all her close family, and seemed to be somewhat isolated in dealing with everyday trials and tribulations. I observed these struggles for Selma up close: at supermarket tills counting out the last of her coins, at home measuring out small batches of minced lamb for the freezer so they could eat that week, or getting three buses instead of one because her weekly pass enabled travel with only one operator. As described in Chap. 4, Selma also had to deal with the stresses of living in inadequate social housing, as well as the pressures of being a single parent supported by state welfare, and the unpleasant encounters that followed from such conditions. The accumulation of these many personal strains took their toll on Selma and other participants, often describing themselves as tired—physically, mentally and of their precarious situation. Stenning (2018) and Wilkinson and Ortega-Alcázar (2018) also write of the embodied impacts of austerity, creating feelings of weariness, exhaustion and being squeezed.

Similarly for Laura, it seemed the rhythm and tempo of daily life was punctuated by everyday acts of getting by, always thinking ahead 'just in case'. Whether making large vats of soup or chilli to feed them for the whole week (as depicted in Fig. 6.1), buying next year's Christmas presents in the Boxing Day sales or monitoring energy use in summer and autumn (so there'd be enough money in the account to cover the winter months), time, energy and consideration were constantly and routinely being invested into the possibility of crisis (Elwood and Lawson 2013; Stacey 1990). Laura also described how being a parent of two 'is probably been harder that I would have thought. But then, I know for other people it's been even harder' (taped discussion, October 2014). This comment exposes how austerity is considered through relational framing and relative experience. As described in Chaps. 3 and 4, Laura relied a lot upon

Fig. 6.1 Laura cooking a vat of soup (illustrated by Claire Stringer, from the *Everyday Austerity* zine by Sarah Marie Hall, see https://everydayausterity.wordpress.com/zine/)

friend and family networks for direct and indirect support with childcare. This is not to say that Laura and other participants were anticipating specific crises; they were not developing 'response-abilities' so much (Haraway 1997; Haraway 2008). Instead, they described crises and their effects as mundane and expected, part and parcel of an already challenging everyday life.

One 'vital' moment of crisis commonly discussed and observed throughout the ethnography related to health. When a serious health problem emerged, participants called upon personal resources of gendered, intergenerational and kinship relations. Zoe described how she, husband Stuart and their two children were 'fairly self-sufficient as a family until there is a problem, like a physical problem, like Ryan is poorly and has to go to hospital, and then we need some help, or Isobel is off school sick or something like that' (taped discussion, January 2014). She further explained that in such a situation:

> I'd probably go to my parents first [for help], I would say they are the most flexible in terms of, they'll just pick it up and run with it and get on with it. If it was an emergency situation, it depends *how* emergency. Because my

> in-laws are around the corner and they're great and they're very very good, they're better in kind of short bursts though. (Zoe, taped discussion, January 2014)

Here, Zoe describes her response to health crises as embedded within everyday practices and relationships (Evans 2014; Johnson-Hanks 2002), with distinct spatial, relational and temporal geographies, as well as differentiating between different levels of crisis and emergency (Wagner-Pacifici 2017). The response is characterised by proximity and mobility ('pick it up and run', 'around the corner'), speed, rhythm and tempo ('flexible', 'short bursts'), as much as by closeness, kinship and social affinity ('parents first', 'in-laws'). Using Larner's (2011) terminology, we can see here that crises can induce new or revised time horizons, or crises temporalities.

While ethnographic observations can often unveil tensions between what participants say, think and do (see Gillis 1996), in this case, Zoe's description was seen through in practice. For example, when daughter Isobel came down with a high temperature and tonsillitis, it was Zoe's parents who looked after her overnight when Zoe and Stuart had a long-anticipated night away. Even though they lived closer by, Stuart's parents 'had not been so forthcoming in offering to help' (field diary, December 2013), showing how crises can become opportunities for exposing relational tensions, or what Stacey (1990) calls familial fragility. This is also related to earlier discussions in Chap. 3, wherein crises can place added stress on everyday social infrastructures and the intimate relations with which they are entangled.

Kerry similarly described a scene of disruption caused by health crises, such as when she was admitted to hospital. This was an unplanned visit and one that disrupted all of the family's usual routines, including our meetings. She was in hospital for a week, 'during which time her mum and sister stepped in to help' (field diary, December 2013). As discussed in Chap. 3, these particular family members were a commonly relied-upon source of practical help and support for Kerry, an everyday social infrastructure, particularly when it came to childcare. On this occasion, possibly because of the severity of the crisis in question, 'even Dan was off work, his boss "surprisingly" gave him time off in kind' (field diary,

December 2013). Kerry described how the pace of everyday life was thrown off during her time in hospital, and required resetting. She spoke about reverting back to familiar daily rhythms and practices once returning home: 'I have a strict routine and when [I was] in the hospital I couldn't wait to get home because they were running riot, I was like "they need this routine"' (Kerry, taped discussion, December 2013). The idea of 'running riot', a metaphor for turbulent, uncontrolled behaviour, conjures spatial imaginaries of movement, chaos and disorder that could only be tempered upon Kerry's return. The temporalities of everyday life can only be understood in conjunction with their disruption, with crises as opportunities for a reflection on and reworking of routines and responsibilities, and when new possibilities (like an empathetic boss) can emerge (French et al. 2009; Hall and Massey 2010; Wagner-Pacifici 2017).

As also noted in Chap. 1, an ethnographic approach is particularly attuned to identifying everyday rhythms of and responses to crisis and conjuncture. It is common to find oneself 'witnessing or commiserating over family crises and tragedies including deaths, severe illnesses, layoffs, evictions, suicide attempts, infidelities, and problems with drugs, alcohol, physical abuse, and the law' (Stacey 1990, p. 33). If ethnography necessitates physical and emotional proximity over time (Hall 2014), then it follows that crises also form part of such research. These instances were referred to by participants as examples of 'family crisis' (Zoe, taped discussion, January 2014) which, when witnessed during ethnography, may also shape the form and direction of our research. For example, Selma made the decision to withdraw from the project after eight months of taking part, due to a combination of the pressures of being a single mother to Mya, and as a result of Mya's recent autism diagnosis. Zoe permanently postponed our final 'thank you' meet up, because Ryan was taken to hospital with a life-threatening illness. And this does not include the many families who could not participate because of ongoing, recent or threats of crises, and the resultant rupturing and dislocation of everyday practices.

Other points or moments of crises observed over the ethnography included partnership dissolution, career changes, house moves, births and deaths, and what these have in common is that they are all so-called vital events in the lifecourse (Johnson-Hanks 2002). These moments of crisis and conjuncture are not only important for how they are marked into lived time, and the changes they make to everyday relationships and practices, but also for what they represent, in hindsight, for their relative qualities. Laura, for instance, regularly reflected upon the lessons learned from getting into heavy credit card debt at a young age, passing this experiential learning on to her partner within shared financial arrangements. 'Rich said it'd be good to have some savings, I said "yeah, but there's no point having savings if we're paying off debt. We might as well pay off the debt first"' (Laura, taped discussion, November 2014). These prior experiences were woven into everyday practices. Nearly every morning after Lucas's school drop-off, she would 'walk to her local newsagents to check her bank balance on the cash point inside, printing out a paper receipt, and studiously note which direct debits, debt repayments, store payments and benefits had entered and exited the account' (field diary, October 2013). This routine enabled Laura to keep up with the daily rhythms and tempos of payments and deposits, to 'know where she is with money', and to exert at least some control in the present for past financial mishandlings (field diary, October 2013). Past personal crises concerning indebtedness therefore continued to shape Laura's everyday temporalities and financial practices (also see García-Lamarca and Kaika 2017; Hall 2016a; Larner 2011).

Thinking further about past, lived experiences and vital events, George and Pauline spoke about how growing up in the shadow of the Second World War and the following years of austerity shaped their attitudes towards money, material things and waste. In a taped discussion, George described how:

> From the way that we grew up, we knew that we didn't have much. If nothing else, we've always been careful [...] brought up in what was a period of austerity ... I was born in '47, and well in the 1950s, having gone through that and knowing what times were like then, and even in to the early Sixties I suppose, it's always taught me to be careful with money because I never had a lot of money to dispose of. (George, taped discussion, August 2015)

After retiring, the imperative to enact these values ramped up, whereby 'Pauline and George were acutely aware that they were no longer able to bring in extra income' (field diary, September 2014). George took 'great pride in his garden; a veritable feast, waiting to be picked, prepared and poached' (field diary, February 2015). Every time I went over to their house, they would be something home-grown and home-made on offer: jams, pickles, pies and puddings. Pauline would often be knitting either clothes or toys to give away (also see Chaps. 3 and 4).

When I asked George to give me a tour of the garden during one of my many visits, 'he pointed out of all sorts of herbs—basil, rosemary, sage, mint, bay and parsley; vegetables—cucumbers, chilli peppers, sweet peppers, runner beans, rocket and marrows; and fruits—tomatoes, raspberries, gooseberries, rhubarb and strawberries—they could live off their garden, if they had to' (field diary, July 2015). I also noted in my field diary how pleased George looked when I took an interest in the garden and started scribbling down his descriptions, including sketching a little annotated map for myself of the garden, and taking a few photographs of his most impressive crops (e.g. see Fig. 6.2). For while a worthy and fulfilling pastime, George's gardening, like Pauline's crafting, was a practice knotted together with past and highly personal experiences of hardship. Crises are, therefore, not only experienced in the present, but can be retold through and woven together with memories, brought forward into ongoing practices and imaginaries of the lifecourses. This is not to say that past experiences of crises are always accurately remembered, or even offer life lessons. However, their recalling can be a way of making familial and financial crises appear more palatable and participants seem 'responseable' (Haraway 2008), a hopeful memory to live with and by, a story told to oneself and others, a silver lining (see Gillis 1996).

Economic crisis and austerity are shown to be situated, knotted within the context of other significant life events and circumstances, in turn shaping everyday understandings and future responses. To further illustrate, I'll draw on the example of married couple Sharon and Bill. They described themselves as financially comfortable, emphasising that this was as a result of working their way up within their respective careers. In the 14 months they took part in the research, their feelings towards economic instability and crisis—including when asked about the impact of austerity—were almost always discussed as relative. Positioned alongside individual and shared experiences of getting by in other situations, they

Fig. 6.2 Greenhouse vegetables grown by George (photograph taken by Sarah Marie Hall)

regularly revisited and referenced Sharon's recent and ongoing battle with breast cancer: a most significant vital conjuncture (Evans 2014; Johnson-Hanks 2002). Though they described being directly impacted by austerity, including the stagnation of Bill's wages—'I've not had a pay rise since I've joined' (taped discussion, August 2014)—they related this to Sharon's cancer. There was 'a sense that nothing could be as difficult as that experience has been, for them both' (field diary, December 2013).

This personal and relational crisis was an everyday conjuncture, revealing who Sharon and Bill could rely on for support and reshaping their social relationships and responsibilities (Haraway 2008). As noted in Chap. 4, Sharon was especially disappointed with her sister Pat, her only sibling, for her lack of support. As well as sharing these concerns with her Reiki master and osteopath, Sharon confided in me that she found her sister 'very very difficult. It was quite an eye-opener, although it was hell going through cancer, it was a real eye-opener' (taped discussion, August 2017). There was also a neighbour who Sharon thought would have knocked by more after being discharged when the bedroom curtains were closed for weeks on end (field diary, December 2013). Sharon since significantly distanced herself from her sister and the neighbour, would not go to either of them for support and was also less inclined to offer it. Over the period in which they took part in the research, Sharon saw her sister (with whom she was once very close) with less frequency and spoke about her less favourably. As well as being a disrupting event, shaping everyday life and imagined futures, this conjuncture was revealing of familial fragility and the interrelational entangled nature of crises.

Crises are absorbed and woven into everyday practices and relationships, often approached with an inventory of personal comparators, life experiences and memories which resonate strongly. While this can provide a sense of hope about getting by, crises are nevertheless also personally affective and can have lasting impacts on social relationships.

A Life Crisis?

As mentioned earlier in this chapter, geographers, demographers and sociologists have long critiqued ideas of the lifecourse as being demarcated by vital events (Hörschelmann 2011; Johnson-Hanks 2002). And yet stages in the lifecourse remain important, as the milestones by which many people measure their success and personal worth (see Bailey 2009; Hopkins and Pain 2007; Pimlott-Wilson 2017). In this sense, economic crisis and austerity can also be the cause of vital, everyday conjunctures, leading to rupture and fragmentation in the things people can do, afford or dream about.

Participants in the ethnography frequently described the affects of living in and through austerity as disruptions in their real and anticipated lifecourse, or a 'life crisis'. They reported strong feeling that their lives and the lives of people they knew were going 'off track', revealing cracks in the modern family system (see Stacey 1990). This can lead to uncertainty about the future and feelings of a very personal crisis. During my fieldwork, I observed many instances of this, including adults returning to childhood homes, or not having the financial independence to leave, or being unable to retire due to the reduced value of pensions. In austere times, questions are raised about how people's lives play out alongside imagined lifecourses, aspirations and expectations, and about the spaces, times and social relations in which they situate their lives. As a result, the reverberations of crises can be personally felt, relational and far-reaching.

The example of Laura and Rich provides a useful illustration. During the course of the ethnography, they experienced a number of vital life events and, at times, vital conjunctures. During her time participating in the research project, Laura returned to work part-time after maternity leave from her second child and became also engaged to Rich, getting married a few months after the end of the ethnography. Laura regularly expressed concerns that her life was not going as she had hoped, as if the pace were too slow. She expressed not wanting to 'wish time away', and yet 'wanted to be married, to own a house and have a fully-fledged career, rather than renting and paying off debt' (field diary, October 2013).

These discussions mirrored notions of both familial fragility and temporal disjuncture introduced earlier in this chapter (Larner 2011; Stacey 1990), giving the sense that the tempos of Laura's realised and imaginary lifecourse were somehow out of sync. This perceived delay in the lifecourse—a rupture in her anticipated life trajectory (see Elwood and Lawson 2013)—has an impact beyond Laura. It directly impacts on her partner Rich and his own experiences and ideas of the future. Laura could only finish her social work course in order to progress from her 'support worker job, with no sort of career plan' (taped discussion, November 2013) if she and Rich were both in paid employment. This was only made possible with the informal childcare offered by family, friends and neighbours (see Chap. 3), thus knotting together personal crises, interrelational responsibilities and shared lifecourse biographies (Bailey 2009; Haraway 2008; Hopkins and Pain 2007).

This has a compounding effect on how Laura talked about the future. She regularly spoke about it as 'likely to involve trying to get out of debt and renting for a while yet' (field diary, November 2013), and sometimes talked about 'maybe having another baby but once their debts are sorted' (field diary, May 2014). If she 'could win an amount, say like win the lottery', she once told me, then 'we could pay off our debt and buy our own house [...] that would solve a lot of our problems' (taped discussion, October 2014). Realistically, however, she envisaged that they would be 'renting for a lot longer but we do want to buy. We want to try and get out of debt and get a pension sorted'. She fully expected that things were 'going to get worse' once 'the full impact of austerity' hit, particularly in terms of cuts to the state services and social infrastructures they relied upon (field diary and taped discussion, November 2014).

All the meanwhile, the likelihood of saving for a mortgage and owning their own home, as a commonplace lifecourse aspiration (see Bailey 2009; García-Lamarca and Kaika 2017; Pimlott-Wilson 2017), was moving further out of arm's reach. She explained:

> A mortgage on this house would be more than we pay in rent. But we couldn't afford to buy this house but we can afford to rent it [...] it's [affording] the deposit. So I think, when we get the course out of the way, get married and then [...] I think my mum and dad will help us out with the deposit. [...] But obviously it will have to be written into their will, that I've had that from them already, so obviously my brother will get an extra thirty grand. You just don't know, do you? You just don't know what's going to happen. (Laura, taped discussion, May 2014)

In this extract, Laura discusses personal and shared biographies simultaneously. Her studies are described a shared task ('we'), as well as an important point in her career progression. This, along with getting married, marks a vital event in her lifecourse. She explains how their only hope for buying a house in the future was if her mum and dad would help them out. But if they were to do this, they would have to compensate Laura's brother in their will, itself a direct reference to vital events in the lifecourse and entwined interpersonal biographies. She also indicates towards the uncertainty of her situation, which is also a common theme of the literature (see Stacey 1990; Wagner-Pacifici 2017) as well as the potential hopefulness of temporal contingencies and the unknown (Elwood and Lawson 2013; Hörschelmann 2011). In this example, everyday financial practices of lending and borrowing were also intergenerational practices (see related discussions in Chaps. 3 and 4; also see Hochstenbach 2018; MacLeavy and Manley 2018). Moreover, they impacted upon Laura's experiences of austerity both in the present and into the future, shaping lived temporalities of austerity and feelings of a personal crisis.

Kerry's reflections on her real and imaginary lifecourse were in some ways remarkably similar to Laura's. When reflecting on the future, she said she expected much of the same. They would continue renting where they were, being unable to buy a house in the school catchment area. She also saw her children growing up, but it 'didn't make sense for her to go back to work with the costs of childcare' (field diary, January 2014), 'unless', she joked, 'I win the lottery' (taped discussion, October 2014). And there was the strong presence of intra-familial resources, intragenerational responsibilities and intertwined biographies, of looking after her nephew because her sister and brother-in-law could not afford formal childcare (see Chaps. 3 and 4 for more background on this example). At the same time, Kerry was worried about them, saying 'she "didn't know how they were going to cope". Her sister earns the same amount as Dan, but unlike Kerry they would only be entitled to child tax credits for one child' (field diary, January 2014). Familial and financial fragilities were laid bare. But when asked to imagine the future differently, she also yearned for financial stability ('bigger house and bigger garden [...] more money'), career prospects ('go back to work'), a 'healthy', hopefully expanded, family ('I want a baby girl'), and a 'nice and thin' body (taped discussion, October 2014). These imaginary elements were quite different to the realities participants saw for themselves, removed from expected or planned lifecourse trajectories.

Further evidence of how personal crises and relational politics of austerity are interconnected can be seen in how participants spoke about crises faced by family and friends, whether or not participants considered these relationships to be 'close'. As discussed in Chap. 3, George and Pauline did not regard their relationships with their sons as particularly intimate. When musing about the future, they expressed explicit concern for their children and grandchildren (also see Shirani et al. 2013). While recognising the impacts on their own lives, realised and imaginary, their narratives crystallised around *future* familial fragility:

George: You know, it's such an uncertain future. I mean, I never had to fight, or go to war or anything like that. Neither of the boys [sons] have. It makes you wonder, with grandchildren, what's around the corner for them at some point? It's a bit of a frightening thought.
Pauline: work and … property and … what are they going to do?
George: […] Things have changed an awful lot in the last, even the last ten years but certainly the last-
Pauline: Our parents did better than their parents, fared better than them. We've fared better than our parents. I can't see how this next generation and the generation after can do better.
George: […] I mean, we were fortunate, getting that first house we did when prices suddenly started rocketing after that and we paid … what, £24,000 for this, was it? It's worth, what? £200,000 now? So we've got that to leave to the boys, we've got the house that they can share between them.
Pauline: If we don't end up in care.
George: Well, if we don't end up in care, because that will eat a big lump in to it. And then the next thing I suppose will be downsizing in due course, when we get too old to maintain this place any longer. (taped discussion, September 2015)

While George and Pauline started by talking about future crises and the potential impact on their children's children, they moved quickly to discuss relational impacts on their own lives. They compared opportunities of employment and homeownership between generations, a reminder of temporal geographies of crises through the lifecourse, and the role of personal and shared comparative experiences. Towards the end of the extract, they acknowledge the certainty of death, and the passing on of financial asserts to their children, but only if they 'don't end up in care'. Personal and relational biographies become entwined with emotional and financial consequences shared across generations, but the possibility of crises lingers in the background.

The passing on of personal crises to kith and kin was also discussed as a source of instability in itself, where personal relationships might come under strain and in turn be reshaped (see Stacey 1990). Sharon and Bill both had siblings with financial instabilities, creating tensions that regularly made their way into my field diaries. When Sharon's sister went on holiday with their dad, he paid for everything, and he always pays for her sister when they meet for a coffee (field diary, August 2014). This serves as an example of how familial fragilities can lead to interpersonal crises. During one of our taped discussions, Sharon and Bill spoke at length about changing familial relationships as a result of these tensions:

Bill: My brother ... He's had to take a pay cut [...] the owner took two hundred pound a month off him. [...] It's a fair chunk. And he's not particularly well paid either. [...]
Sharon: He's not well paid ... so yeah, he's really, really struggled.
Bill: Because the [work] wasn't there, money wasn't coming through, so ... he didn't get his bonus to go with that so it's all-
Sharon: So yeah, he's really been hit by it. [...]
Bill: Mum's probably helped him out.
Sharon: His mum's supporting him.
Bill: Mother's probably helped him out with bits ... well, probably more than she thinks, actually. [...]
Sharon: Well, [Pat] hasn't had a pay rise, she's a [public sector worker] as well. So she has been affected to an extent. But she has got deeper pockets and shorter arms. [...] She's surviving very well because dad comes round and does this and does that and pays for this. [...] It's taking the piss out of my dad. I don't begrudge it and I don't want him to spend anything on me, because he did me the greatest honour of giving me away at our wedding and there is nothing more he can ever top for me. And I don't want him to give me any money and I keep saying "it's your money, you earned it, you spend it". (taped discussion, August 2014)

Both Sharon's sister and Bill's brother have been affected by economic changes during austerity, specifically in the reduction or stagnation of wages. The relational elements of personal crises can be seen in how family members (in this example, Sharon's father and Bill's mother) have offered financial support, emerging as forms of everyday social and intergenerational infrastructures (also see Chap. 3).

While Sharon and Bill have not been financially implicated in this, they are emotionally engaged and personally proximate to the situation. Both expressed frustration, anger and resentment regarding their adult siblings' lack of financial independence and the impact on their elderly parents, becoming 'animated and flustered' during the discussion (field diary, August 2014). Their descriptions were woven within the same narrative, movingly seamlessly from one sibling to the other, with Sharon and Bill repeating one another and finishing off each other's sentences. Sharon also compares her father's spending on her sister to being 'given away' at her wedding, further entangling stories of financial and familial fragilities with past experiences and vital events.

In all the examples above, austerity and crisis are revealed to have personal impacts on experiences and imaginations of the lifecourse, the effects of which can also rebound as an interpersonal experience, part of both personal and shared biographies. Struggles with paying off debt, a housing boom and a lack of employment opportunities—linked to the recent period of austerity and economic crisis—were also conjunctural moments, as well as sources of familial and structural fragility.

Conclusion

With this chapter I have illustrated how conceptualisations of crises and conjuncture can be extended and enriched by focusing on familial relationships, personal and shared biographies, and lifecourse geographies. Using ideas across economic and social theory, I have developed current literatures on austerity and economic crisis at the personal scale, including how these events are responded to in everyday life. I have also argued that austerity and economic crises in fact constitute and provide a temporality for everyday life, both knotted and woven together, punctuated and disrupted. Developing this theoretical framework with the application of ethnographic findings, the impacts of austerity have been shown to be affective, emotional and relational, not only in how families respond but also in how they imagine their personal and shared future lifecourses.

Economic crises and austerity can be particularly revealing of the fragilities within familial, intimate and personal relationships. Questions are raised about how people image themselves, and the relationships, spaces and times in which they situate their lives—previously, presently and prospectively. Personal inventories of other important life experiences, relational comparators and memories, of social, emotional, intergenerational or financial hardship, also resonate strongly. Likewise, crises have been shown to be part of the everyday, as well as future imaginaries, manifesting as a very personal crisis. Everyday conjunctures and family fragilities are two sides of the same coin. Crises can form out of both, offering possibilities for change and continuity.

Bibliography

Bailey, A. J. (2009). Population Geography: Lifecourse Matters. *Progress in Human Geography, 33*(3), 407–418.

Christophers, B. (2015). Geographies of Finance II: Crisis, Space and Political-Economic Transformation. *Progress in Human Geography, 39*(2), 205–213.

Christophers, B. (2018). Intergenerational Inequality? Labour, Capital and Housing Through the Ages. *Antipode, 50*(1), 101–121.

Di Feliciantonio, C. (2016). Subjectification in Times of Indebtedness and Neoliberal/Austerity Urbanism. *Antipode, 48*(5), 1206–1227.

Edwards, R., & Weller, S. (2010). Trajectories from Youth to Adulthood: Choice and Structure for Young People Before and During Recession. *Twenty-First Century Society, 5*(2), 125–136.

Elwood, S., & Lawson, V. (2013). Whose Crisis? Spatial Imaginaries of Class, Poverty, and Vulnerability. *Environment and Planning A, 45*, 103–108.

Evans, R. (2014). Parental Death as a Vital Conjuncture? Intergenerational Care and Responsibility Following Bereavement in Senegal. *Social & Cultural Geography, 15*, 547–570.

Fields, D. (2017). Unwilling Subjects of Financialisation. *International Journal of Urban and Regional Research, 41*(4), 588–603.

Fields, D., Libman, K., & Saegert, S. (2010). Turning Everywhere, Getting Nowhere: Experiences of Seeking Help for Mortgage Delinquency and Their

Implications for Foreclosure Prevention. *The International History Review, 20*(4), 647–686.

French, S., & Leyshon, A. (2010). "These F@#king Guys": The Terrible Waste of a Good Crisis. *Environment and Planning A, 42*, 2549–2559.

French, S., Leyshon, A., & Thrift, N. (2009). A Very Geographical Crisis: The Making and Breaking of the 2007–2008 Financial Crisis. *Cambridge Journal of Regions, Economy and Society, 2*, 287–302.

García-Lamarca, M., & Kaika, M. (2017). "Mortgaged Lives": The Biopolitics of Debt and Housing Financialisation. *Transactions of the Institute of British Geographers, 41*, 313–327.

Gillis, J. R. (1996). *A World of Their Own Making: Myth, Ritual, and the Quest for Family Values*. New York: Basic Books.

Hall, S. M. (2014). Ethics of Ethnography with Families: A Geographical Perspective. *Environment and Planning A, 46*(9), 2175–2194.

Hall, S. M. (2016a). Everyday Family Experiences of the Financial Crisis: Getting by in the Recent Economic Recession. *Journal of Economic Geography, 16*(2), 305–330.

Hall, S. M. (2016b). Moral Geographies of Family: Articulating, Forming and Transmitting Moralities in Everyday Life. *Social & Cultural Geography, 17*(8), 1017–1039.

Hall, S. M., & Holdsworth, C. (2016). Family Practices, Holiday and the Everyday. *Mobilities, 11*(2), 284–302.

Hall, S., & Massey, D. (2010). Interpreting the Crisis. *Soundings, 44*(44), 57–71.

Haraway, D. J. (1997). *Modest_Witness@Second_Millennium: Femaleman_Meets_Oncomouse: Feminism and Technoscience*. New York: Routledge.

Haraway, D. J. (2008). *When Species Meet*. Minneapolis, MN: University of Minnesota Press.

Hochstenbach, C. (2018). Spatializing the Intergenerational Transmission of Inequalities: Parental Wealth, Residential Segregation, and Urban Inequality. *Environment and Planning A, 50*(3), 689–708.

Hopkins, P., & Pain, R. (2007). Geographies of Age: Thinking Relationally. *Area, 39*(3), 287–294.

Hörschelmann, K. (2011). Theorising Life Transitions: Geographical Perspectives. *Area, 43*(4), 378–383.

Johnson-Hanks, J. (2002). On the Limits of Life Stages in Ethnography: Toward a Theory of Vital Conjunctures. *American anthropologist, 104*(3), 865–880.

Larner, W. (2011). C-change? Geographies of Crisis. *Dialogues in Human Geography, 1*(3), 319–335.

MacLeavy, J., & Manley, D. (2018). (Re)discovering the Lost Middle: Intergenerational Inheritances and Economic Inequality in Urban and Regional Research. *Regional Studies, 52*(10), 1435–1446.

Pimlott-Wilson, H. (2017). Individualising the Future: The Emotional Geographies of Neoliberal Governance in Young Peoples' Aspirations. *Area, 49*(3), 288–295.

Shirani, F., Butler, C., Henwood, K., Parkhill, K., & Pidgeon, N. (2013). Disconnected Futures: Exploring Notions of Ethical Responsibility in Energy Practices. *Local Environment, 18*(4), 455–468.

Sidaway, J. (2008). Subprime Crisis: American Crisis or Human Crisis. *Environment and Planning D, 26*, 195–198.

Smart, C. (2007). *Personal Life*. Cambridge: Polity Press.

Stacey, J. (1990). *Brave New Families: Stories of Domestic Upheaval in Late-Twentieth-Century America*. Berkeley, CA: University of California Press.

Stenning, A. (2018). Feeling the Squeeze: Towards a Psychosocial Geography of Austerity in Low-to-Middle Income Families. *Geoforum*. https://doi.org/10.1016/j.geoforum.2018.09.035.

van Lanen, S. (2017). Living Austerity Urbanism: Space–Time Expansion and Deepening Socio-Spatial Inequalities for Disadvantaged Urban Youth in Ireland. *Urban Geography, 38*(10), 1603–1613.

Wagner-Pacifici, R. (2017). *What Is an Event?* Chicago, IL: The University of Chicago Press.

Wilkinson, E., & Ortega-Alcázar, I. (2018). The Right to Be Weary? Endurance and Exhaustion in Austere Times. *Transactions of the Institute of British Geographers, 44*(1), 155–167.

7

Conclusion

With the preceding chapters I have made the case for a relational approach to everyday life in austerity. Exploring everyday austerity's impacts on family, friendship and intimate relations, and where they intersect, offers fresh comprehensions and conceptualisations of contemporary socio-economic change. Austerity is a deeply personal and social condition, with impacts that spread across and between everyday relationships, spaces and temporal perspectives. Based upon a rich two-year ethnography in the context of austerity in the UK, weaving together the experiences of families and communities in Argleton, I have crafted my conceptual framework from the ground up.

Throughout this book, and addressing the questions posed in Chap. 1, I have shown austerity to be lived and felt on the ground, though with distinctly uneven socio-economic consequences. This is particularly the case for gendered labour, care and responsibilities. I have also identified how everyday relationships are subject to change and continuity in times of austerity. Some of these might be galvanised by conviviality and togetherness, others tainted by arguments and awkwardness, which in turn shape how people respond to austerity. Austerity has been shown to have lasting impacts on personal and shared experiences, both in terms of

S. M. Hall, *Everyday Life in Austerity*, Palgrave Macmillan Studies in Family and Intimate Life, https://doi.org/10.1007/978-3-030-17094-3_7

day-to-day practices and the lives people imagine themselves living. With this final chapter, I offer an overview of my contributions, and present suggestions for further work on everyday austerity.

Thinking Relationally About Austerity

Opening with a discussion of the dual and intersecting meanings of austerity, in Chap. 1, I positioned the importance of situating austerity as both a set of fiscal policies and as a condition that is social and economic, personal and relational. This focus on the personal and relational gives rise to thinking about the social relationships that form the basis of everyday life. Where austerity has typically been approached 'from above', such as by studying financial institutions, fiscal policies or urban governance (e.g. Aalbers 2009; Christophers 2015; Peck 2012), I reframe and rescale austerity debates around personal and relational lives, to build theory 'from below'. My interest in austerity is not centred around one specific policy or even specific social groups, but instead positions everyday personal and relational impacts of austerity at the core of my investigation. My approach has been strongly guided by feminist ideas and principles, from the authors cited and the terminology employed, to the methods, voices and experiences that make up the empirical study.

By looking at impacts on and in everyday life, and acknowledging that cuts fall in different ways upon different groups, I have sought to capture the diversity and unevenness of austerity as a set of policies and as a condition. Thinking relationally about austerity means that relative experiences are acknowledged and accounted for, from those witnessing spending cuts at a distance, to those feeling them at the sharpest end. I distinguish between living in and living with austerity, that is, the difference between living in a social context where austerity policies are being implemented, and living with austerity in the most intimate elements of daily life. With an ethnographic approach to the everyday experiences of families and communities, this book provides evidence of the textured and colourful ways that people get by in austere times, weaving in their lived experiences, memories and voices. These are by no means all hopeful, romantic or nostalgic. The impacts of austerity can just as often lead to tensions, awkwardness and hostility. To filter out these accounts, to offer only the positive stories, is to present a selective and dishonest account of everyday austerity.

In Chap. 2, I detailed what a relational approach to everyday life might look like, and what it can achieve. I argued that, when taken together, a focus on family, friends and intimate relations can bring forth geographically sensitive understandings of everyday austerity. This involves paying close attention to geographies *of* everyday life, by attending to questions of difference through, across and between spaces. It also involves exploring geographies *in* everyday life, by addressing the interactions, relationships and spatial practices that configure and are configured by the everyday. This also reveals the capacity for austerity to sharpen, blur or refract the boundaries of kinship, friendship and a whole range of 'intimate others' as the everyday context in which economic change plays out. Here we are also reminded of the value of developing geographical work on family, friend and intimate relationships, and crucially the links between them.

It is, no doubt, an impossible task to cover all elements of everyday life. As stated in Chap. 1, my intention with this book is not to provide a one-size-fits-all 'major theory' (Katz 1996). Rather, it is to interrogate and push the boundaries of relational thinking, and to apply it to the real world (Massey 1991; Massey 2004). Bringing this relational approach to everyday austerity, applying it as I have to everyday practices like caring or mobility, also helps to unpick the interrelationality of austerity. Austerity is situated within and across everyday relationships, reconfiguring these relationships through and across space. Family, friendship and intimacy are also argued to be reconstituted by austerity. With Chap. 3, I began to flesh out how austerity cuts through, across and between everyday life.

Using the metaphor of the tapestry to evoke imaginaries of female skilled labour, Chap. 3 sheds lights on the social infrastructures that undergird everyday relationships and practices, but which come under intense strain under austerity. Working through literature on politics of care and gendered labour, entwined with burgeoning ideas about social infrastructures, I stitched together the concept of everyday social infrastructures. Carefully woven fabrics of familial and extra-familial relationships, everyday social infrastructures rest on the notion of relationality. Care and support in everyday life are made possible by the warps and wefts of relations and practices. In austerity, cuts to social infrastructures hit the hardest: to welfare, education, health, local government and social care as sectors that mainly employ and are used by women (also see Pearson and Elson 2015). Framing everyday social infrastructures as a political responsibility and necessity then requires a re-evaluation of what and whom are impacted by austerity.

Intergenerational and gendered infrastructures are essential for everyday acts of childcare, according to sometimes complex patterns of friends, family and other intimate relations. Messy undersides to the tapestry of care were also exposed, such as where relationships can fray as a result of increased burdens on these social infrastructures due to austerity measures. It is because everyday social infrastructures are embroidered within personal relationships that these tapestries can also become entangled with interrelational tensions, power dynamics and relational inequalities. These same qualities can be seen in fieldwork encounters, too. In times of austerity, researchers may become woven into the everyday care infrastructures of participants' lives and emerge as an intimate relation. Fieldwork can then also become a relational space of austerity, where differences and similarities are played out and tested.

Continuing the theme of intimacy, Chap. 4 revealed how everyday relationships within and between family, friends and other intimate relations can be changed or reshaped by austere conditions. Intimacy and austerity were also shown to be entangled, or what I term austere intimacies and intimate austerities: the impacts of austerity on intimate relations, and the ways in which austerity is intimately felt and lived with, respectively. Playing with geographical concepts of closeness and distance, proximity and propinquity, ideas and writings on intimacy typically capture an array of physical, corporeal, material, emotional, social and personal relations (e.g. see Morgan 2009; Twigg 2000; Zelizer 2005). I argue that these are not exclusive, that they do not necessarily coexist. By considering a wider array of intimacies beyond family and friendship to include other types of intimate relations, I argue that everyday austerity might be seen a little differently. I illustrated this with the following four themes.

Monetary arrangements are one means by which to examine intimacy in austerity, particularly when the dual condition of austerity leads to restrictions on personal and national finances. Money is commonly exchanged within intimate relationships, or for intimate practices, like care work, domestic work and body-work; and such intimate exchanges can also lead to further intimacies. These monetary arrangements have strong potential to shape (for good or bad) the relationships in which they are grounded, particularly when austerity places pressure on their availability and maintenance. My ethnographic observations also highlighted the role of momentary encounters as part of the fabric of everyday austerity. Fleeting moments of connection can be sources of advice and comfort, and can also be the basis upon which further intimacies flourish. They can also be awkward, difficult and exposing; intimate encounters are not always welcomed. With regard to more-than-human intimacies and material proximities, I pushed further at the boundaries of relational thinking. Animal encounters can soften or sharpen the impact of austerity cuts in various ways. Material things can also facilitate intimacy through exchange, and can present opportunities for ongoing social relations and intimacies.

Chapter 5 continued to develop a relational approach to everyday austerity, on the basis that 'the personal is political' (Hanisch 1970). Giving greater value to lived experiences and everyday inequalities, this is as much about rethinking what counts as political as it is about questioning whose voices are heard. These are well-founded ideas within feminist theory, including feminist geography, and this chapter brought this work together with emerging ideas about quiet politics. Subtle, unfussy everyday acts that might go almost unnoticed or provoke little further thought have political potential in times of austerity (also see Askins 2014; Horton and Kraftl 2009; Pottinger 2017). These quietly political acts also offer new ways of understanding relational spaces of austerity, where social distances and interpersonal differences might be reconfigured, confronted or reinforced.

Smiles, nods and passing conversations are examples of quiet politics that I reflect upon, where relational spaces of togetherness and solidarity can be built. In many instances, gatherings such as coffee mornings or play groups provided spaces for connection and conviviality, counsel and care in the context of austerity. Expanding upon the current literature, I also made the case for conceptualising micro-aggressions as another type of quiet politics. Coloured instead by exclusion or hostility, micro-aggressions were shown to have deeply personal and provocative consequences. Their quietness was also described as operating in two interconnected ways. By definition, micro-aggressions are dismissible and subtle, and deniable if challenged, but they can also have the effect of silencing those on the receiving end (see Domosh 2015; Joshi et al. 2015). In austerity, social relations and relational spaces are just as likely to be reshaped by aggressive as by convivial politics. I also reflected upon the politics of presence, particularly as an ethnographer doing research on and in austerity. Through co-presence, being with participants to share in and hear their everyday experiences, fieldwork can also be a relational space for quiet politics (albeit with new challenges in austere environments).

From relational politics to relational biographies, with Chap. 6, I brought previously disparate areas of scholarship—around financial crisis and austerity, familial crises, and vital life events, conjunctures and lifecourses—into conversation with one another (e.g. Hall and Massey 2010; Johnson-Hanks 2002; Stacey 1990). Crises are shown to be part and parcel of everyday austerity, providing a sense of rhythm and tempo, punctuating daily life and putting stresses on personal relationships. Crises also presented opportunities for change or continuity, to reflect or rework everyday relationships and practices, but were also often deeply unsettling. Austerity was also conceptualised as a life crisis in and of itself, rupturing and fragmenting real and anticipated lifecourse trajectories, again with relational implications. Lifecourses impacted by austerity are both personal and relational, with shared biographies woven together, as well as with ideas of the future.

Synthesising theories of familial and economic crises in this way, and applying these concepts to ethnographic findings, had a number of effects. The current naming and framing of crisis-talk remains disconnected from the ways in which crises are lived and experienced. Rescaling theoretical frameworks towards personal crises, everyday conjunctures and family fragilities offers possibilities for lived experiences to 'talk up' to social, economic and political transformations and policy-making. It brings about a revised epistemological focus that sees crises as not always ground-breaking, horizon-shifting, paradigm-shaking events (see Castree 2010; Larner 2011), but also as intimately embedded in everyday lives as they are lived. Crises are personally affective, they can lead to rupture, fragmentation and disjuncture, having lasting personal and relational impacts. Economic crises and austerity are almost always and inevitably felt as a personal crisis. They are a vital conjuncture, the culmination of circumstance, opening up the wounds of old memories and creating new ones, compromising familial and financial fragility. It seems pertinent, then, to question the future of and futures in everyday austerity when, as some have claimed, austerity is over.

Austerity Is Over?

From when I started my fieldwork for this project to the time of writing, the discourses, policies and ideologies of austerity in the UK have been shifting. While they were originally purported to be a necessary response to the Global Financial Crisis and period of recession in the UK, as a means of ensuring financial recovery with the reduction of the national deficit (see Elwood and Lawson 2013; Hall 2015; Hinton and Goodman 2010), more recently the politics of austerity have become less powerful—or perhaps just less useful (also see Raynor 2018). Over the last few years, possibly as a response to growing public dissatisfaction with prolonged austerity (nine years and counting), senior figures in UK government have repeatedly made claims that austerity is over (e.g. see Mikhailova and Hymas 2018; Watts 2017).

These claims turned out to be a hollow promise, and by applying the dual and intersecting definitions of austerity, this becomes further apparent. Taking the notion of austerity as a fiscal policy, of cutting public spending in order to reduce the deficit, the claim that austerity is over is highly questionable. Recent government budget announcements have offered little in the way of reversing austerity cuts or reinvesting in those areas that have been hammered by a series of damaging policies, such as welfare, social care and education. Analysis of the most recent UK budget at the time of writing (the Autumn Budget 2018) reveals that 'there was more money for local physical rather than social infrastructure with £420 million to repair potholes, £150 million to improve traffic hot spots and £680 million for the transforming cities fund' (Women's Budget Group 2018, p. 2). Overall, 'none of the announcements were enough to make up for the sustained underfunding of public services since 2010. Spending cuts were not reversed' (ibid., p. 22).

Secondly, and significantly, neither does the claim stand up next to the definition of austerity as a condition of simplicity and self-restraint, which I have argued throughout this book to be a personal and relational condition. Lived experiences of austerity have impacted millions of people in the UK, with fiscal cuts bleeding into fabric of everyday life. This book has charted how the relational implications of austerity can have deep and lasting emotional, material, financial and social consequences. Whether temporary or irrevocable, everyday relationships have been reconfigured directly and indirectly because of austerity. Conceptualising everyday life in austerity with a relational approach reveals how family, friend and intimate relationships have been become forged and fraught, tamed and tested. As Chap. 6 in particular shows, economic, social and personal changes under austerity have impacted whole lifecourses and biographies.

In refuting the argument that austerity is over, we must ask the question: over for whom? Austerity is a condition that exacerbates already-existing inequalities and social differences within society. This book has highlighted the gendered burdens that come with increased pressure on care work, within and across everyday spaces such as community, home, work and leisure. And it impacts on multiple people at the same time, reverberating across and within families, friendship groups, communities and generations. The idea that austerity is over suggests that the effects cease to exist, vanishing into thin air. How can this be, when work opportunities, housing options, financial security and caring responsibilities have for many people, including participants within my ethnography, been fundamentally shaped by austerity? And what about longer-term prospects, hopes and dreams, the future lives imagined and lived? Are these over too? What are the personal, relational and political implications of this, and is the ending of austerity evenly distributed?

It stands to reason that the personal and relational implications of austerity will have long-lasting impacts on many people's everyday lives for years, even decades, to come. I foresee that these concerns will shape critically engaged social science research for a long time, or at least they should. While there can be a temptation for some scholars to study phenomena that are distant, unusual, even exceptional, this can have the effect of missing that which stands before our very eyes. Using doorstep ethnographies, the methodological approach I adopt within the research for this book, makes it difficult not to take note of social and economic change where it impacts on everyday lives as they are lived.

Future austerity research should also be attuned to future lives and the consequences of austerity through and over time, space and relationships. By this, I do not mean only far-reaching, long-term futures (though these are important), but everyday life at a more gentle pace. This includes the ways in which lived experiences and ongoing lifecourses intersect with ideas of the future, particularly personal and shared biographies. This might involve tracing and tracking the decisions people make about where to live and who to live with, the types of relationships they develop or dissolve, and how they plan or respond to vital events like births and deaths. Similarly, the ways in which the experience of everyday austerity works as a sort of relational comparator during other crises may also be of interest. How these experiences differ between people, and at different scales, is important for meaningful social science research that speaks back to and challenges austerity as an uneven and discriminative condition. Academics and activists alike cannot afford to be complacent about everyday austerity, or the tools we currently possess to comprehend it. We must continually strive for nuanced and conceptually considerate approaches, situated within everyday lives, to address the injustices it produces.

These issues raise some political challenges for scholars. An investment of time and resources from individuals, institutions and funders is required for research that engages in meaningful, long-term and in-depth studies of contemporary and future crises. With this comes questions about the future of academic research on austerity. While I have no doubt that longitudinal and ethnographic research should be applied to understanding everyday relationships in times of socio-economic change, whether it will be is another matter. These approaches are costly, time consuming and often energy draining; they do not offer a quick or easy fix. At the same time, crises occur within academic institutions and everyday academic life. An increasingly competitive research funding landscape and growing pressures on scholars to teach, research, perform leadership roles and undertake engagement activities (also see Christopherson et al. 2014) makes long-term, fine-grained projects less attractive and practically feasible. These empirical approaches are also thought unlikely to offer the faster and within-budget results that other approaches might promise, and as a result are less frequently chosen.

Readers can, therefore, take this as a plea for conceptually informed, empirically grounded, detailed and ethically sensitive research on austerity and crisis to continue. There might be hurdles and risks with this approach, but there is so much to be gained from the rich and textured contributions this work can make and the meaningful impact it can have. One-off interviews or short-term observations could never have provided the detailed stories upon which the ideas in this book have been built. Placing the experiences and voices of those affected by social and economic change at the very heart of our research, and finding ways for these to be shared and amplified are as important as ever. Austerity is not just out there, it is also in here. It is lived, intimate and so very personal.

Bibliography

Aalbers, M. (2009). The Sociology and Geography of Mortgage Markets: Reflections on the Financial Crisis. *International Journal of Urban and Regional Research, 33*(2), 281–290.

Askins, K. (2014). A Quiet Politics of Being Together: Miriam and Rose. *Area, 46*(4), 353–354.

Castree, N. (2010). The 2007–9 Financial Crisis: Narrating and Politicising a Calamity. *Human Geography, 3*(1), 34–48.

Christophers, B. (2015). Geographies of Finance II: Crisis, Space and Political-Economic Transformation. *Progress in Human Geography, 39*(2), 205–213.

Christopherson, S., Gertler, M., & Gray, M. (2014). Universities in Crisis. *Cambridge Journal of Regions, Economy and Society, 7*, 209–215.

Domosh, M. (2015). How We Hurt Each Other Every Day and What We Might Do About It. *Association of American Geographers Newsletter*. Retrieved December 14, 2018, from http://news.aag.org/2015/05/how-we-hurt-each-other-every-day/.

Elwood, S., & Lawson, V. (2013). Whose Crisis? Spatial Imaginaries of Class, Poverty, and Vulnerability. *Environment and Planning A, 45*, 103–108.

Hall, S. M. (2015). Everyday Ethics of Consumption in the Austere City. *Geography Compass, 9*(3), 140–151.

Hall, S., & Massey, D. (2010). Interpreting the Crisis. *Soundings, 44*(44), 57–71.

Hanisch, C. (1970). The Personal Is Political. In S. Firestone & Koedt (Eds.), *Notes from the Second Year* (pp. 76–78). New York: Published by Editors.

Hinton, E., & Goodman, M. (2010). Sustainable Consumption: Developments, Considerations and New Directions. In M. R. Redclift & G. Woodgate (Eds.), *The International Handbook of Environmental Sociology* (pp. 245–261). London: Edward Elgar.

Horton, J., & Kraftl, P. (2009). Small Acts, Kind Words and "Not Too Much Fuss": Implicit Activisms. *Emotion, Space and Society, 2*(1), 14–23.

Johnson-Hanks, J. (2002). On the Limits of Life Stages in Ethnography: Toward a Theory of Vital Conjunctures. *American anthropologist, 104*(3), 865–880.

Joshi, S., McCutcheon, P., & Sweet, E. (2015). Visceral Geographies of Whiteness and Invisible Microaggressions. *ACME: An International E-Journal for Critical Geographies, 14*(1), 298–323.

Katz, C. (1996). Towards Minor Theory. *Environment and Planning D: Society and Space, 14*, 487–499.

Larner, W. (2011). C-change? Geographies of Crisis. *Dialogues in Human Geography, 1*(3), 319–335.

Massey, D. (1991, June). A Global Sense of Place. *Marxism Today*, pp. 24–29.

Massey, D. (2004). Geographies of Responsibility. *Geografiska Annaler B, 86*(1), 5–18.

Mikhailova, A., & Hymas, C. (2018). "Austerity is Over," Says Philip Hammond as £12 Billion Windfall Sees Spending Increase. *The Telegraph*. Retrieved December 19, 2018, from www.telegraph.co.uk/politics/2018/10/29/austerity-says-philip-hammond-12-billion-windfall-sees-spending/.

Morgan, D. (2009). *Acquaintances: The Space Between Intimates And Strangers: The Space Between Intimates and Strangers*. Maidenhead: McGraw-Hill Education (UK).

Pearson, R., & Elson, D. (2015). Transcending the Impact of the Financial Crisis in the United Kingdom: Towards Plan F—A Feminist Economic Strategy. *Feminist Review, 109*, 8–30.

Peck, J. (2012). Austerity Urbanism: American Cities Under Extreme Economy. *City, 16*(6), 626–655.

Pottinger, L. (2017). Planting the Seeds of a Quiet Activism. *Area, 49*(2), 215–222.

Raynor, R. (2018). Intervention—Changing the Question from "The End of Austerity" to "What Ends in Austerity?" *Antipode Foundation*. Retrieved December 19, 2018, from https://antipodefoundation.org/2018/11/19/what-ends-in-austerity/.

Stacey, J. (1990). *Brave New Families: Stories of Domestic Upheaval in Late-Twentieth-Century America*. Berkeley, CA: University of California Press.

Twigg, J. (2000). Carework as a Form of Bodywork. *Ageing and Society, 20*(4), 389–411.

Watts, J. (2017). Theresa May Signals Austerity Is Over and Overhaul of Brexit Plans. *The Independent*. Retrieved July 31, 2017, from www.independent.co.uk/news/uk/politics/theresa-may-austerity-brexit-plans-uk-leave-eu-hard-soft-latest-tax-cuts-welfare-benefit-a7787001.html.

Women's Budget Group. (2018). A "Jam Tomorrow" Budget': Women's Budget Group Response to Autumn Budget 2018. Retrieved December 19, 2018, from https://wbg.org.uk/wp-content/uploads/2018/11/WBG-2018-Autumn-Budget-full-analysis.pdf.

Zelizer, V. (2005). *The Purchase of Intimacy*. Princeton, NJ: Princeton University Press.

Bibliography

Aalbers, M. (2009). The Sociology and Geography of Mortgage Markets: Reflections on the Financial Crisis. *International Journal of Urban and Regional Research, 33*(2), 281–290.

Ahmed, S. (2004). *The Cultural Politics of Emotion*. Edinburgh: Edinburgh University Press.

Ahmed, S. (2017). *Living a Feminist Life*. Croydon: Duke University Press.

Aitken, S. C. (1998). *Family Fantasies and Community Space*. New Brunswick, NJ: Rutgers University Press.

Allan, G. (1989). *Friendship: Developing a Sociological Perspective*. Brighton: Harvester and Wheatsheaf.

Anderson, B., & McFarlane, C. (2011). Assemblage and Geography. *Area, 43*(2), 124–127.

Andrews, G. J., & Chen, S. (2006). The Production of Tyrannical Space. *Children's Geographies, 4*(2), 239–250.

Askins, K. (2014). A Quiet Politics of Being Together: Miriam and Rose. *Area, 46*(4), 353–354.

Askins, K. (2015). Being Together: Everyday Geographies and the Quiet Politics of Belonging. *ACME: An International E-Journal for Critical Geographies, 14*(2), 470–478.

Bailey, A. J. (2009). Population Geography: Lifecourse Matters. *Progress in Human Geography, 33*(3), 407–418.

S. M. Hall, *Everyday Life in Austerity*, Palgrave Macmillan Studies in Family and Intimate Life, https://doi.org/10.1007/978-3-030-17094-3

Ballas, D., Dorling, D., & Hennig, B. (2017). Analysing the Regional Geography of Poverty, Austerity and Inequality in Europe: A Human Cartographic Perspective. *Regional Studies, 51*(1), 174–185.

Barnett, C., & Land, D. (2007). Geographies of Generosity: Beyond the "Moral Turn". *Geoforum, 38*, 1065–1075.

Bartos, A. E. (2013). Friendship and Environmental Politics in Childhood. *Space and Polity, 17*(1), 17–32.

Bayat, A. (2000). From "Dangerous Classes" to "Quiet Rebels": Politics of the Urban Subaltern in the Global South. *International Sociology, 15*(3), 533–557.

Beck, U., & Beck-Gernsheim, E. (2002). *Individualization*. London: Sage.

Bell, S., & Coleman, S. (1999). *The Anthropology of Friendship*. Oxford: Berg.

Binnie, J., Edensor, T., Holloway, J., Millington, S., & Young, C. (2007). Mundane Mobilities, Banal Travels. *Social & Cultural Geography, 8*(2), 165–174.

Blake, M. K. (2007). Formality and Friendship: Research Ethics Review and Participatory Action Research. *Acme, 6*(3), 411–421.

Blunt, A. (2005). Cultural Geography: Cultural Geographies of Home. *Progress in Human Geography, 29*(4), 505–515.

Bornat, J., & Bytheway, B. (2010). Late Life Reflections on the Downturn: Perspectives from The Oldest Generation. *Twenty-First Century Society, 5*(2), 183–192.

Bott, E. (1957). *Family and Social Network: Roles, Norms, and External Relationships in Ordinary Urban Families*. London: Tavistock Publications.

Bowlby, S. (2011). Friendship, Co-presence and Care: Neglected Spaces. *Social & Cultural Geography, 12*(6), 605–622.

Bowlby, S. (2012). Recognising the Time-Space Dimensions of Care: Caringscapes and Carescapes. *Environment and Planning A, 44*, 2101–2118.

Bradley, H. (1986). Work, Home and the Restructuring of Jobs. In K. Purcell, S. Wood, A. Waton, & S. Allen (Eds.), *The Changing Experience of Employment: Restructuring and Recession* (pp. 95–113). London: Macmillan.

Braithwaite, A. (2002). The Personal, the Political, Third Wave and Postfeminisms. *Feminist Theory, 3*(3), 335–344.

Braun, B. (2006). Environmental Issues: Global Natures in the Space of Assemblage. *Progress in Human Geography, 30*(5), 644–654.

Brewster, L. (2014). The Public Library as Therapeutic Landscape: A Qualitative Case Study. *Health & Place, 26*, 94–99.

Bridge, G. (1997). Towards a Situated Universalism: On Strategic Rationality and "Local Theory". *Environment and Planning D: Society and Space, 15*, 633–639.

Bridge, G., & Smith, A. (2003). Intimate Encounters: Culture—Economy—Commodity. *Environment and Planning D: Society and Space, 21*, 257–268.

Broadbent, S. (2009). How the Internet Enables Intimacy. *Technology, Entertainment, Design (TED) Talks*. Retrieved August 28, 2015, from www.ted.com/talks/stefana_broadbent_how_the_internet_enables_intimacy.

Brown, G. (2015). Marriage and the Spare Bedroom Tax: Exploring the Sexual Politics of Austerity in Britain. *ACME: An International e-Journal for Critical Geographies, 14*(4), 975–988.

Browne, K. (2003). Negotiations and Fieldworkings: Friendship and Feminist Research. *ACME: An International E-Journal for Critical Geographies, 2*(2), 132–146.

Bunnell, T., Yea, S., Peake, L., Skelton, T., & Smith, M. (2012). Geographies of Friendships. *Progress in Human Geography, 36*(4), 490–507.

Burrell, K. (2011). Opportunity and Uncertainty: Young People's Narratives of "Double Transition" in Post-Socialist Poland. *Area, 43*(4), 413–419.

Burrell, K. (2017). The Recalcitrance of Distance: Exploring the Infrastructures of Sending in Migrants' Lives. *Mobilities, 12*(6), 813–826.

Butterworth, J., & Burton, J. (2013). Equality, Human Rights and the Public Service Spending Cuts: Do UK Welfare Cuts Violate the Equal Right to Social Security? *Equal Rights Review, 11*, 26–45.

Cahill, C. (2007). The Personal is Political: Developing New Subjectivities Through Participatory Action Research. *Gender, Place & Culture, 14*(3), 267–292.

Castree, N. (2009). Crisis, Continuity and Change: Neoliberalism, the Left and the Future of Capitalism. *Antipode, 41*(1), 185–213.

Castree, N. (2010). The 2007–9 Financial Crisis: Narrating and Politicising a Calamity. *Human Geography, 3*(1), 34–48.

Charles, N. (2000). *Feminism, the State and Social Policy*. Basingstoke: Palgrave.

Charles, N., & Davies, C. A. (2008). My Family and Other Animals. *Sociological Research Online, 13*(5), 4.

Christophers, B. (2015). Geographies of Finance II: Crisis, Space and Political-Economic Transformation. *Progress in Human Geography, 39*(2), 205–213.

Christophers, B. (2018). Intergenerational Inequality? Labour, Capital and Housing Through the Ages. *Antipode, 50*(1), 101–121.

Christopherson, S., Gertler, M., & Gray, M. (2014). Universities in Crisis. *Cambridge Journal of Regions, Economy and Society, 7*, 209–215.

Clayton, J., Donovan, C., & Macdonald, S. J. (2016). A Critical Portrait of Hate Crime/Incident Reporting in North East England: The Value of Statistical Data and the Politics of Recording in an Age of Austerity. *Geoforum, 75*, 64–74.

Cloke, P., May, J., & Williams, A. (2016). The Geographies of Food Banks in the Meantime. *Progress in Human Geography*. https://doi.org/10.1177/0309132516655881.

Coakley, L. (2002). "All Over the Place, in Town, in the Pub, Everywhere": A Social Geography of Women's Friendships in Cork. *Irish Geography, 35*(1), 40–50.

Cohen, R. L. (2010). When It Pays to Be Friendly: Employment Relationships and Emotional Labour in Hairstyling. *Sociological Review, 58*(2), 197–218.

Conradson, D. (2003). Geographies of Care: Spaces, Practices, Experiences. *Social & Cultural Geography, 4*(4), 451–454.

Conradson, D., & Latham, A. (2005). Friendship, Networks and Transnationality in a World City: Antipodean Transmigrants in London. *Journal of Ethnic and Migration Studies, 31*(2), 287–305.

Cox, R., & Narula, R. (2003). Playing Happy Families: Rules and Relationships in Au Pair Employing Households in London, England. *Gender Place and Culture, 10*, 333–344.

Crang, M. (1994). It's Showtime: On the Workplace Geographies of Display in a Restaurant in Southeast England. *Environment and Planning D: Society & Space, 12*, 675–704.

Daly, M., & Lewis, J. (2000). The Concept of Social Care and the Analysis of Contemporary Welfare States. *British Journal of Sociology, 51*(2), 281–298.

Davidson, M., & Ward, K. (2014). "Picking Up the Pieces": Austerity Urbanism California and Fiscal Crisis. *Cambridge Journal of Regions, Economy and Society, 7*(1), 81–97.

Davies, C. A. (2008). *Reflexive Ethnography: A Guide to Researching Selves and Others*. London: Routledge.

de Certeau, M. (1984). *The Practice of Everyday Life*. Berkeley, CA: University of California Press.

Derickson, K. D. (2016). Urban Geography II: Urban Geography in the Age of Ferguson. *Progress in Human Geography, 41*(2), 230–244.

Devault, M. (1991). *Feeding the Family: The Social Organisation of Caring as Gendered Work*. London: The University of Chicago Press.

Dicken, P. (2004). Geographers and 'Globalization': (Yet) Another Missed Boat? *Transactions of the Institute of British Geographers, 29*, 5–26.

Di Feliciantonio, C. (2016). Subjectification in Times of Indebtedness and Neoliberal/Austerity Urbanism. *Antipode, 48*(5), 1206–1227.

Domosh, M. (1997). Geography and Gender: The Personal and the Political. *Progress in Human Geography, 21*(1), 81–87.

Domosh, M. (1998). Geography and Gender: Home, Again? *Progress in Human Geography, 22*(2), 276–282.

Domosh, M. (2015). How We Hurt Each Other Every Day and What We Might Do About It. *Association of American Geographers Newsletter*. Retrieved December 14, 2018, from http://news.aag.org/2015/05/how-we-hurt-each-other-every-day/.

Donald, B., Glasmeier, A., Gray, M., & Lobao, L. (2014). Austerity in the City: Economic Crisis and Urban Service Decline? *Cambridge Journal of Regions. Economy and Society, 7*(1), 3–15.

Duffy, M. (2011). *Making Care Count: A Century of Gender, Race, and Paid Care Work*. London: Rutgers University Press.

Dyck, I. (2005). Feminist Geography, the "Everyday", and Local-Global Relations: Hidden Spaces of Place-Making. *The Canadian Geographer, 49*, 233–245.

Edwards, J. (2000). *Born and Bred: Idioms of Kinship and New Reproductive Technologies in England*. Oxford: Oxford University Press.

Edwards, R., & Gillies, V. (2004). Support in Parenting: Values and Consensus Concerning Who To Turn To. *Journal of Social Policy, 33*(4), 627–647.

Edwards, R., & Gillies, V. (2012). Farewell to Family? Notes on an Argument for Retaining the Concept. *Families, Relationships and Societies, 1*(1), 63–69.

Edwards, R., & Weller, S. (2010). Trajectories from Youth to Adulthood: Choice and Structure for Young People Before and During Recession. *Twenty-First Century Society, 5*(2), 125–136.

Ellegard, K., & De Pater, B. (1999). The Complex Tapestry of Everyday Life. *GeoJournal, 48*(3), 149–153.

Elwood, S., & Lawson, V. (2013). Whose Crisis? Spatial Imaginaries of Class, Poverty, and Vulnerability. *Environment and Planning A, 45*, 103–108.

Emerson, R., Fretz, R., & Shaw, C. (1995). *Writing Ethnographic Fieldnotes*. Chicago, IL: University of Chicago Press.

Emmel, N., & Hughes, K. (2010). "Recession, It's All the Same to Us Son": The Longitudinal Experience (1999–2010) of Deprivation. *Twenty-First Century Society, 5*(2), 171–181.

Engelen, E., & Falconbridge, J. (2009). Introduction: Financial Geographies—The Credit Crisis as an Opportunity to Catch Economic Geography's Next Boat? *Journal of Economic Geography, 9*, 587–595.

England, K. V. L. (1994). Getting Personal: Reflexivity Positionality and Feminist Research. *The Professional Geographer, 46*, 80–89.

England, K. (2010). Home, Work and the Shifting Geographies of Care. *Ethics, Place & Environment, 13*(2), 131–150.

England, K., & Dyck, I. (2011). Managing the Body Work of Home Care. *Sociology of Health & Illness, 33*(2), 206–219.

Etherington, D., & Jones, M. (2017) *Devolution, Austerity and Inclusive Growth in Greater Manchester: Assessing Impacts and Developing Alternatives*. Hendon: CEEDR, Middlesex University. Retrieved July 13, 2018, from www.mdx.ac.uk/__data/assets/pdf_file/0030/368373/Greater-Manchester-Report.pdf.

Eurofound. (2014). *Third European Quality of Life Survey—Quality of Life in Europe: Families in the Economic Crisis*. Luxembourg: Publications Office of the European Union.

Evans, R. (2012). Sibling Caringscapes: Time-Space Practices of Caring Within Youth-Headed Households in Tanzania and Uganda. *Geoforum, 43*(4), 824–835.

Evans, R. (2014). Parental Death as a Vital Conjuncture? Intergenerational Care and Responsibility Following Bereavement in Senegal. *Social & Cultural Geography, 15*, 547–570.

Fields, D. (2017). Unwilling Subjects of Financialisation. *International Journal of Urban and Regional Research, 41*(4), 588–603.

Fields, D., Libman, K., & Saegert, S. (2010). Turning Everywhere, Getting Nowhere: Experiences of Seeking Help for Mortgage Delinquency and Their Implications for Foreclosure Prevention. *The International History Review, 20*(4), 647–686.

Finch, J., & Mason, J. (1993). *Negotiating Family Responsibilities*. London: Routledge.

Fisher, B., & Tronto, J. (1990). Toward a Feminist Theory of Caring. In E. Abel & M. Nelson (Eds.), *Circles of Care* (pp. 36–54). Albany: SUNY Press.

Fodor, E. (2006). A Different Type of Gender Gap: How Women and Men Experience Poverty. *East European Politics and Societies: And Cultures, 20*(1), 14–39.

Fox, E. (2006). Animal Behaviours, Post-Human Lives: Everyday Negotiations of the Animal-Human Divide in Pet-Keeping. *Social and Cultural Geography, 7*(4), 525–537.

French, S., & Leyshon, A. (2010). "These F@#king Guys": The Terrible Waste of a Good Crisis. *Environment and Planning A, 42*, 2549–2559.

French, S., Leyshon, A., & Thrift, N. (2009). A Very Geographical Crisis: The Making and Breaking of the 2007–2008 Financial Crisis. *Cambridge Journal of Regions, Economy and Society, 2*, 287–302.

García-Lamarca, M., & Kaika, M. (2017). "Mortgaged Lives": The Biopolitics of Debt and Housing Financialisation. *Transactions of the Institute of British Geographers, 41*, 313–327.

Gardiner, M. (2000). *Critiques of Everyday Life*. London and New York: Routledge.

Garthwaite, K. (2016). *Hunger Pains: Life Inside Foodbank Britain*. Bristol: Policy Press.

Giddens, A. (1992). *The Transformation of Intimacy: Sexuality, Love and Eroticism in Modern Societies*. Cambridge: Polity.

Gillies, V. (2005). Meeting Parents' Needs? Discourses of "Support" and "Inclusion" in Family Policy. *Critical Social Policy, 25*, 70–90.

Gillis, J. R. (1996). *A World of Their Own Making: Myth, Ritual, and the Quest for Family Values*. New York: Basic Books.

Greer-Murphy, A. (2017). Austerity in the United Kingdom: The Intersections of Spatial and Gendered Inequalities. *Area, 49*(1), 122–124.

Gregson, N., & Rose, G. (1997). Contested and Negotiated Histories of Feminist Geographies. In Women and Geography Study Group (Ed.), *Feminist Geographies: Explorations of Diversity and Difference*. Harlow: Addison Wesley Longman.

Hackney, F. (2013). Quiet Activism and the New Amateur: The Power of Home and Hobby Crafts. *Design and Culture, 5*, 169–193.

Hall, S. M. (2009). "Private Life" and "Work Life": Difficulties and Dilemmas When Making and Maintaining Friendships with Ethnographic Participants. *Area, 41*, 263–272.

Hall, S. (2010). Geographies of Money and Finance I: Cultural Economy, Politics and Place. *Progress in Human Geography, 35*, 234–245.

Hall, S. M. (2014). Ethics of Ethnography with Families: A Geographical Perspective. *Environment and Planning A, 46*(9), 2175–2194.

Hall, S. M. (2015). Everyday Ethics of Consumption in the Austere City. *Geography Compass, 9*(3), 140–151.

Hall, S. M. (2016a). Everyday Family Experiences of the Financial Crisis: Getting by in the Recent Economic Recession. *Journal of Economic Geography, 16*(2), 305–330.

Hall, S. M. (2016b). Moral Geographies of Family: Articulating, Forming and Transmitting Moralities in Everyday Life. *Social & Cultural Geography, 17*(8), 1017–1039.

Hall, S. M. (2016c). Family Relations in Times of Austerity: Reflections from the UK. In S. Punch, R. Vanderbeck, & T. Skelton (Eds.), *Geographies of Children and Young People: Families, Intergenerationality and Peer Group Relations*. Berlin: Springer.

Hall, S. M. (2017). Personal, Relational and Intimate Geographies of Austerity: Ethical and Empirical Considerations. *Area, 49*(3), 303–310.

Hall, S. M., & Holdsworth, C. (2016). Family Practices, Holiday and the Everyday. *Mobilities, 11*(2), 284–302.

Hall, S. M., & Holmes, H. (2017). Making Do and Getting By? Beyond a Romantic Politics of Austerity and Crisis. *Discover Society*, p. 44. Retrieved from https://discoversociety.org/2017/05/02/making-do-and-getting-by-beyond-a-romantic-politics-of-austerity-and-crisis/.

Hall, S. M., & Jayne, M. (2016). Make, Mend and Befriend: Geographies of Austerity, Crafting and Friendship in Contemporary Cultures of Dressmaking. *Gender, Place & Culture, 23*(2), 216–234.

Hall, S., & Massey, D. (2010). Interpreting the Crisis. *Soundings, 44*(44), 57–71.

Hall, S. M., McIntosh, K., Neitzert, E., Pottinger, L., Sandhu, K., Stephenson, M.-A., Reed, H., & Taylor, L. (2017). *Intersecting Inequalities: The Impact of Austerity on Black and Minority Ethnic Women in the UK*. London: Runnymede and Women's Budget Group. Retrieved from www.intersecting-inequalities.com.

Hammersley, M., & Atkinson, P. (1983). *Ethnography: Principles in Practice*. London: Routledge.

Hanisch, C. (1970). The Personal Is Political. In S. Firestone & Koedt (Eds.), *Notes from the Second Year* (pp. 76–78). New York: Published by Editors.

Hanisch, C. (2006). *The Personal Is Political: The Women's Liberation Movement Classic with a New Explanatory Introduction*. Retrieved April 10, 2018, from http://www.carolhanisch.org/CHwritings/PIP.html.

Hankins, K. (2017). Creative Democracy and the Quiet Politics of the Everyday. *Urban Geography*. https://doi.org/10.1080/02723638.2016.1272197.

Haraway, D. J. (1997). *Modest_Witness@Second_Millennium: Femaleman_Meets_Oncomouse: Feminism and Technoscience*. New York: Routledge.

Haraway, D. J. (2008). *When Species Meet*. Minneapolis, MN: University of Minnesota Press.

Harker, C., & Martin, L. L. (2012). Familial Relations: Spaces, Subjects, and Politics. *Environment and Planning A, 44*(4), 768–775.

Harrison, E. (2013). Bouncing Back? Recession, Resilience and Everyday Lives. *Critical Social Policy, 33*(1), 97–113.

Heath, S., & Calvert, E. (2013). Gifts, Loans and Intergenerational Support for Young Adults. *Sociology, 47*, 1120–1135.

Held, V. (1993). *Feminist Morality: Transforming Culture, Society and Politics*. Chicago, IL: University of Chicago Press.

Hemmings, S., Silva, E., & Thompson, K. (2002). Accounting for the Everyday. In T. Bennett & D. Watson (Eds.), *Understanding Everyday Life* (pp. 271–315). Oxford: Blackwell Publishers.

Henwood, K., Shirani, F., & Coltart, C. (2010). Fathers and Financial Risk-Taking During the Economic Downturn: Insights from a QLL Study of Men's Identities-in-the-Making. *Twenty- First Century Society, 5*(2), 137–147.

Herbert, S. (2000). For Ethnography. *Progress in Human Geography, 24*, 550–568.

Hinton, E., & Goodman, M. (2010). Sustainable Consumption: Developments, Considerations and New Directions. In M. R. Redclift & G. Woodgate (Eds.), *The International Handbook of Environmental Sociology* (pp. 245–261). London: Edward Elgar.

Hitchen, E. (2016). Living and Feeling the Austere. *New Formations, 87*, 102–118.

HM Treasury. (2015). *Summer Budget 2015*. Retrieved July 13, 2015, from http://www.gov.uk/government/publications/summer-budget-2015/summer-budget-2015.

Hochschild, A. R. (1983). *The Managed Heart: Commercialization of Human Feeling*. Berkeley, CA: University of California Press.

Hochstenbach, C. (2018). Spatializing the Intergenerational Transmission of Inequalities: Parental Wealth, Residential Segregation, and Urban Inequality. *Environment and Planning A, 50*(3), 689–708.

Holdsworth, C. (2013). *Family and Intimate Mobilities*. Basingstoke: Palgrave Macmillan.

Holloway, S. L. (1998). Local Childcare Cultures: Moral Geographies of Mothering and the Social Organisation of Pre-school Education. *Gender, Place & Culture, 5*, 29–53.

Holloway, S. L., & Pimlott-Wilson, H. (2014). "Any Advice is Welcome Isn't It?": Neoliberal Parenting Education, Local Mothering Cultures, and Social Class. *Environment and Planning A, 46*(1), 94–111.

Holmes, H. (2015). Transient Craft: Reclaiming the Contemporary Craft Worker. *Work, Employment and Society, 29*(3), 479–495.

Holmes, H. (2018a). New Spaces, Ordinary Practices: Circulating and Sharing Within Diverse Economies of Provisioning. *Geoforum, 88*, 134–147.

Holmes, H. (2018b). Material Affinities: "Doing" Family Through the Practices of Passing On. *Sociology, 53*(1), 174–191.

Holmes, H. (2018c). Transient Productions; Enduring Encounters: The Crafting of Bodies and Friendships in the Hair Salon. In L. Price & H. Hawkins (Eds.), *Geographies of Making, Craft and Creativity*. London: Routledge.

hooks, b. (1981). *Ain't I a Woman? Black Women and Feminism*. Boston: South End Press.

Hopkins, P., & Pain, R. (2007). Geographies of Age: Thinking Relationally. *Area, 39*(3), 287–294.

Hörschelmann, K. (2011). Theorising Life Transitions: Geographical Perspectives. *Area, 43*(4), 378–383.

Hörschelmann, K., & van Blerk, L. (2012). *Children, Youth and the City*. Abingdon: Routledge.

Horton, J. (2016). Anticipating Service Withdrawal: Young People in Spaces of Neoliberalisation, Austerity and Economic Crisis. *Transactions of the Institute of British Geographers, 41*(4), 349–362.

Horton, J. (2017). Young People and Debt: Getting on with Austerities. *Area, 49*(3), 280–287.

Horton, J., & Kraftl, P. (2009). Small Acts, Kind Words and "Not Too Much Fuss": Implicit Activisms. *Emotion, Space and Society, 2*(1), 14–23.

Howard, A. L. (2014). *More than Shelter: Activism and Community in San Francisco Public Housing*. Minneapolis, MN: University of Minnesota Press.

Hubbard, P. (2001). Sex Zones: Intimacy, Citizenship and Public Space. *Sexualities, 4*(1), 51–71.

Hyndman, J. (2004). Mind the Gap: Bridging Feminist and Political Geography Through Geopolitics. *Political Geography, 23*(3), 307–322.

Jackson, A. (Ed.). (1987). *Anthropology at Home*. London: Tavistock Publications.

Jackson, P. (2009). Introduction: Food as a Lens on Family Life. In P. Jackson (Ed.), *Changing Families, Changing Food* (pp. 1–16). Basingstoke: Palgrave Macmillan.

Jackson, L. (2016). Intimate Citizenship? Rethinking the Politics and Experience of Citizenship as Emotional in Wales and Singapore. *Gender, Place & Culture, 23*(6), 817–833.

Jackson, L., Harris, C., & Valentine, G. (2017). Rethinking Concepts of the Strange and the Stranger. *Social & Cultural Geography, 18*(1), 1–15.

James, A., & Curtis, P. (2010). Family Displays and Personal Lives. *Sociology, 44*(6), 1163–1180.

Jamieson, L. (1997). *Intimacy: Personal Relationships in Modern Societies*. Cambridge: Polity Press.

Jamieson, L. (1999). Intimacy Transformed? A Critical Look at the 'Pure Relationship'. *Sociology, 33*(3), 477–494.

Jarvis, H. (2005). Moving to London Time. *Time & Society, 14*(1), 133–154.

Jayne, M., & Leung, H. H. (2014). Embodying Chinese Urbanism: Towards a Research Agenda. *Area, 46*(3), 256–267.

Jenkins, R. (1984). Bringing It All Back Home: An Anthropologist in Belfast. In C. Bell & H. Roberts (Eds.), *Social Researching: Politics, Problems, Practice* (pp. 147–164). London: Routledge and Kegan Paul.

Jensen, T., & Tyler, I. (2012). Austerity Parenting: New Economies of Parent-Citizenship. *Studies in the Maternal, 4*(2), 1–5.

Johnson, L., & Longhurst, R. (2010). *Space, Place and Sex: Geographies of Sexualities*. Plymouth: Rowman and Littlefield.

Johnson-Hanks, J. (2002). On the Limits of Life Stages in Ethnography: Toward a Theory of Vital Conjunctures. *American anthropologist, 104*(3), 865–880.

Jones, M. (2009). Phase Space: Geography, Relational Thinking, and Beyond. *Progress in Human Geography, 33*(4), 487–506.

Joshi, S., McCutcheon, P., & Sweet, E. (2015). Visceral Geographies of Whiteness and Invisible Microaggressions. *ACME: An International E-Journal for Critical Geographies, 14*(1), 298–323.

JRF. (2015). *The Cost of the Cuts: The Impact on Local Government and Poorer Communities*. Retrieved July 17, 2015, from http://www.jrf.org.uk/sites/files/jrf/CostofCuts-Full.pdf.

Jupp, E. (2013a). Enacting Parenting Policy? The Hybrid Spaces of Sure Start Children's Centres. *Children's Geographies, 11*(2), 173–187.

Jupp, E. (2013b). "I Feel More at Home Here than in My Own Community": Approaching the Emotional Geographies of Neighbourhood Policy. *Critical Social Policy, 33*, 532–553.

Jupp, E. (2017). Home Space, Gender and Activism: The Visible and the Invisible in Austere Times. *Critical Social Policy, 37*(3), 348–366.

Katz, C. (1996). Towards Minor Theory. *Environment and Planning D: Society and Space, 14*, 487–499.

Kirwan, S. F., McDermont, M. A., & Clarke, J. (2016). Imagining and Practising Citizenship in Austere Times: The Work of Citizens Advice. *Citizenship Studies, 20*(6–7), 764–778.

Kitson, M., Martin, R., & Tyler, P. (2011). The Geographies of Austerity. *Cambridge Journal of Regions. Economy and Society, 4*(3), 289–302.

Kraftl, P., & Horton, J. (2007). "The Health Event": Everyday, Affective Politics of Participation. *Geoforum, 38*(5), 1012–1027.

Krumer-Nevo, M. (2017). Poverty and the Political: Wresting the Political Out of and Into Social Work Theory, Research and Practice. *European Journal of Social Work, 20*(6), 811–822.

Lambie-Mumford, H., & Green, M. A. (2015). Austerity, Welfare Reform and the Rising Use of Food Banks by Children in England and Wales. *Area*. https://doi.org/10.1111/area.12233.

Langley, P. (2008). *The Everyday Life of Global Finance: Saving and Borrowing in America*. Oxford: Oxford University Press.

Larner, W. (2011). C-change? Geographies of Crisis. *Dialogues in Human Geography, 1*(3), 319–335.

Lawson, V. (2007). Geographies of Care and Responsibility. *Annals of the Association of American Geographers, 97*(1), 1–11.

Leach, R., Phillipson, C., Biggs, S. and Money, A. (2013) 'Babyboomers, consumption and social change: the bridging generation?', *International Review of Sociology, 23*(1), 104–122.

Lee, R., Clark, G. L., Pollard, J., & Leyshon, A. (2009). The Remit of Financial Geography—Before and After the Crisis. *Journal of Economic Geography, 9*, 723–747.

Lefebvre, H. (1991). *Critique of Everyday Life Volume I [1947]*. New York: Verso.

Lewis, C. (2018). Making Community Through the Exchange of Material Things. *Journal of Material Culture, 23*(3), 295–311.

Longhurst, R. (2008). The Geography Closest In—The Body … The Politics of Pregnability. *Australian Geographical Studies, 32*(2), 214–223.

Longhurst, R., Ho, E., & Johnston, L. (2008). Using "The Body" as an "Instrument of Research": Kimch'i and Pavlova. *Area, 40*(2), 208–217.

Lumsden, K. (2009). "Don't Ask a Woman to Do Another Woman's Job": Gendered Interactions and the Emotional Ethnographer. *Sociology, 43*(3), 497–513.

MacLeavy, J. (2011). A "New" Politics of Austerity, Workfare and Gender? The UK Coalition Government's Welfare Reform Proposals. *Cambridge Journal of Regions, Economy and Society, 4*, 355–367.

MacLeavy, J., & Manley, D. (2018). (Re)discovering the Lost Middle: Intergenerational Inheritances and Economic Inequality in Urban and Regional Research. *Regional Studies, 52*(10), 1435–1446.

Madge, C., & O'Connor, H. (2006). Parenting Gone Wired: Empowerment of New Mothers on the Internet? *Social & Cultural Geography, 7*(2), 199–220.

Mann, J. (2015). Towards a Politics of Whimsy: Yarn Bombing the City. *Area, 47*(1), 65–72.

Martin, R. (2011). The Local Geographies of the Financial Crisis: From the Housing Bubble to Economic Recession and Beyond. *Journal of Economic Geography, 11*, 587–618.

Massey, D. (1991, June). A Global Sense of Place. *Marxism Today*, pp. 24–29.

Massey, D. (2004). Geographies of Responsibility. *Geografiska Annaler B, 86*(1), 5–18.

May, V. (2011). *Sociology of Personal Life*. Basingstoke: Palgrave Macmillan.

McDowell, L. (2012). Post-Crisis, Post-Ford and Post-Gender? Youth Identities in an Era of Austerity. *Journal of Youth Studies, 15*(5), 573–590.

McDowell, L. (2017). Youth, Children and Families in Austere Times: Change, Politics and a New Gender Contract. *Area, 49*(3), 311–316.

McDowell, L., Ray, K., Perrons, D., Fagan, C., & Ward, K. (2005). Women's Paid Work and Moral Economies of Care. *Social & Cultural Geography, 6*, 219–235.

McEwan, C., & Goodman, M. (2010). Place Geography and the Ethics of Care: Introductory Remarks on the Geographies of Ethics, Responsibility and Care. *Ethics, Place and Environment, 13*(2), 103–112.

Mikhailova, A., & Hymas, C. (2018). "Austerity is Over," Says Philip Hammond as £12 Billion Windfall Sees Spending Increase. *The Telegraph*. Retrieved December 19, 2018, from www.telegraph.co.uk/politics/2018/10/29/austerity-says-philip-hammond-12-billion-windfall-sees-spending/.

Millar, J., & Ridge, T. (2013). Lone Mothers and Paid Work: The "Family-Work Project". *International Review of Sociology, 23*(3), 564–577.

Milligan, C. (2003). Location or Dis-Location? Towards a Conceptualization of People and Place in the Care-Giving Experience. *Social & Cultural Geography, 4*(4), 455–470.

Mitchell, K. (2007). Geographies of Identity: The Intimate Cosmopolitan. *Progress in Human Geography, 31*(5), 706–720.

Mizen, P., & Ofosu-Kusi, Y. (2010). Asking, Giving, Receiving: Friendship as Survival Strategy Among Accra's Street Children. *Childhood, 17*(4), 441–454.

Morgan, D. (2009). *Acquaintances: The Space Between Intimates And Strangers: The Space Between Intimates and Strangers*. Maidenhead: McGraw-Hill Education (UK).

Morgan, D. (2011). *Rethinking Family Practices*. Basingstoke: Palgrave Macmillan.

Morris, J. (1992). Personal and Political: A Feminist Perspective on Researching Physical Disability. *Disability, Handicap & Society, 7*(2), 157–166.

Morrison, C., Johnston, L., & Longhurst, R. (2012). Critical Geographies of Love as Spatial, Relational and Political. *Progress in Human Geography, 37*(4), 505–521.

Morris-Roberts, K. (2001). Intervening in Friendship Exclusion? The Politics of Doing Feminist Research with Teenage Girls. *Ethics, Place & Environment, 4*(2), 147–153.

Morris-Roberts, K. (2004). Girls' Friendships, "Distinctive Individuality" and Socio-Spatial Practices of (Dis)identification. *Children's Geographies, 2*(2), 237–255.

Moss, P. (2001). Writing One's Life. In P. Moss (Ed.), *Placing Autobiography in Geography* (pp. 1–21). Syracuse, NY: Syracuse University Press.

Mountz, A., Bonds, A., Mansfield, B., Loyd, J., Hyndman, J., Walton-Roberts, M., Basu, R., Whitson, R., Hawkins, R., Hamilton, T., & Curran, W. (2015).

For Slow Scholarship: A Feminist Politics of Resistance Through Collective Action in the Neoliberal University. *ACME, 14*(4), 1235–1259.

Mullings, B., Peake, L., & Parizeau, K. (2016). Cultivating an Ethic of Wellness in Geography. *The Canadian Geographer, 60*(2), 161–167.

Nash, C. (2005). Geographies of Relatedness. *Transactions of the Institute of British Geographers, 30*(4), 449–462.

Nast, H. J. (2006). Critical Pet Studies? *Antipode, 38*(5), 894–906.

Neal, S., & Vincent, C. (2013). Multiculture, Middle Class Competencies and Friendship Practices in Super-Diverse Geographies. *Social & Cultural Geography, 14*(8), 909–929.

Nelson, G. D. (2018). Mosaic and Tapestry: Metaphors as Geographical Concept Generators. *Progress in Human Geography*. https://doi.org/10.1177/0309132518788951.

Newman, M., Woodcock, A., & Dunham, P. (2006). "Playtime in the Borderlands": Children's Representations of School, Gender and Bullying Through Photographs and Interviews. *Children's Geographies, 4*(3), 289–302.

Oakley, A. (1981). Interviewing Women: A Contradiction in Terms. In H. Roberts (Ed.), *Doing Feminist Research* (pp. 30–61). London: Routledge.

Oswin, N., & Olund, E. (2010). Governing Intimacy. *Environment and Planning D: Society and Space, 28*(1), 60–67.

Pahl, R. (1984). *Divisions of Labour*. Oxford: Blackwell.

Pahl, R. (2000). *On Friendship*. Cambridge: Polity Press.

Pain, R. (2004). Social Geography: Participatory Research. *Progress in Human Geography, 28*(5), 652–663.

Pain, R., & Smith, S. (2008). *Fear: Critical Geopolitics and Everyday Life*. Abingdon: Ashgate.

Pain, R., & Staeheli, L. (2014). Introduction: Intimacy Geo-politics and Violence. *Area, 46*(4), 344–347.

Parrenas, R. (2005). Long Distance Intimacy: Class, Gender and Intergenerational Relations Between Mothers and Children in Filipino Transnational Families. *Global Networks, 5*(4), 317–336.

Pearson, R., & Elson, D. (2015). Transcending the Impact of the Financial Crisis in the United Kingdom: Towards Plan F—A Feminist Economic Strategy. *Feminist Review, 109*, 8–30.

Peck, J. (2012). Austerity Urbanism: American Cities Under Extreme Economy. *City, 16*(6), 626–655.

Pessar, P. R., & Mahler, S. J. (2003). Transnational Migration: Bringing Gender In. *International Migration Review, 37*(3), 812–846.

Pike, A., Coombes, M., O'Brien, P., & Tomaney, J. (2018). Austerity States, Institutional Dismantling and the Governance of Subnational Economic Development: The Demise of the Regional Development Agencies in England. *Territory, Politics, Governance*, 6(1), 118–144.

Pimlott-Wilson, H. (2017). Individualising the Future: The Emotional Geographies of Neoliberal Governance in Young Peoples' Aspirations. *Area, 49*(3), 288–295.

Pimlott-Wilson, H., & Hall, S. M. (2017). Everyday Experiences of Economic Change: Repositioning Geographies of Children, Youth and Families. *Area, 49*(3), 258–265.

Pinkerton, J., & Dolan, P. (2007). Family Support, Social Capital, Resilience and Adolescent Coping. *Child and Family Social Work, 12*(3), 219–228.

Pollard, J. S. (2013). Gendering Capital: Financial Crisis, Financialization and an Agenda for Economic Geography. *Progress in Human Geography, 37*, 403–423.

Popke, J. (2006). Geography and Ethics: Everyday Mediations Through Care and Consumption. *Progress in Human Geography, 30*(4), 504–512.

Pottinger, L. (2017). Planting the Seeds of a Quiet Activism. *Area, 49*(2), 215–222.

Pottinger, L. (2018). Growing, Guarding and Generous Exchange in an Analogue Sharing Economy. *Geoforum, 96*, 108–118.

Powdermaker, H. (1966). *Stranger and Friend: The Way of an Anthropologist.* New York: WW Norton & Company.

Power, E. (2008). Furry Families: Making a Human-Dog Family Through Home. *Social & Cultural Geography, 9*(5), 535–555.

Power, A., & Hall, E. (2018). Placing Care in Times of Austerity. *Social & Cultural Geography, 19*(3), 303–313.

Pratt, G. (1997). Stereotypes and Ambivalence: The Construction of Domestic Workers in Vancouver, British Columbia. *Gender, Place and Culture, 4*(2), 159–178.

Price, P. L. (2012). Race and Ethnicity II: Skin and Other Intimacies. *Progress in Human Geography, 37*(4), 578–586.

Pugh, R. (2018). Who Speaks for Economic Geography? *Environment and Planning A: Economy and Society, 50*(7), 1525–1531.

Raynor, R. (2018). Intervention—Changing the Question from "The End of Austerity" to "What Ends in Austerity?" *Antipode Foundation*. Retrieved December 19, 2018, from https://antipodefoundation.org/2018/11/19/what-ends-in-austerity/.

Reed-Danahay, D. (2009). Anthropologists, Education, and Autoethnography. *Reviews in Anthropology, 38*(1), 28–47.

Rhodes, D. (2017). North of England Hit Hardest by Government Cuts. *BBC News*. Retrieved July 13, 2018, from www.bbc.co.uk/news/uk-england-42049922.

Roberts, H. (Ed.). (1981). *Doing Feminist Research*. London: Routledge.

Robinson, V., Hockey, J., & Meah, A. (2004). "What I Used to Do … On My Mother's Settee": Spatial and Emotional Aspects of Heterosexuality in England. *Gender, Place & Culture, 11*(3), 417–435.

Rose, G. (1995). *Love's Work*. New York: New York Review Books.

Rose, G. (1997). Situating Knowledges: Positionality, Reflexivities and Other Tactics. *Progress in Human Geography, 21*, 305–320.

Round, J., Williams, C. C., & Rodgers, P. (2008). Everyday Tactic of Spaces of Power: The Role of Informal Economies in Post-Soviet Ukraine. *Social & Cultural Geography, 9*, 171–185.

Scott, S. (2009). *Making Sense of Everyday Life*. Cambridge: Polity Press.

Shirani, F., Butler, C., Henwood, K., Parkhill, K., & Pidgeon, N. (2013). Disconnected Futures: Exploring Notions of Ethical Responsibility in Energy Practices. *Local Environment, 18*(4), 455–468.

Sidaway, J. (2008). Subprime Crisis: American Crisis or Human Crisis. *Environment and Planning D, 26*, 195–198.

Skeggs, B. (2004). *Class, Self and Culture*. London: Routledge.

Skelton, T. (2000). "Nothing to Do, Nowhere to Go?": Teenage Girls and 'Public' Space in the Rhondda Valleys, South Wales. In S. L. Holloway & G. Valentine (Eds.), *Children's Geographies: Playing, Living, Learning* (pp. 69–85). London: Routledge.

Skop, E. (2015). Conceptualizing Scale in the Science of Broadening Participation of Underrepresented Groups in Higher Education. *The Professional Geographer, 67*(3), 427–437.

Slater, T. (2013). Your Life Chances Affect Where You Live: A Critique of the 'Cottage Industry' of Neighbourhood Effects Research. *International Journal of Urban and Regional Research, 37*(2), 367–387.

Smart, C. (2007). *Personal Life*. Cambridge: Polity Press.

Smith, D. M. (1999). Geography, Community and Morality. *Environment and Planning A, 31*, 19–35.

Smith, S. (2005). States, Markets and an Ethic of Care. *Political Geography, 25*, 1–20.

Smith, D. P. (2011). Geographies of Long-Distance Family Migration: Moving to a "Spatial Turn". *Progress in Human Geography, 35*(5), 652–668.

Smith, A., & Stenning, A. (2006). Beyond Household Economies: Articulations and Spaces of Economic Practice in Post-Socialism. *Progress in Human Geography, 30*(2), 190–213.

Spencer, L., & Pahl, R. (2006). *Rethinking Friendship: Hidden Solidarities Today.* Princeton, NJ: Princeton University Press.

Stacey, J. (1988). Can There Be a Feminist Ethnography? *Women's Studies International Forum, 11*(1), 21–27.

Stacey, J. (1990). *Brave New Families: Stories of Domestic Upheaval in Late-Twentieth-Century America.* Berkeley, CA: University of California Press.

Staeheli, L., Ehrkamp, P., Leitner, H., & Nagel, C. (2012). Dreaming the Ordinary: Daily Life and the Complex Geographies of Citizenship. *Progress in Human Geography, 36*(5), 628–644.

Stenning, A. (2005). Post-Socialism and the Changing Geographies of the Everyday in Poland. *Transactions of the Institute of British Geographers, 30,* 113–127.

Stenning, A. (2018). Feeling the Squeeze: Towards a Psychosocial Geography of Austerity in Low-to-Middle Income Families. *Geoforum.* https://doi.org/10.1016/j.geoforum.2018.09.035.

Stenning, A., & Hall, S. M. (2018). Loneliness and the Politics of Austerity. *Discover Society*, p. 62. Retrieved from https://discoversociety.org/2018/11/06/on-the-frontline-loneliness-and-the-politics-of-austerity/.

Strong, S. (2018). Food Banks, Actually Existing Austerity and the Localisation of Responsibility. *Geoforum.* https://doi.org/10.1016/j.geoforum.2018.09.025.

Tarrant, A. (2010). Constructing a Social Geography of Grandparenthood: A New Focus for Intergenerationality. *Area, 42*(2), 190–197.

Tarrant, A. (2013). Grandfathering as Spatio-Temporal Practice: Conceptualizing Performances of Ageing Masculinities in Contemporary Familial Carescapes. *Social & Cultural Geography, 14*(2), 192–210.

Tarrant, A. (2018). Care in an Age of Austerity: Men's Care Responsibilities in Low-Income Families. *Ethics & Social Welfare, 12*(1), 34–48.

Thomson, R., Hadfield, L., Kehily, M. J., & Sharpe, S. (2010). Family Fortunes: An Intergenerational Perspective on Recession. *21st Century Society, 5,* 149–157.

Tipper, B. (2011). "A Dog Who I Know Quite Well": Everyday Relationships Between Children and Animals. *Children's Geographies, 9*(2), 145–165.

Torres, R. M. (2018). A Crisis of Rights and Responsibility: Feminist Geopolitical Perspectives on Latin American Refugees and Migrants. *Gender, Place & Culture*. https://doi.org/10.1080/0966369X.2017.1414036.

Tronto, J. (1993). *Moral Boundaries: A Political Argument for an Ethic of Care*. London: Routledge.

Twigg, J. (2000). Carework as a Form of Bodywork. *Ageing and Society, 20*(4), 389–411.

Twigg, J. (2006). *The Body in Health and Social Care*. Basingstoke: Palgrave Macmillan.

Valentine, G. (1993). Desperately Seeing Susan: A Geography of Lesbian Friendships. *Area, 25*(2), 109–116.

Valentine, G. (1998). "Sticks and Stone May Break My Bones": A Personal Geography of Harassment. *Antipode, 30*(4), 305–332.

Valentine, G. (2008a). The Ties that Bind: Towards Geographies of Intimacy. *Geography Compass, 2*(6), 2097–2110.

Valentine, G. (2008b). Living with Difference: Reflections on Geographies of Encounter. *Progress in Human Geography, 32*(3), 323–337.

Valentine, G., & Hughes, K. (2011). Geographies of 'Family' Life: Interdependent Relationships Across the Life Course in the Context of Problem Internet Gambling. In L. Holt (Ed.), *Geographies of Children, Youth and Families: An International Perspective* (pp. 121–135). London: Routledge.

Valentine, G., Jayne, M., & Gould, M. (2012). Do as I Say, Not as I Do: The Affective Space of Family Life and the Generational Transmission of Drinking Cultures. *Environment and Planning A, 44*(4), 776–792.

Valentine, G., Piekut, A., & Harris, C. (2015). Intimate Encounters: The Negotiation of Difference Within the Family and Its Implications for Social Relations in Public Space. *The Geographical Journal, 181*(3), 280–294.

van Blerk, L. (2011). Managing Cape Town's Street Children/Youth: The Impact of the 2010 World Cup Bid on Street Life in the City. *South African Geographical Journal, 93*(1), 29–37.

Vanderbeck, R. M. (2007). Intergenerational Geographies: Age Relations, Segregation and Re-engagements. *Geography Compass, 1*(2), 200–221.

van Lanen, S. (2017). Living Austerity Urbanism: Space–Time Expansion and Deepening Socio-Spatial Inequalities for Disadvantaged Urban Youth in Ireland. *Urban Geography, 38*(10), 1603–1613.

Volger, C. M. (1994). Money in the Household. In M. Anderson, F. Bechhofer, & J. Gershuny (Eds.), *The Social and Political Economy of the Household* (pp. 225–262). Oxford: Oxford University Press.

Wagner-Pacifici, R. (2017). *What Is an Event?* Chicago, IL: The University of Chicago Press.

Waight, E. (2018). "Hand-Me-Down" Childrenswear and the Middle-Class Economy of Nearly New Sales. In A. Ince & S. M. Hall (Eds.), *Sharing Economies in Times of Crisis: Practices, Politics and Possibilities* (pp. 96–109). London: Routledge.

Waters, J. L. (2002). Flexible Families? "Astronaut" Households and the Experiences of Lone Mothers in Vancouver, British Columbia. *Social & Cultural Geography, 3*(2), 117–134.

Waters, J. L. (2005). Transnational Family Strategies and Education in the Contemporary Chinese Diaspora. *Global Networks, 5*, 359–377.

Watts, J. (2017). Theresa May Signals Austerity Is Over and Overhaul of Brexit Plans. *The Independent*. Retrieved July 31, 2017, from www.independent.co.uk/news/uk/politics/theresa-may-austerity-brexit-plans-uk-leave-eu-hard-soft-latest-tax-cuts-welfare-benefit-a7787001.html.

Weeks, J., Heaphy, B., & Donovan, C. (2001). *Same Sex Intimacies: Families of Choice and Other Life Experiments*. London: Routledge.

Wellman, B. (1990). The Place of Kinfolk in Personal Community Networks. *Marriage & Family Review, 15*(1/2), 195–228.

Wellman, B. (2001). Physical Space and Cyberplace: The Rise of Personalized Networking. *International Journal of Urban and Regional Research, 25*(2), 227–252.

White, S. (2017). Spain Veers Away from Austerity in Compromise Budget. *CNBC*. Retrieved July 31, 2017, from www.cnbc.com/2017/03/31/reuters-america-spain-veers-away-from-austerity-in-compromise-budget.html.

Wilkinson, E., & Ortega-Alcázar, I. (2017). A Home of One's Own? Housing Welfare for 'Young Adults' in Times of Austerity. *Critical Social Policy, 37*(3), 1–19.

Wilkinson, E., & Ortega-Alcázar, I. (2018). The Right to Be Weary? Endurance and Exhaustion in Austere Times. *Transactions of the Institute of British Geographers, 44*(1), 155–167.

Wilson, H. F. (2013). Collective Life: Parents, Playground Encounters and the Multicultural City. *Social & Cultural Geography, 14*(6), 625–648.

Wilson, H. F. (2017). On Geography and Encounter: Bodies, Borders, and Difference. *Progress in Human Geography, 41*(4), 45–471.

Women's Budget Group. (2018). A "Jam Tomorrow" Budget': Women's Budget Group Response to Autumn Budget 2018. Retrieved December 19, 2018, from https://wbg.org.uk/wp-content/uploads/2018/11/WBG-2018-Autumn-Budget-full-analysis.pdf.

Woodward, S. (2015). The Hidden Lives of Domestic Things: Accumulations in Cupboards, Lofts and Shelves. In E. Casey & Y. Taylor (Eds.), *Intimacies, Critical Consumption and Diverse Economies* (pp. 216–231). Basingstoke: Palgrave Macmillan.

Young, M., & Willmott, P. (1957). *Family and Kinship in East London*. London: Routledge and Kegan Paul.

Zelizer, V. (2005). *The Purchase of Intimacy*. Princeton, NJ: Princeton University Press.

Index

S. M. Hall, *Everyday Life in Austerity*, Palgrave Macmillan Studies in Family and Intimate Life, https://doi.org/10.1007/978-3-030-17094-3

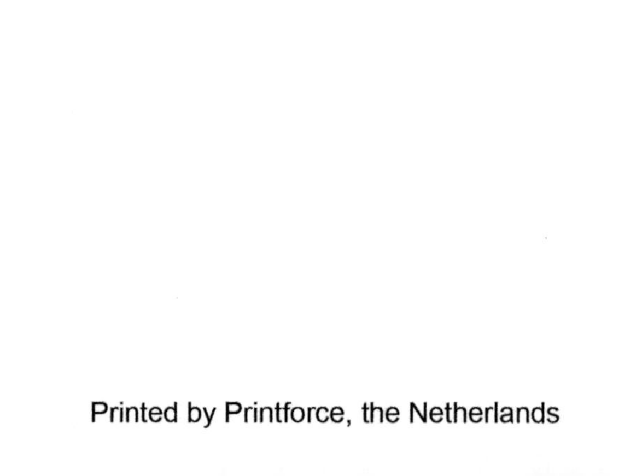

Printed by Printforce, the Netherlands